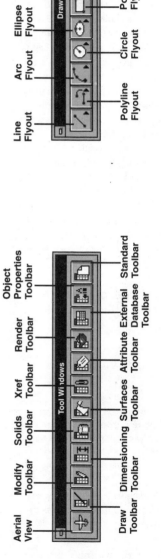

Draw

Line Flyout
Arc Flyout
Ellipse Flyout
Point Flyout
Hatch Flyout
Text Flyout
Polyline Flyout
Circle Flyout
Polygon Flyout
Block Flyout

Tool Windows

Object Properties Toolbar

Aerial View
Modify Toolbar
Solids Toolbar
Xref Toolbar
Render Toolbar
Standard Toolbar
Draw Toolbar
Dimensioning Toolbar
Surfaces Toolbar
Attribute Toolbar
External Database Toolbar

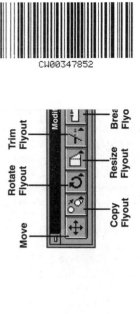

Modify

Move
Rotate Flyout
Trim Flyout
Copy Flyout
Resize Flyout
Break Flyout

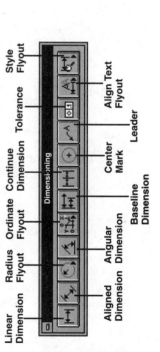

Dimensioning

Linear Dimension
Radius Flyout
Ordinate Flyout
Continue Dimension
Tolerance
Style Flyout
Aligned Dimension
Angular Dimension
Baseline Dimension
Center Mark
Leader
Align Text Flyout

For every kind of computer user, there is a SYBEX book.

All computer users learn in their own way. Some need straightforward and methodical explanations. Others are just too busy for this approach. But no matter what camp you fall into, SYBEX has a book that can help you get the most out of your computer and computer software while learning at your own pace.

Beginners generally want to start at the beginning. The **ABC's** series, with its step-by-step lessons in plain language, helps you build basic skills quickly. For a more personal approach, there's the **Murphy's Laws** and **Guided Tour** series. Or you might try our **Quick & Easy** series, the friendly, full-color guide, with **Quick & Easy References**, the companion pocket references to the **Quick & Easy** series. For hardware novices, there's the **Your First** series.

The **Mastering and Understanding** series will tell you everything you need to know about a subject. They're perfect for intermediate and advanced computer users, yet they don't make the mistake of leaving beginners behind. You may even want to check into our **Secrets & Solutions** series.

SYBEX even offers special titles on subjects that don't neatly fit a category—like our **Pushbutton Guides**, our books about the Internet, the latest computer games, and a wide range of books for Macintosh computers and software.

SYBEX books are written by authors who are expert in their subjects. In fact, many make their living as professionals, consultants or teachers in the field of computer software. And their manuscripts are thoroughly reviewed by our technical and editorial staff for accuracy and ease-of-use.

So when you want answers about computers or any popular software package, just help yourself to SYBEX.

For a complete catalog of our publications, please write:

SYBEX Inc.
2021 Challenger Drive
Alameda, CA 94501
Tel: (510) 523-8233/(800) 227-2346 Telex: 336311
Fax: (510) 523-2373

The SYBEX Instant Reference Series

Instant References are available on these topics:

AutoCAD Release 12 for Windows

CorelDRAW 4

DOS 6.2

Excel 5 for Windows

Internet

Lotus 1-2-3 Release 4 for Windows

Lotus 1-2-3 Release 5 for Windows

Microsoft Access 2

OS/2 2.1

Paradox 4.5 for Windows

Paradox 4.5 for DOS

PC Tools 8

Quattro Pro 5 for Windows

SQL

Windows 3.1

Windows NT

Microsoft Word for Windows, Version 2.0

Word 6 for Windows

WordPerfect 5.1 for Windows

WordPerfect 5.1 for DOS

WordPerfect 6 & 6a for Windows

WordPerfect 6 for DOS

AutoCAD® 13
Instant Reference

George Omura
Paul W. Richardson

SYBEX®

San Francisco • Paris • Düsseldorf • Soest

Acquisitions Editor: Kristine Plachy
Developmental Editor: Richard Mills
Editor: Peter Weverka
Project Editor: Michelle Khazai
Technical Editor: B. Robert Callori
Book Designer: Ingrid Owen
Technical Art: Cuong Le, John Corrigan
Desktop Publisher: Deborah A. Bevilacqua
Production Assistants: Emily Smith, David Nash
Indexer: Nancy Guenther
Cover Designer: Design Site
Cover Photographer: Mark Johann
Photo Art Direction: Ingalls + Associates

Library of Congress Card Number: 94-68874
ISBN: 0-7821-1474-1

Manufactured in the United States of America
10 9 8 7 6 5 4 3 2 1

Acknowledgments

My role in the creation of this book was a small one. I am greatly indebted to those who were able to pull this book together with a minimal amount of input on my part. My thanks go to those at SYBEX who have helped in the creation of this edition of *AutoCAD Instant Reference*. In particular, I'd like to thank the following people: Richard Mills, developmental editor, who laid the groundwork for this latest edition; Michelle Khazai, project editor, whose constant support and direction kept this project on track; Peter Weverka, editor, for his unflagging attention to issues of style and form; and, of course, the team in the production department who did all the "real" work: Cuong Le, illustrator; Deborah Bevilacqua, desktop publisher; and Emily Smith and David Nash, production assistants.

I'd also like to thank B. Robert Callori for his continued involvement in this book. Robert gave his insight and careful review to this edition. The staff at Autodesk also provided much needed support: Lisa Senauke made sure we had the right software, and Art Cooney gave advice and technical support for those nagging questions.

Finally, special thanks go to coauthor Paul Richardson, along with Christine Meredith, of Technical Publications, for updating this edition of the book. While I may have provided the background material, they made the painstaking effort of adding the features of Release 13 to this book. Many thanks to you both.

G.O.

Introduction

This book is designed to give you quick and comprehensive answers to your questions about AutoCAD functions and commands. Whether the command you've just issued does not work as you intended or you need a concise guide to using a feature you've never tried before, *AutoCAD 13 Instant Reference* will help you solve the problem quickly so you can get on with your work. All of the main program's features are here—the basic commands as well as the built-in functions you may not use every day. (Auxiliary programs like the Advanced Modeling Extension are not covered.)

Who Should Read This Book

This book is for users who have some basic knowledge of AutoCAD—people who already have an idea of what they need to know but just aren't sure of the precise steps involved. It is equally useful both for casual AutoCAD users who need basic information fast and experienced users who need a refresher on specific commands. The information in the book is directed specifically to AutoCAD Release 13.

This book is for users of both AutoCAD for Windows and AutoCAD for DOS.

If you are new to AutoCAD, read *Mastering AutoCAD Release 13 for DOS* (SYBEX, 1995), or *Mastering AutoCAD Release 13 for Windows* (SYBEX, 1995), which offer a tutorial approach and contain a wealth of tips and techniques for both beginning and advanced users.

How This Book Is Organized

This book presents commands and features in alphabetical order. Most entries offer the following information:

1. The *name* of the command or feature appears as a header in a shaded box. These names are in alphabetical order. Commands that are new to Release 13 are identified in the shaded box by the word "New." A few commands are available only in the Windows environment, and you'll see the words "Windows Only" at the top of these command entries.

2. A short paragraph or two then follows, explaining the command's *purpose*.

3. Unless the procedure is completely obvious, *instructions* on using the command follow a head that takes the form *To Do Such-and-Such:*. The instructions take you through the prompts and/or dialog-box settings that AutoCAD displays. The instructions tell you what information Auto-CAD requires to complete the command. Differences between Windows and DOS procedures, if any, are explained.

4. Many AutoCAD commands present choices, or options. Short descriptions of these options, and notes on how to select them as well, are presented in the Options section. The Windows and DOS options are almost always the same, but if there are any discrepancies, they are explained.

5. The *Notes* section describes command restrictions and interactions with other commands, and provides special tips or warnings.

6. *See Also* directs you to related entries for further information.

We have also used the following typographic conventions. When a command needs to be typed in, it appears in **boldface.** *Italic* text is used for command options, system variables, and file names. You'll see a separate Prompt: typeface for AutoCAD prompts.

Working from the Command Line

All AutoCAD commands can be started by typing the command at the command prompt. Most commands will either execute immediately or prompt you for further information. These prompts appear on the **Command:** line at the bottom of the screen or in a dialog box that pops open. If you prefer the command-line approach, you can use the *Filedia* or *Cmddia* system variables to turn off the dialog box in most cases. *Filedia* controls dialog boxes pertaining to file and directory management, and *Cmddia* controls all other commands. To turn *Filedia* OFF, simply type **Filedia** and set the value to zero (0). You can change *Filedia* or *Cmddia* as often as you wish, according to how you want to work. To change *Filedia*, simply type **Filedia** at the command line and enter a different value.

Working with AutoCAD Dialog Boxes

Dialog boxes allow you to see at one time all the options necessary for an operation. Make sure that *Filedia* and *Cmddia* are set to ON (1). If Filedia is OFF and you only wish to override it for the current command, type a ~ (tilde) at any prompt asking for a file name.

When a dialog box opens, the cursor changes from a crosshair to an arrow, which you then position on the item you want by moving and clicking a mouse (or some other point-and-click device) or by pressing the **Tab** key on your keyboard (which moves the cursor from one item to the next). You can also press and hold the Alt key on your keyboard and type the letter that is underscored in the item you want to pick. For example, typing Alt-P will activate the Pattern edit box for keyboard entry. The following dialog box operations are standard throughout the AutoCAD dialog-box system:

- To make a cursor *pick*, click the arrow on the item you want to pick.

- To type information in an *edit box*, click the arrow inside the edit box to place the cursor where you want it.

- To move a *slide bar*, drag the arrow in the direction you want (hold the mouse button down while moving the mouse).

- To toggle a *radio button* or *check box*, simply click on it.

- To expand a *pop-up list*, double-click on it.

- To view an *image tile*, double-click on it.

- To pick an *icon*, double-click on it.

Working with the Windows Toolbars

AutoCAD Release 13 for Windows comes with a set of standard toolbars. Frequently used commands are grouped on the toolbars for easy access. Toolbars can be docked on any side of the Auto-CAD window or left floating in the drawing workspace. Each command (or subgroup of commands) is represented by a distinctive icon. To identify a command on a toolbar, rest your pointing device on the icon. A *Tool Tip* will appear below the icon showing the icon's name. At the same time, a short description of its function appears in the status bar.

To start a command, simply click on the icon (or button) and follow the prompts or provide information as required in the dialog box. When you click on an icon with a ➤ in the bottom-left corner, yet another mini-toolbar (called a *flyout*) appears, offering more choices within the command group. Click on the flyout icon you require to activate the command. Note that any flyout icon you choose becomes the "default" and will appear on top of the flyout in the future.

Features New to Release 13

Here are the features new to AutoCAD Release 13.

Text

The new **Mtext** command allows you to create multiline (or paragraph) text objects. You can change the attributes of the text—that is, you can underline or change its font, height, and color. The new **Spell** command lets you spell-check the words. Besides standard .SHX font files, AutoCAD now supports PostScript Type 1 fonts and TrueType fonts. Stacked fractions are also available with this release.

Dimensioning

In Release 13, the **DIM** and **DIM1** commands have been retired, although they are still supported for compatibility purposes. Dimensioning commands are now full commands. The *Dimension Style* facility introduced in Release 11 has been expanded to include *Dimension Style Families*. Now you can define one dimension style with variations for different dimension types, including linear, radial, angular, and leader. The new **Leader** command lets you create a leader object, which may be curved (spline), annotated with multiline text, and have an arrowhead. AutoCAD now has Geometric Dimensioning and Tolerancing (GD&T). Release 13 also provides support for international design and drafting standards (ANSI, ISO, and JIS) with respect to dimensioning elements.

Hatching

Release 13 has improved boundary creation and selection techniques. You can hatch complex groupings of objects. The new **Hatchedit** command allows you to update the hatch properties of most objects without having to re-create them. A full set of ISO standard hatches is included with Release 13.

Linetypes

Linetype definition has been extended to include more complex definitions than the dash-dot-space sequences previously offered. You can now create complex linetypes with text or shapes (.SHP files). The standard linetype file now contains a full set of ISO linetype definitions. Linetype scaling on a *per object* basis is also available.

Drawing and Editing

The **Trim** and **Extend** commands can now be used in the context of *implied* boundaries and intersections, so objects can be trimmed or extended to the point where they *would* intersect with a boundary or cutting edge. Both **Fillet** and **Chamfer** can be performed either with or without trimming. All of these commands, and the **Break** command as well, can be performed successfully even if the objects are not in a plane parallel to the UCS. The new **Lengthen** command

allows you to change the length of any object by dragging it or by
entering a value or increment at the command prompt. Object selection has been improved by the introduction of "cycling." When
two or more 2D or 3D objects are superimposed, you can now cycle
through the objects and select the one you want.

Geometry Improvements

Release 13 introduces a true NURBS spline curve and a true ellipse
object. The new spline is easy to edit with the **Splinedit** command,
and an ellipse can be trimmed to an elliptical arc. Both objects can
be exploded without losing their smooth curves. As a result of
these improvements, it is now possible to **Explode** non-uniformly
scaled blocks. New geometry commands include **Mline**, **Ray**, and
Xline. The multiline feature allows you to draw sets of parallel
lines, define multiline styles (using **Mlstyle**), and add vertices and
the intersections (using **Mledit**). Two new line objects, **Ray** and
Xline, have been added so you can create infinite lines for construction purposes. The new **Group** command allows you to relate and
save a number of objects in a more complex *named* object.

External References

You can access external references in *overlay* mode without actually
making the external reference a part of the current drawing. Now
different members of a work group can access data without actually owning it, which avoids circularity problems in Xrefs.

Solid Modeling

Prior to Release 13, solid modeling was available only in the
AutoDESK Advanced Modeling Extension (AME). With Release 13, a
full range of solid modeling commands have been implemented.

Windows OLE

Object Linking and Embedding in Release 12 was a one-way operation, but with Release 13, AutoCAD can act as an OLE client as well
as a server. You can import objects via the Windows Clipboard
from any Windows application that supports OLE.

ABOUT

About identifies your AutoCAD version and serial numbers and displays the *Acad.MSG* message file. On the command line, use **About** (or **'About**, to use transparently).

To Access AutoCAD Information

Choose ➤ Help ➤ About AutoCAD.

 NOTES   The *Acad.MSG* file can be customized using any word processor that saves files in the ASCII format.

ACAD.INI
Windows Only

Acad.INI is an ASCII file that contains system and environment settings made in the Options ➤ Preferences options. It also contains the macros stored in the toolbar buttons. You can edit Acad.INI using the Windows Notepad application. Settings for toolbars and buttons can now be found in the Acad.MNS file.

See Also   Preferences, Tbconfig, Toolbar

ACAD.PGP

Acad.PGP is the ProGram Parameters ASCII file that contains information needed to launch a DOS program from within AutoCAD; it is also the location for command alias definitions. Most of the commands in the Utility-External Commands menu need this file. For example, if you use a word processor, specifying the alias in *Acad.PGP* allows you to execute it as an AutoCAD command.

NOTES Each external command has a maximum of five parts. The first item in each entry is the command name to be entered at the AutoCAD command prompt. The second item is the actual command as it would be entered at the DOS prompt. Next is the amount of memory in bytes to allocate to the command. AutoCAD Release 12 and 13 do not use the value of this field—it is retained for compatibility with previous releases, and should be set to 0 for Release 13. The fourth item specifies the prompt, if there is any, that appears after the command is issued. An asterisk (optional) preceding the prompt tells AutoCAD to accept spaces within the user's response. The fifth part can be used to enter a statement, similar to **Files to delete:** to clarify the prompt; if no prompt is needed, this item can be blank. The last item is a return code, usually 0. The primary return codes are listed below:

0 = Screen remains in text mode.

1 = Loads the file *$cmd.DXB* when the command is terminated.

2 = Creates a block with the name from the prompt. Block objects will be taken from the file *$cmd.DXB*. This return code must be used in conjunction with return code 1.

4 = Restores previous screen mode (text or graphics).

The command alias format is simple. The first item is the alias. It is followed by a comma, a space, an asterisk, and the name of the command being aliased.

Use **Reinit** to reinitialize the *Acad.PGP* file if you edit it and want to activate those changes in the current drawing session.

 **See Also** Reinit, Shell/sh

ALIGN

Align relocates an object in two or three dimensions so that it aligns with another object, using up to three source and three destination points. The command line is **Align**.

To Align Objects

1. In **Windows**, choose Modify toolbar ➤ Rotate flyout ➤ Align button. In **DOS**, choose Modify ➤ Align.

2. **Select objects:** Pick objects to move.

3. **1st source point:** Select first source point of object.

4. **1st destination point:** Select first destination point where object is to be realigned.

5. Either press ↵ at the second prompt to move the object directly from the source point to the destination point, or relocate the object in two or three dimensions by specifying the second and third pairs of points at the subsequent prompts.

OPTIONS

2d Rotations in 2D occur in the XY plane of the current UCS (user coordinate system).

3d Rotations in 3D use the two destination points and the second source point defined by the first source and destination points.

APERTURE

Aperture sets the size of the Osnap (object snap) target box to your preference. The equivalent dialog box command is **Ddosnap**.

To Set the Size of the Osnap Target Box

1. In **Windows**, choose Osnap toolbar ➤ Running Object Snap. In **DOS**, enter **Aperture** (or **Àperture**, to use transparently) at the command line.

2. Object snap target height (1–50 pixels) <10>: Enter desired size of osnap target in pixels. Default settings may vary depending on your display.

Using the Object Snap toolbar will open the Running Object Snap dialog box, allowing you to use the Aperture size slider bar to visually set the Osnap box size.

See Also   Ddosnap; Ddselect; Grips; Osnp; *System Variables:* Aperture

APPLOAD

Appload displays a dialog box for loading AutoLISP files or loading and unloading ADS and Rx applications. The command line is **Appload**.

To Load AutoLISP Applications

Choose Tools ➤ Applications.

 **OPTIONS**

File… Opens the Select LISP/ADS/.Rx dialog box and allows you to search for files to add.

Remove Deletes files from list box.

Load Loads files from list box.

Unload Removes ADS, AutoLISP, or Rx applications.

Save List Saves current applications shown in list box to the Appload.dfs file.

 NOTES Files listed on DOS systems and Windows are limited to AutoLISP (.LSP), AutoCAD Development System (.EXE and .EXP), and .ARX file extensions.

⊙ See Also AutoLISP

ARC

Arc allows you to draw an arc using a variety of methods. Depending upon the method chosen, the system prompts shown below will vary with the options chosen. The command line is **Arc**.

To Draw an Arc

1. In **Windows**, choose Draw toolbar ➤ Arc flyout ➤ (preset options). In **DOS**, choose Draw ➤ Arc ➤ (preset options).

2. Center/<Start point>: Use the mouse to pick the start point of the arc or select **C** for more options.

3. Center/End/<Second point>: Pick the second point of the arc, or select **C** or **E** for more options.

4. Angle/Length of Chord/End point: Pick the end point of the arc.

 **OPTIONS**

Angle Enters an arc in terms of degrees or current angular units. You are prompted for the Included angle:. You can enter an angle value or use the cursor to visually select an angle.

Center Enters the location of an arc's center point. At the prompt Center:, enter a coordinate or pick a point with your cursor.

Direction Enters a tangent direction from the start point of an arc. At the prompt Direction from start point:, either enter a relative coordinate or pick a point with your cursor.

End Enters the end point of an arc. At the prompt End point:, enter a coordinate or pick a point with your cursor.

Length Enters the length of an arc's chord. At the prompt Length of chord:, enter a length or drag and pick a length with your cursor.

Radius Enters an arc's radius. At the prompt Radius:, enter a radius or pick a point that defines a radius length.

Start point Enters the beginning point of an arc.

NOTES If you select Arc from the pull-down menu in **DOS**, the Arc Cascading menu appears, with ten preset arc options. For example, *S,E,D* allows you to select the start point, the end point, and the direction of the arc. Figure 1 illustrates how these options draw arcs.

If you press ↵ at the first prompt of the Arc command or select the Arc Continue button on the Windows toolbar, AutoCAD uses the most recent point entered for a line or arc as the first point of the new arc. It then prompts you for a new end point. An arc is drawn tangent to the last line or arc drawn.

If you select the Arc button via the toolbar in **Windows**, the button bar allows you to select the same preset arc options. You can convert arcs to polyline arcs with the **Pedit** command. You can also lengthen existing arcs using the **Lengthen** command.

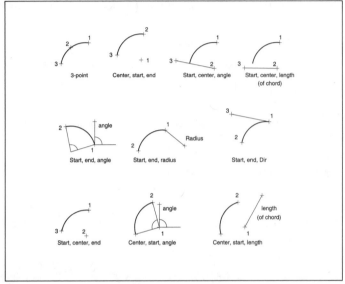

Figure 1: The Arc menu/flyout options and their meanings

See Also   Change, Elev, Ellipse, Lengthen, UCS

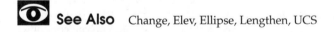

AREA

Area carries out an area calculation based on dimensions that you specify by defining line segments, by selecting lines and polylines, or by doing both. The command line is **Area**.

To Calculate an Area

1. In **Windows**, choose Object Properties toolbar ➤ Inquiry toolbar ➤ Area button. In **DOS**, choose Assist ➤ Inquiry ➤ Area.

2. <First point>/Object/Add/Subtract: Pick first point or enter option.

3. Next Point: Pick the next point.

4. Continue picking points until you have defined the area, then press ↵ to display the calculated area and perimeter in the following format:

   ```
   Area = <Calculated area>, Perimeter =
   <Perimeter>
   ```

 **OPTIONS**

Next point Continues selecting points until you have defined the area to be calculated. Once you have defined the area, press ↵ at the **Next Point:** prompt.

Object Selects a circle or polyline for area calculation. If you pick an open polyline, AutoCAD will calculate the area of the polyline as if its two end points were closed.

Add Keeps a running count of areas. Normally, Area returns you to the command prompt as soon as an area has been calculated. If you enter the Add mode, you are returned to the Area command prompt once an area has been calculated, and you can continue to add area values to the current area.

Subtract Subtracts areas from a running count of areas.

Return Exits the command.

NOTES Area does not calculate areas for arcs. To find the area of a shape that includes arcs, you must convert the arc areas into polylines (see **Pedit**) before you issue the Area command. Then issue the command, select the *Object/Entity* option, and pick the polyline—Area will calculate the area of the polyline. Add all the polyline areas to rectangular areas to arrive at the total area. Use Bpoly to create a closed polyline automatically. Area only calculates areas in a plane parallel to the current user coordinate system.

 See Also   Bhatch; Dblist; List; Pedit; *System Variables: Area*

ARRAY/3DARRAY

Use Array to make multiple copies of an object or group of objects in a row-and-column matrix, a single row or column, or a circular array (to form such objects as teeth in a gear or the numbers on a circular clock). The command line is **Array** or **3Darray**.

To Create Object Arrays

1. In **Windows**, choose Modify toolbar ➤ Copy flyout ➤ Array Options flyout. In **DOS**, choose Construct ➤ Array or Construct ➤ 3Darray.

2. Select objects: Pick objects to array.

3. Rectangular or Polar array (R/P): Enter desired array type.

If you select the **Rectangular** option or enter **R** at the **Rectangular or Polar array:** prompt, you are given the following series of prompts:

a. Number of rows (---) <1>: Enter the number of rows.

b. Number of columns (||||) <1>: Enter the number of columns.

c. Unit cell or distance between rows (---): Enter the numeric distance between rows or depth of cell (see *Unit cell* option below).

d. Distance between columns (||||): Enter the numeric distance between columns.

If you select the **Polar** option or enter **P** at the Rectangular or Polar array: prompt, you are given the following prompts:

 a. **Center point of array:** Pick the center of rotation.

 b. **Number of items:** Enter number of items in the array, including the originally selected objects.

 c. Angle to fill <360>: Enter the angle the array is to occupy. Use a negative value to indicate a clockwise array.

 d. Rotate objects as they are copied? <Y>: Enter **N** if the arrayed objects are to maintain their current orientation.

Array/3Darray

If you are using the 3Darray command (with the *Rectangular* option), you will also be prompted for **Number of levels** (…):. When using the *Polar* option, you will need to specify a **Second point on axis of rotation:** as well as the center point of the array.

 OPTIONS

Rectangular   Copies the selected objects in an array of rows and columns. You are then prompted for the number of rows and columns and the distance between them.

Polar   Copies the selected objects in a circular array. You are prompted first for the center point of the array and then for the number of items in the array. You are asked whether you want to rotate the objects as they are copied. If you press ↵ without entering a value at the **Number of items:** prompt, you will be prompted for the angle between items.

Unit cell   Enter the size of the rectangular unit cell by picking two points dynamically or with an Osnap mode. After picking the first point, you are prompted to select **Other corner:** of the unit cell.

NOTES   Usually, row-and-column arrays are aligned with the X and Y axes of your current user coordinate system. To create an array at any other angle, set the **Snap** command's *Rotate* option to the desired angle. Rectangular arrays will be rotated by the snap angle. The *Snapang* system variable also allows you to set the cursor rotation angle. The order in which you select the two points for the *Unit cell* option determines the direction of the array.

 **See Also** Minsert; Select; Snap; *System Variables:* Snapang, 3Darray

---

ASE

ASE is an application that links AutoCAD to external database files. You can modify database files from within AutoCAD and link AutoCAD objects to database records. Use ASE to access dBASE III+, dBASE IV, Fox Pro 2.5, Microsoft ODBC, Informix, Oracle, and Paradox 4.5 files.

To Use the ASE Application

In **Windows**, Choose External Database toolbar ➤ Administration/Rows/Links/Select Objects/Import Links/SQL Editor buttons. In **DOS**, choose Tools ➤ External Database ➤ Administration/Rows/Links/Select Objects/Import Links/SQL Editor.

OPTIONS

The following options appear in the External Database menu and toolbar. The command line equivalent of each menu or toolbar option is shown in parentheses.

Adminstration Allows you to set up the ASE environment. You first specify the type of database (*Database Object*) to connect to, and define the path to the actual database table (*Catalog/Schema/Table*). You may set a *User Name* and *Password*, and select an *Isolation level* to determine whether data in different transactions by different users is interleaved or isolated. Once the database object has been defined, use the *Set by*

option to define a *Link Path Name* by selecting key columns in the
database, and to select AutoCAD (*Graphical*) objects for linking
(**Aseadmin** command).

Rows...   Displays the current Database Object Settings and allows
you to *Select Objects* and view and edit rows in the database via the
Edit Rows subdialog box. This command option is also used to edit
and delete links to selected rows in the database, and create selection sets and displayable attributes (**Aserows** command).

Links...   Allows you select AutoCAD objects and edit or delete
their database links. You may delete specific links or all links
(**Aselinks** command).

Select Objects   Allows you to create a selection set based on a combination of graphic and nongraphic data. You may define search criteria
based on database information via the *Select* option by entering a selection statement in the Condition field. You may then select Auto-
CAD (*Graphical*) objects and compare the selection sets using the
Union/Intersect/Subtract A-B/Subtract B-A logical operators. Depending on the logical operation selected, the final selection set will
contain all objects that belong in each selection set; only those that
meet both sets of selection parameters; or a set based on subtraction of
one set from the other (**Aseselect** command).

Export Links...   Allows you to select AutoCAD objects and their
linked database information, and export this information into a text
file in a variety of formats. Available export formats are space-
delimited (SDF), comma-delimited (CDF), and native database formats. These export tables can be used to generate reports using the
appropriate report-writing software. A separate table is generated
for each *Link Path Name* (**Aseexport** command).

SQL Editor...   Allows you to interact with the external databases
via SQL statements. This method allows you to generate more complex queries and edits than are available via the AutoCAD external
database commands. You may enter SQL statements directly into
the SQL Editor dialog box, or load and run saved SQL statements
(**Asesqled** command).

ATTDEF

Attdef creates an attribute definition that allows you to store text and numeric data with a block. When you insert a block containing an attribute definition into a drawing, you are prompted for the data that is to be stored with the block. Use Attdef to work from the command line and **Ddattdef** to work from the Attribute Definition dialog box. The **Ddattdef** command provides the added feature of aligning your new attribute definition below the previous one. Later you can use **Ddatte** to view the data and edit attributes. The **Attext** or **Ddattext** command extracts attribute data into an ASCII text file. You can control the format of the extracted file for easy export to a database manager, spreadsheet, or word processing program.

To Create an Attribute Definition with Attdef

1. At the command line, enter **Attdef**.

2. Attribute modes--Invisible:N Constant:N Verify:N Preset:N Enter (ICVP) to change, RETURN when done: Enter **I**, **C**, **V**, or **P** to toggle an option on or off, or press ↵ to go to the next prompt.

3. Attribute tag: Enter the attribute name.

4. Attribute prompt: Enter the prompt to be displayed for attribute input.

5. Default attribute value: Enter the default value for attribute input.

6. Justify/Style/<Start point>: Enter coordinates or pick with the cursor to indicate the location of attribute text, or select an option to determine orientation or style of the attribute text.

7. Height (2.000): Enter the attribute text height. This prompt appears only if the current text style height is set to 0.

8. Rotation angle <0>: Enter the angle of the attribute text.

💡 OPTIONS

Invisible   Makes the attribute invisible when inserted.

Constant   Gives the attribute a value that you cannot change.

Verify   Allows review of the attribute value after insertion.

Preset   Automatically inputs the default attribute value on insertion. Unlike the Constant option, it lets you change the input value of a preset attribute by using the **Ddatte** or **Attedit** commands. See **Dtext** for *Attdef* options related to location, style, and orientation of attributes.

📝 **NOTES**   Use **Change** or **Ddedit** to edit the attribute definition before making the attribute into a block. When inserting a block with attributes, the prompt sequence is determined by the order selected during creation of the block.

👁 **See Also**   Attedit; Attdisp; Attext; Block; Change; Chprop; Ddatte; Ddattext; Ddedit; Dtext; Insert; *System Variables:* Aflags, Attdia, Attreq

ATTDISP

Attdisp allows you to control the display and plotting of all attributes in a drawing. You can force attributes to be visible or invisible according to their display mode. The command line is **Attdisp** (or **'Attdisp** to use transparently).

To Set Attribute Display Using Attdisp

1.   Choose Options ➤ Display ➤ Attribute Display.

2.   Normal/ON/OFF <Normal>: Enter **ON**, **OFF**, or ↵ for your selection.

ATTEXT

...ts attribute information into external ASCII text files.
...bring these files into database or spreadsheet pro-
...lysis. Attext allows you to choose from three standard
...spreadsheet file formats.

Attext Conversion

... command line, enter **Attext**.

...SDF or DXF Attribute extract (or Objects)? <C>:
...format of extracted file or press ↵ to select specific
...utes for extraction.

...*Filedia* system variable is set to 1, the Select Template
...ialog list box will appear to pick a template file, and
...reate Extract File dialog list box will then open to
...the extract file.

...*Filedia* system variable is set to 0, the command-line
...ots are as follows:

...DXF Attribute extract (or Objects)? <C>: Enter for-
...ted file or press ↵ to select specific attributes for ex-
...objects. Enter the name of the external template file.
...ame <drawing name>: Enter the name of the file to
...icted information.

...ONS

...-delimited file) Creates an ASCII file using commas to
...Each attribute is treated as a field of a record, and all the
...block are treated as one record. Character fields are en-
...es. Some database programs such as dBASE III, III Plus,
...id this format without any alteration.

...elimited format) Creates an ASCII file using spaces
...ds. Each attribute is treated as a field of a record, and

 **OPTIONS**

Normal Hides attributes that are set to be invisible. All other attributes are displayed.

ON Displays all attributes, including those set to be invisible.

OFF Hides all attributes, whether or not they are set to be invisible.

 NOTES If autoregeneration is on (see **Regenauto**), your
drawing will regenerate when you complete the command, and the
display of attributes will reflect the option you select. If autoregeneration is off, the drawing will not regenerate until you issue **Regen**.

See Also Attdef; Regen; Regenauto; *System Variables:*
Aflags, Attmode

ATTEDIT

Attedit edits attribute values after you have inserted them in a
drawing. You can edit attributes individually or globally. The command line is **Attedit**.

To Edit Attribute Values with Attedit

1. In **Windows**, choose Attribute toolbar ➤ Edit Attribute
    Globally button. In **DOS**, choose Modify ➤ Attribute ➤
    Edit Globally.

2. Edit attributes one at a time? <Y>: Enter **Y** for individual
    or **N** for global attribute editing. Depending on your re-
    sponse, you may see one or more additional prompts
    before the Block name: prompt below. These prompts
    are self-explanatory; respond to them to move on to the
    following.

3. Block name specification <*>: Press ↵, or enter a block name to restrict the attribute edits to a specific block, or enter a wildcard filter list to limit it to a group of blocks.

4. Attribute tag specification <*>: Press ↵, or enter an attribute tag to restrict attribute edits to a specific attribute, or enter a wildcard filter list.

5. Attribute value specification <*>: Press ↵, or enter a value to restrict attribute edits to a specific attribute value, or enter a wildcard to filter a list.

6. In most cases, the next prompt asks you to select attributes. Pick the attributes you want to edit. If you elected in Step 1 to edit the attributes one at a time, an X appears on the first attribute to be edited, and you will see the following prompt:

   • Value/Position/Height/Angle/Style/Layer/Color/Next/<N>: The options in this prompt are discussed below.

 OPTIONS

Y (at first prompt) Allows you to edit attribute values one at a time and change an attribute's position, height, angle, text style, layer, and color.

N (at first prompt) Allows you to modify attribute values globally. If you select this option, you are asked whether you want to edit only visible attributes.

Value Changes the value of the currently marked attribute(s).

Position Moves an attribute.

Height Changes the height of attribute text.

Angle Changes the attribute angle.

Style Changes the attribute text style.

Layer Changes the layer that the attribute is on.

Color Changes the attribute code or by name. See **Color/**

Next Displays the next sequ

 NOTES If you ch answer all of the prompts (y prompted to select attributes an X marks the first attribute move the marking X to the n

By entering **V** at the Value/ ceed to either change or rep *Replace*, the default option, value. The new attribute val return to the Value/Position, you are prompted for a spec for a new string to replace tl tions of an attribute's value tribute value.

If you choose to edit only vis first prompt), you are promp visually pick the attributes t string to change the replacer the prompts, AutoCAD cha enter **N** at the prompt Visible select attributes. Instead, Au the attributes in the drawing ible. The Select attribute pr rectly to the prompt Change

When answering the attribu wildcard characters (the ques ers) to "filter" a group of attri attribute edits to attributes tl slash) at the Attribute val Ddatte Attribute dialog box l

 See Also Attext, Wildcard characters

Attext conver You can then grams for ana database and

To Do an

1. At the

2. CDF, S Enter attrib

3. If the File d the Cr name

4. If the prom

CDF, SDF or mat of extrac traction from **Extract file** r hold the extr

 **OPT**

CDF (comma delimit fields. attributes in a closed in quo and IV can re

SDF (space-c to delimit fie

all attributes in a block are treated as one record. The field values are given a fixed width, and character fields are not given special treatment. If you open this file using a word processor, the attribute values appear as rows and columns (the rows are the records and the columns are the fields).

DXF (data-exchange format) Creates an abbreviated AutoCAD DXF file that contains only the block reference, attribute, and end-of-sequence objects. **Objects:** prompts you to select objects. You can then select specific attributes to extract. Once you are done with the selection, the **Attribute extract:** prompt reappears.

NOTES Before you can extract attribute values with Attext, you need to create a *template file*, an external ASCII file containing a list of attribute tags you wish to extract. Template files, which have the extension .TXT, also contain a code describing the characteristics of the attributes associated with each tag. The code denotes character and numeric values as well as the number of characters for string values or the number of placeholders for numeric values. For example, if you expect the value entered for a numeric attribute whose tag is *cost* to be five characters long with two decimal places, include the following line in the template file:

```
cost N005002
```

The *N* indicates that this attribute is a numeric value. The next three characters indicate the number of digits the value will hold. The last three characters indicate the number of decimal places the number will require. If you want to extract a character attribute, you might include the following line in the template file:

```
name C030000
```

The C denotes a character value. The next three characters indicate the number of characters you expect for the attribute value. The last three characters in character attributes are always zeros, because character values have no decimal places.

Follow the last line in the template file by a ↵, or you will receive an error message when you try to use the template file.

You can also extract information about the block that contains the attributes. Table 1 shows the format you use in the template file to

extract block information. A template file containing these codes
must also contain at least one attribute tag because AutoCAD must
know which attribute it is extracting before it can tell what block
the attribute is associated with.

Table 1: Template Tags and Codes for Extracting Information
about Blocks

Tag	Code	Description
BL:LEVEL	Nxxx000	Level of nesting for block
BL:NAME	Cxxx000	Block name
BL:X	N$xxxxxx$	X value for block insertion point
BL:Y	N$xxxxxx$	Y value for block insertion point
BL:Z	N$xxxxxx$	Z value for block insertion point
BL:NUMBER	Nxxx000	Block counter
BL:HANDLE	Cxxx000	Block handle
BL:LAYER	Cxxx000	Name of layer block is on
BL:ORIENT	N$xxxxxx$	Block rotation angle
BL:XSCALE	N$xxxxxx$	Block X scale
BL:YSCALE	N$xxxxxx$	Block Y scale
BL:ZSCALE	N$xxxxxx$	Block Z scale
BL:XEXTRUDE	N$xxxxxx$	X value for block extrusion direction
BL:YEXTRUDE	N$xxxxxx$	Y value for block extrusion direction
BL:ZEXTRUDE	N$xxxxxx$	Z value for block extrusion direction

Note: Italicized x's indicate adjustable numeric variables.

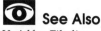 **See Also**   Attdef; Attedit; Ddattdef; Ddattext; *System Variables:* Filedia

Attredef allows you to redefine an existing block and delete and/or update the associated attributes. The command line is **Attredef**.

To Redefine Block Attributes

1.   In **Windows,** choose Attribute toolbar ➤ Redefine Attribute button. In **DOS,** choose Modify ➤ Attribute➤ Redefine

2.   Name of Block you wish to redefine: Enter the block name.

3.   Select objects: Select objects and attribute definitions.

4.   Insertion base point of new Block: Pick a new insertion point for block.

 NOTES   When you assign new attributes to an existing block reference, they are given default values; existing attributes keep their old values. If an old attribute is not included in the new block definition, it will be deleted from the block reference.

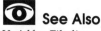 **See Also**   Attedit, Ddattdef, Ddatte

AUDIT

Use Audit to check a drawing file for errors or corrupted data. If errors are detected, AutoCAD will optionally correct them. The command line is **Audit**.

To Use Audit

1. Choose **File ➤ Management ➤ Audit**.

2. Fix errors detected? <N>: Select **Y** to correct any errors found. Selecting **N** reports errors but will not fix them.

If no errors are detected, a screen display like the following will be appear:

```
4  Blocks audited
Pass 1 4 objects audited
Pass 2 4 objects audited
total errors found 0 fixed 0
```

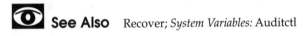 **NOTES**   Audit creates an ASCII file that contains a report of the audit and any action taken. The file has the extension .ADT. The information presented by the Audit command may not be important to most users. However, it may help your AutoCAD dealer or Autodesk's product support department to diagnose a problem with a file.

See Also   Recover; *System Variables:* Auditctl

AUTOLISP

AutoLISP is a programming language embedded in AutoCAD. It allows you to automate repetitive tasks and add your own custom commands to AutoCAD. AutoLISP enables you to link applications written in C to AutoCAD. Several AutoLISP programs are provided with AutoCAD, and others can be obtained from computer bulletin boards such as the Autodesk forum on CompuServe.

To Use AutoLISP

1. Enter your AutoLISP program code directly through the command prompt, or write your code with a word processor and store it as an ASCII file with the file name extension .LSF.

2. If you save your program code as a file on disk, use the AutoLISP *Load* function to load your program while in the AutoCAD drawing editor or issue the **Appload** command. The following example shows the syntax for the *Load* function at the command line:

    ```
    (load "drive/directory/file name") ↵
    ```

    You can leave off the drive and directory information if either your DOS path or the *Acad* environment variable points to the directory that holds the AutoLISP programs.

3. You can also open the Appload dialog box and save the LISP file in the list box, then activate it by selecting *Load*.

4. Once a program file is loaded, you can use it by entering its name through the keyboard, just like a standard AutoCAD program. You don't have to load the file again while in the current editing session.

NOTES You can combine your favorite AutoLISP programs into a single file called *Acad.LSP*. Place this file in your AutoCAD directory. It will be loaded automatically every time you open a drawing file. AutoLISP code can also be embedded in the Auto-CAD menu system. For information on how to edit an AutoCAD menu file, consult *Mastering AutoCAD Release 13 by George Omura (SYBEX, 1995).*

 **See Also**   Appload

BASE

When you insert one drawing into another, Base sets the drawing's *base point,* a point of reference for insertion. You select the base point in relation to the world coordinate system (WCS). The default base point for all drawings is the WCS origin point at coordinate 0,0,0.

To Set a Base Point

1.   At the command line, enter **Base** (or **'Base**, to use transparently).

2.   Base point <0.0000,0.0000,0.0000>: Enter the coordinates of a point or pick a point.

 **See Also**   Block; Ddinsert; Insert; Select; Wblock; *System Variables:* Insbase

BHATCH

Bhatch opens a dialog box with hatching options. It enables you to fill an enclosed boundary defined by lines, arcs, circles, and poly-lines with a predefined pattern or a simple hatch pattern by point-ing to it. Or you can make the hatch pattern "associative" so that it is updated when the boundary is changed. The pattern can also be previewed before being applied. The command line is **Bhatch**.

To Use the Bhatch Dialog Box

1. In **Windows**, choose Draw Toolbar ➤ Hatch flyout ➤ Hatch button. In **DOS**, choose Draw ➤ Hatch.

2. Pick the appropriate options from the Bhatch dialog box.

 OPTIONS

Pattern Type Allows you to set hatch patterns using *Pre-defined* stored patterns from the *ACAD.PAT* file, *User-Defined* single line patterns, or *Custom* patterns. An onscreen graphic allows you to cy-cle through the predefined patterns by simply clicking on the graphic. A full set of ISO standard hatch patterns is included in the ACAD.PAT file.

Pattern Properties Allows you to change the pattern *Scale*, *Angle*, and *Spacing*. You may optionally *Double* (cross-hatch) the hatch pat-tern or *Explode* it. If an ISO hatch pattern has been selected, you may select an *ISO Pen Width* to produce ISO-related scaling.

Boundary controls aspects of boundary definition. *Pick Points* prompts you to pick a point within the bounded area. Selecting text contained within a bounded area creates an imaginary rectangle around the text and prevents it from being hatched. If Island Detec-tion (below) is enabled, objects within the boundary are defined as "islands." *Select Objects* allows you to select objects or use **Osnap** modes to define the area to be hatched. *Remove Islands* removes from the boundary set "islands" defined by the *Pick Points* option.

View Selections highlights boundaries and objects selected for the hatching area, then returns you to the dialog box.

Inherit Properties Allows you to select an existing associative hatch object and apply its properties to the current hatch pattern.

Preview Hatch Displays a preview of the hatch pattern, then returns you to the dialog box.

Advanced Options Allows you to control the method AutoCAD uses to define the boundary set or to make a new boundary set. *Style* allows you to set boundary options by selecting from a list box, or visually by clicking on an on-screen icon. *Ray Casting* determines how AutoCAD finds the enclosed border for the hatch pattern when you pick a point. You can also *Retain Boundaries* as a polyline; if you don't choose this option, it is erased after the hatch pattern is created. *Island Detection* allows you to specify whether objects within the outermost boundary are to be hatched or to be treated as "islands."

Associative Associates the hatch pattern with the hatch boundary object, so that it will adjust its shape when the object boundary is changed.

Apply Applies the selected pattern to the bounded area.

NOTES You cannot copy a hatch pattern created with a version of AutoCAD earlier than Release 12. Hatched boundaries can be defined by a line, arc, circle, 2D or 3D polyline, 3D face, and viewport objects. Areas in nested blocks can also be hatched.

See Also Hatch; *System Variables:* Hpang, Hpbound, Hpdouble, Hpname, Hpscale, Hpspace

BLIPMODE

When you draw with AutoCAD, tiny crosses called *blips* appear wherever you select points. These blips are not part of your drawing; they merely help you locate the points that you have selected. You can use Blipmode to suppress these blips if you don't want them.

To Reset Blipmode

1. At the command line, enter **Blipmode** (or **'Blipmode**, to use transparently).

2. ON/OFF <current setting>: Enter **ON** or **OFF**.

 **OPTIONS**

ON   Displays blips when you enter points.

OFF   Suppresses blips when you enter points.

 See Also   Ddrmodes; *System Variables:* Blipmode

BLOCK

Block groups a set of drawing objects together to act as a single object. You can then insert, copy, mirror, move, rotate, scale, or save the block as an external file. The command line is **Block**.

To Create a Block

1. In **Windows**, choose Draw toolbar ➤ Block flyout ➤ Block button. In **DOS**, choose Construct ➤ Block.

2. Block name (or ?): Enter the name for the block. Enter a question mark to list existing blocks.

3. Insertion base point: Enter a coordinate value or pick a point to set the base point of the block.

4. Select objects: Pick objects to include in the block. The objects you select will disappear, but you can restore them as individual objects by using the **Oops** command. If your block includes attributes, select each one in the order you wish them to appear in the dialog box.

NOTES Blocks exist only within the drawing in which they are created. However, you can convert them into drawing files with the **Wblock** command. Blocks can contain other nested blocks. You can include attributes in blocks to allow the input and storage of information with the block; see **Attdef**.

If you attempt to create a block that has the same name as an existing block, you will see the prompt:

```
Block <name> already exists.
Redefine it? <N>
```

To redefine the existing block, enter **Y**. The Block command proceeds as usual and replaces the existing block with the new one. If the existing block has been inserted into the drawing, the new block appears in its place. If **Regenauto** has been turned off, the new block will not appear until you issue a **Regen** command.

To insert an exploded block into a drawing, preface the block name with an asterisk.

See Also Attedit, Attdisp, Attext, Attredef, Ddatte, Insert, Regen, Regenauto, Wblock, Wildcard characters, Xbind, Xref,

BOUNDARY

Boundary makes a region or polyline boundary from overlapping objects. It displays a dialog box to automatically create a polyline boundary from enclosed objects by picking a point within the area. The command line is **Boundary**.

To Create an Enclosed Polyline or Region

1. In **Windows**, choose Draw Toolbar ➤ Polygon flyout ➤ Boundary button. In **DOS**, choose Construct ➤ Boundary.

2. Specify the object type (polyline or region), and define the boundary set and other parameters.

3. Click on the Pick Points button in the Boundary Creation dialog box. Pick a point within the connected objects. This highlights the boundary, then joins the objects into a polyline or region.

 NOTES Boundary uses the same options and parameters as the **Bhatch** command. Refer to **Bhatch** for further details.

See Also Area, Bhatch, Pedit, Polygon, Psfill, Region

BREAK

Break erases a line, trace, circle, or arc, or a polyline between two points.

To Use Break

1. In **Windows**, choose Modify toolbar ➤ Break flyout ➤ (Preset options). In **DOS**, choose Modify ➤ Break ➤ (Preset options).

2. Select object: Pick an object to be broken.

3. Enter second point (or F for first point): Pick second point of break or enter **F** to specify first and second points.

 **OPTIONS**

1 Point Breaks an object in one place, at the point of selection.

1 Point/Select Allows you to select the object first, and then specify the break point.

2 Points Allows you to break an object in two places. The *first* break is at the point of selection.

2 Points/Select Allows you select the object, and then specify the *first* break point.

 **NOTES** If you use the cursor to pick the object, the "pick" point becomes the first point of the break. Pick the second point of the break or enter **F** to specify a different first break point. If you selected the object using a window, crossing window, wpolygon, cpolygon, fence, or a *Last* or *Previous* option, you are automatically prompted for a first and second point.

Break does not work on three-dimensional faces, blocks, solids, text, or shapes. When breaking circles, you must use the proper break-point selection sequence:

- A counterclockwise sequence causes the break to occur between the two break points.

- A clockwise sequence causes the segment between the two points to remain and the rest of the circle to disappear.

See Also Change, Trim

N E W

CAL

Cal is an on-line calculator. It stores calculated values as variables that can be recalled any time during the current editing session. It can be used transparently to supply values in response to command prompts. Cal also allows you to translate between World and UCS coordinates. The command line is **Cal** (or **'Cal**, to use transparently).

To use the Calculator

1. In **Windows**, choose Standard toolbar ➤ Object Snap flyout ➤ Calculator button. In **DOS**, choose Tools ➤ Calculator.

2. >>**Expression:** Enter the desired mathematical expression.

NOTES Cal evaluates vector (point), real, or integer expressions. The expressions can access existing geometry using the object snap functions such as Cen, End, and Ins. You may insert AutoLISP variables into the arithmetic expression and assign the value of the expression back to an AutoLISP variable. You may use these arithmetic and vector expressions in any AutoCAD command that expects points, vectors, or numbers.

CHAMFER

Chamfer joins two unparallel lines with an intermediate line or bevel, or adds intermediate lines between the line segments of a two-dimensional polyline. The command line is **Chamfer**.

To Use Chamfer

1. In **Windows**, choose Modify toolbar ➤ Feature Flyout ➤ Chamfer button. In **DOS**, choose Construct ➤ Chamfer.

2. **Polyline/Distance/Angle/Trim/Method<select first line>:** Pick first line.

3. **Select second line:** Pick second line.

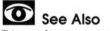 **OPTIONS**

Polyline Allows you to chamfer all line segments within a polyline. This option prompts you to select a two-dimensional polyline. All the joining polyline segments are then chamfered.

Distance Allows you to specify the length of the chamfer. This option prompts you for the first and second chamfer distance. These are the distances measured from the intersection point of the two lines to the beginning of the chamfer.

Angle Allows you to specify the angle of the bevel from a selected point on the line segment.

Trim Allows you to toggle the Trim option on or off, and set it as a temporary default. Turning Trim off allows you to add a bevel while retaining the original line segments.

Method Allows you to establish a default method of chamfering, either by distance or angle.

See Also Fillet; *System Variables:* Chamfera, Chamferb, Trimmode

CHANGE

Change can alter several properties of an object. You can change all the properties of lines. Move line end points by selecting a point at the first prompt. If you select several lines, all of the end points closest to the selected point are moved to the new point. If the Ortho mode is on, the lines become parallel and their end points align with the selected point.

You can change the color, layer, or line type of arcs, circles, and polylines. You can also change the rotation angle or layer assignment of a block. The command line is **Change**.

To Change the Properties of an Object

1. In **Windows**, choose Modify toolbar ➤ Resize flyout ➤ Point button. In **DOS**, choose Modify ➤ Point.

2. Select objects: Select objects to be changed.

3. Properties/<change point>: Enter **P** to change the property of the selected object(s), or select a line and change its end point.

4. Change what property (Color/Elev/LAyer/LType/ ltScale/Thickness) ?): Enter the desired option.

5. Depending on what you have selected to change, some or all of the following prompts will appear:

- Enter text insertion point: Pick new location for text.

- New style or RETURN for no change: Enter style for text. The style must have previously been created using the **Style** command.

- New height <height>: Enter new height.

- New rotation angle <0>: Enter new rotation angle.

- New text <text>: Enter new text.

- New tag <tag name>: Enter new attribute tag name.

- New prompt <prompt>: Enter new attribute prompt.

- New default value <value>: Enter new attribute value.

OPTIONS

Color Prompts you for color to change selected objects to.

Properties Changes the color, elevation, layer, line type, or thickness of an object.

Elev Prompts you for a new elevation in the object's Z axis.

LAyer Prompts you for a new layer.

LType Prompts you for a new line type.

LtScale Prompts you for a new LtScale value for the selected object(s).

Thickness Prompts you for a new thickness in the object's Z axis.

 NOTES The *Thickness* option will extrude into the Z axis a two-dimensional line, arc, circle, or polyline. This option does not work on blocks, however. *Elev* changes an object's location in the Z axis.

When you change an object's color, the object no longer has the color of the layer on which it resides. This can be confusing in complex drawings. To make an object the same color as its layer, enter **Bylayer** at the *Color* prompt.

See Also Chprop, Color, Ddmodify, Select

CHPROP

Chprop works like the **Change** command except that Chprop allows you to change the properties of all object types regardless of their three-dimensional orientation. However, the *Elev* option is not offered—use the **Move** command instead. The equivalent dialog box command is **Ddchprop**.

To Change an Object's Properties

1. At the command line, enter **Chprop**.

2. Select objects: Select objects whose properties you wish to modify.

3. Change what property (Color/LAyer/lType/LtScale/ Thickness)?: Enter the option.

 **OPTIONS**

Color Prompts you for a color to which selected objects will be changed.

LAyer Prompts you for a new layer.

LType Prompts you for a new line type.

LtScale Prompts you for a new LtScale value for the selected object(s).

Thickness Prompts you for new thickness in the object's Z axis.

 See Also   Change, Color, Ddchprop, Elev, Select

CIRCLE

Circle offers several methods for drawing circles, the default being to choose a center point and enter or pick a diameter or radius. The command line is **Circle**.

To Draw a Circle

1. In **Windows**, choose Draw toolbar ➤ Circle flyout. In **DOS**, choose Draw ➤ Circle.

2. Circle 3P/2P/TTR/<Center point>: Pick a center point, then provide a diameter or radius by dynamically picking or entering a value.

 **OPTIONS**

3P (3 Point) Allows you to define a circle based on three points. Once you select this option, you are prompted for a first, second, and third point. The circle will be drawn to pass through these points.

2P (2 Point)   Allows you to define a circle's diameter based on two points. Once you select this option, you are prompted to select the first and second point. The two points will be the opposite ends of the diameter.

TTR (Tangent, Tangent, Radius)   Allows you to define a circle based on two tangent points and a radius. The tangent points can be on lines, arcs, or circles.

COLOR/COLOUR

Color/Colour sets the color of objects being drawn. Once you select a color, all objects will be given the selected color regardless of their layers, unless you specify *Bylayer* as the color. Objects you drew before using the Color command are not affected. This dialog box equivalent is **Ddcolor**.

To Set the Color of Objects

1.   Enter **Color** or **Colour** at the command line (or **'Color** or **'Colour**, to use transparently).

2.   New object color <current default>: Enter the color.

 **OPTIONS**

Bylayer   Gives objects the color of the layer on which they are placed. It is the default color setting.

Byblock   Works on objects used in blocks. If such an object is assigned the Byblock color, it will take on the color of the layer in which the block is placed.

Table 2 shows the color names that AutoCAD recognizes, and their number codes. You can enter any of these names or numbers—in fact, you can enter any number from 1 to 255. The color that is displayed depends on your display adapter and monitor, but the first seven colors are the same for most display systems.

Table 2: Color Names Recognized by AutoCAD

Color Name	Color Number
Red	1
Yellow	2
Green	3
Cyan	4
Blue	5
Magenta	6
White	7

Command Name	Color
Bylayer	Color of the layer on which the object is located
Byblock	Color of the layer on which the block is located

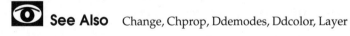 **NOTES**   Assign colors carefully, especially if you use them to distinguish different layers. The Color... subdialog box is accessible also through the Object Properties toolbar.

See Also   Change, Chprop, Ddemodes, Ddcolor, Layer

COMPILE

You can create your own text fonts and shapes by compiling a shape/font description file. This file is an ASCII file that uses a special system of codes to describe your fonts or shapes. Compile displays a dialog box listing ASCII files with .SHB or .PFB extensions for converting into a form that lets AutoCAD read the descriptions and include them in a drawing. The command line is **Compile**.

To Compile Your Own Text Fonts

1.   Choose Tools Menu ➤ Compile.

- When the *Filedia* system variable is set to 1, Compile opens the Select Shape or Font File dialog box, displaying .SHP extensions for Shape files or .PFB extensions for PostScript files. Enter a Shape/Font file name into the *File:* box to compile into a .SHX extension.

- When *Filedia* is set to 0 and Compile is entered at the command line, the following prompt appears:

2.   Enter NAME of shape file: Enter the shape or font file name.

CONFIG

Use Config to configure AutoCAD for specific input and output devices and display systems. You can also control plotting optimization and aspect ratio, screen aspect ratio, network capabilities, the location of temporary files, and much more.

To Configure AutoCAD

1. Choose Options ➤ Configure.

2. A screen appears showing the current configuration. Press ↵ to go to the Configuration menu.

3. Enter the number of the configuration option you wish to access.

4. After you have gone through the configuration, you are returned to the Configuration menu. You can enter the number of another configuration option or enter **0** to exit the Configuration menu and return to the main menu.

5. After you enter 0, you are prompted to save the configuration changes you have just made. Press ↵ to accept the changes or enter **N** to cancel the changes and return to the previous settings.

 OPTIONS

0. Exit to drawing editor Lets you exit the Configuration menu. You are then asked whether you want to save your configuration changes.

1. Show current configuration Displays the current configuration.

2. Allow detailed configuration Gives you access to more detailed configuration options. These include plotter optimization and the control of the display colors on color systems.

3. Configure video display Lets you control the aspect ratio of your drawing editor screen. You can also turn on or off the various parts of the drawing editor screen. You can control the colors shown in the drawing editor if you select option 2 before picking this option.

4. Configure digitizer Lets you control the sensitivity of your pointing device. If you use a digitizer, you can change the puck configuration. Port assignments can also be controlled through this option.

40   Config

5. Configure Plotter   Allows multiple configurations, displaying a menu to add, delete, change, or rename a plotting or printing device. Lets you adjust the plotter output aspect ratio and change post assignments. If you use option 2 before issuing this option, you can also control pen optimization. Most of the other options can also be changed using the **Plot** command. To adjust the aspect ratio, draw a square that measures 5 units by 5 units. Use this square to help adjust the plotter aspect ratio. When the *Cmddia* system variable is set to 1, the Plot command displays a Device and Default Selection... subdialog box that allows you to view, save, get, or change configurations prior to plotting.

6. Configure system console   This option is not applicable to IBM-type computers.

7. Configure operating parameters   Lets you control a variety of default settings and network features, as follows:

Alarm on error   Turns on a beep sound when errors occur.

Initial drawing setup   Lets you use a prototype drawing file other than the standard Acad.DWG.

Default plot file name   Lets you specify a plot-to-file file name extension.

Plot spooler directory   Lets you specify a directory in which to store your plot files. (Some plot-spooling software can periodically check a directory and automatically plot new files that appear there.)

Placement of temporary files   Lets you specify where Auto-CAD is to place temporary files. For non-386 versions, directing AutoCAD to store temporary files in a RAM disk can improve overall speed. This option is also useful in networks.

Network node name   Lets you segregate temporary files by specifying a unique file name extension. This is useful when several people are working on files in the same directory of a network server.

Automatic save feature   Lets you save your drawing to a name of your choice for set time intervals.

Full-time CRC (Cyclic Redundancy Check) validation   Lets you control an error-checking mechanism built into AutoCAD.

Automatic audit after DXFIN or DXBIN Controls the auditing of imported files of the DXF or DXB file type (see **Audit**).

Login name Used to specify the default login name of AutoCAD nodes on a network or stand-alone station.

File locking Lets you control the file-locking function of AutoCAD and allows updating of server authorization codes when network nodes are added.

 **NOTES** When you first install AutoCAD, you are asked to specify a video display, pointing device, and plotter. If you change your display or input/output hardware, you must run the appropriate configuration option to inform AutoCAD of the change.

See Also Plot

COPY

Copy copies a single object or a set of objects. The command line is **Copy**.

To Copy

1. In **Windows**, choose the Modify toolbar ➤ Copy flyout ➤ Copy Object button. In **DOS**, choose Construct ➤ Copy.

2. Select objects: Select objects to be copied.

3. <Base point or displacement>/Multiple: Pick the reference or "base" point for copy or enter **M** for multiple copies. The M option instructs AutoCAD that you wish to make several copies and prompts you for the base point again.

4.   Second point of displacement: Pick the copy distance and direction in relation to the base point or enter the displacement value.

 **OPTIONS**

Multiple   Allows you to make several copies of the selected objects. The second point is repeated until you press ↵ or Ctrl-C.

NOTES   AutoCAD assumes you want to make copies within the current user coordinate system (UCS). However, you can make copies in three-dimensional space by entering **0,0,0** as the base point and the desired X,Y,Z coordinates as the second point, or by using the **Osnap** overrides to pick objects in three-dimensional space.

If you press ↵ at the Second point: prompt without entering a point value, the selected objects may be copied to an area that is off your current drawing. To recover, use the **Undo** command. For multiple copying using grips, see **Move**.

See Also   Array, Grips, Move, Multiple, Select

CUT and PASTE

Windows Only

The Cut and Paste facility allows you to copy and transfer information between AutoCAD and other Windows applications using the Windows Clipboard, while retaining the ability to edit the information in the source application. It also lets you exchange graphics between multiple AutoCAD sessions.

To Cut or Copy to the Clipboard

1. Select the object(s) or view you wish to Cut/Copy.

2. Choose Edit ➤ Cut, Copy, or Copy View.

 OPTIONS

Cut   Cuts selected objects to the Windows Clipboard. Cutting deletes the selected objects from the current drawing and stores them
on the Clipboard for pasting into another drawing or application.
The Cut command can also be activated by choosing Standard toolbar ➤ Cut, using the control key sequence Ctrl-X, or by using **Cut-
clip** at the command line.

Copy   Lets you copy all or part of an AutoCAD drawing to another
application via the Windows Clipboard. The copied object does not
retain any link to the original. It is *embedded* in the other application
(see **OLE**). The Copy command can also be activated by choosing
Standard toolbar ➤ Copy, using the control key sequence Ctrl-C, or
by using **Copyclip** at the command line.

Copy View   Lets you copy a selected view or viewport to the Clipboard and *link* it to another drawing or application (see **OLE**). The
linked view retains a connection to the source. If the source view is
changed, you may update the linked copy by updating the link (see
Olelinks). The Copy View command can also be activated by using
Copylink at the command line.

Copyhist   Allows you to copy the current command line history
(all of the text in the AutoCAD text window) to the Clipboard. At
the command line, use **Copyhist**.

To Paste Objects from the Clipboard

Choose Edit ➤ Paste or Paste Special.

 **OPTIONS**

Paste   Lets you paste AutoCAD objects (usually from another drawing), text and other Windows file formats (bitmap, metafile, and multimedia) from the Clipboard into an AutoCAD drawing. Graphic objects are inserted at the top-left corner of the drawing area. You may click on them and drag them into position or resize them using the object "handles." Pasted Text is inserted at the top-left corner and becomes an Mtext object. Once objects have been inserted, you can edit them in their native applications by double-clicking on them in AutoCAD. The Paste command can also be activated by using the control key sequence Ctrl-V or by using **Pasteclip** at the command line.

Paste Special   Lets you insert objects from the Windows Clipboard, link objects to their source application, and/or convert the file format. When you start the Paste Special command, the Paste Special dialog box opens, showing the following information and options: Source shows the name of the application in which the Clipboard object was created; the Paste and Paste Link radio buttons allow you select whether to simply insert the object into the drawing or to maintain a *link* with the source file (see **OLE**); the As List box lists the file formats you can use to paste the Clipboard object into the current drawing; the *Convert* option converts Windows metafile format into AutoCAD format for future editing. The Paste Special command can also be activated by using **Pastespec** at the command line.

 See Also   Insertobj, OLE, Olelinks

DBLIST

Dblist lists the properties of all objects in a drawing.

To Display Drawing Information

Enter **Dblist** at the command prompt.

 **NOTES** When you invoke Dblist, the screen switches to Text mode and the list of objects pauses at each screen of text. Press Enter to continue. Dblist is similar to the **List** command.

 See Also List

DDATTDEF

Ddattdef opens the Attribute Definition dialog box that lets you create attribute definitions that can store textual and numeric data with a block. The command line is **Ddattdef**.

To Create an Attribute Definition

1. In **Windows**, choose Attribute toolbar ➤ Ddattdef button. In **DOS**, choose Construct ➤ Attribute.

2. Provide information as needed in the dialog box(es).

OPTIONS

Mode Sets Invisible, Constant, Verify, and Preset modes.

Attribute Sets Tag name, input Prompt, and default Value.

Insertion Point Allows you to Pick Point or enter the XYZ coordinates.

Text Options Sets text Justification, Text Style, Height, or Rotation.

Align below previous attribute Locates an attribute tag below a previously defined attribute.

NOTES Use **Change** or **Ddedit** to edit the attribute definition. Attribute tags are always displayed in uppercase.

See Also Attdef, Change, Ddedit

DDATTE

Ddatte displays the Edit Attributes dialog box that lets you view
and edit the attribute values of a single block. The equivalent
command-line prompt is **Attedit**. The command line is **Ddatte**.

To Edit Attribute Values

1. In **Windows**, choose Attributes toolbar ➤ Ddatte button.
    In **DOS**, choose Modify ➤ Attribute ➤ Edit…

2. Select block: Pick the block containing the attribute(s) to edit.

3. The Edit attributes dialog box appears containing the attrib-
    ute prompts and values. Enter new attribute text or edit the
    existing attribute text by positioning the cursor at the appro-
    priate location, deleting text, and typing your correction.

See Also Attdef, Attedit, Attext, Ddattdef, Ddattext,
Multiple

DDATTEXT

Ddattext displays an Attribute Extraction dialog box allowing you
to convert attributes into external ASCII text files. These files can

then be imported into database or spreadsheet programs. The equivalent command-line prompt is **Attext**.

To Convert Attributes to ASCII

1. In **Windows**, enter **Ddattext** at the command line. In **DOS**, choose File ➤ Export ➤ Attributes...

2. File Format: Pick CDF, SDF, or DXF format for the extracted file.

3. Select Objects: Temporarily exits the dialog box, allowing you to select the attribute entities.

4. Template File...: Opens the standard file dialog box, displaying a list box showing all .TXT files from which to make a selection for the corresponding edit box. A .TXT file extension is automatically assigned to the file name in the edit box if you don't enter an extension.

5. Output File...: Opens the Output File subdialog box, displaying a list box showing all .TXT files from which to make a selection for the corresponding edit box. When a template file name is selected, the current drawing file name is automatically assigned to the file name in the edit box but with a .TXT extension.

NOTES The *Template File...* button is disabled when the DXF format is active.

See Also Attdef, Attedit, Attext, Ddattdef, Multiple

DDCHPROP

Ddchprop opens the Change Properties dialog box that lets you change properties of all object types. The equivalent command-line prompt is **Chprop.** The command line is **Ddchprop.**

To Change an Object's Properties

1. At the command line, enter **Ddchprop.**

2. **Select objects:** Select the object(s) whose properties you wish to modify.

 **OPTIONS**

Color Opens the Select Color dialog box to set object colors. (See **Color/Colour.**)

Layer... Opens the Select Layer dialog box, displaying a list of layer names to make a selection.

Linetype... Opens the Select Linetype dialog box, displaying *Bylayer, Byblock,* and a list of linetypes to make a selection.

Ltscale/Linetype Scale: Edit box to change selected object's LtScale value.

Thickness: Edit box to change an object's 3D thickness.

See Also Change; Chprop; Color; Ddemodes; Ddlmodes; Layer; Linetype; *System Variables*: Thickness

DDCOLOR

N E W

Ddcolor opens the Select Color dialog box and allows you to set the color for new objects. Once you select a color, all objects will be given the selected color regardless of their layers, unless you specify *Bylayer* as the color.

To Set the Object Color

1. In **Windows**, choose Object Properties ➤ Color Control button. In **DOS**, choose Data ➤ Color.

2. **Select objects:** Select the object(s) whose color you wish to set.

 **OPTIONS**

Bylayer   Gives objects the color of the layer on which they are placed. It is the default color setting.

Byblock   Works on objects used in blocks. If such an object is assigned the By block color, it will take on the color of the layer in which the block is placed.

 See Also   Color, DDemodes, Layer

DDEDIT

Ddedit changes a text or attribute definition. Ddedit displays a line of text in a dialog box for editing and viewing. You can position a cursor to delete single characters, make corrections, or add to the text. The equivalent command-line prompt is **Change**. The command line is **Ddedit**.

To Edit Text Objects

1. In **Windows**, choose Modify toolbar ➤ Special Edit flyout ➤ Text Edit button. In **DOS**, choose Modify ➤ Edit Text.

2. <Select a TEXT or ATTDEF object>/Undo: Pick the line of text or attribute definition to edit.

3. Depending upon your object selection, the Edit Text dialog box will open (with a *Text* edit box) or the Edit Attribute Definition dialog box will open (with the *Tag*, *Prompt*, and *Default* edit boxes).

 **OPTIONS**

Text Edit box for revising text.

Tag Edit box to change the tag name.

Prompt Edit box to change the attribute prompt.

Default Edit box to change the attribute value.

NOTES Every time you finish editing one line of text, AutoCAD will then prompt you to select another text or Attdef object rather than return you to the command prompt. To exit the Ddedit command, press ↵ twice (do not enter any text at the last **Text:** or **Attdef:** prompt).

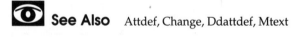 **See Also** Attdef, Change, Ddattdef, Mtext

DDEMODES

Ddemodes opens the Object Creation Modes dialog box that sets several object creation modes including default color, linetype, elevation, and thickness of objects being drawn, as well as the current default layer, text style, and linetype scale. You can also use the equivalent **Color**, **Linetype**, **Elev**, **Layer**, and **Style** commands to set these modes individually. The command line is **Ddemodes** (or **'Ddemodes**, to use transparently).

To Open the Ddemodes Dialog Box

1. In **Windows**, choose Object Properties toolbar ➤ Object Creation... In **DOS**, choose Data ➤ Object Creation...

2. Provide information as needed in the dialog box(es).

 **OPTIONS**

Color... Opens the Select Color dialog box to set the current default color for objects being drawn. (See **Color** or **Ddcolor**.)

Layer... Opens the Layer Control subdialog box to select and edit layer settings.

Linetype... Opens the Select Linetype subdialog box displaying linetypes to set the current default linetype for objects being drawn.

Text Style... Opens the Select Text Style subdialog box to show and set the current default text style. A list box appears with the currently loaded text styles. You cannot create new text styles in this dialog box; you must use the **Style** command to create a text style. The *Show All...* button displays the entire symbol set. The text font, height, width, obliging angle, and orientation are also identified.

LtScale/Linetype Scale Edit box to change the LtScale value of the objects being drawn.

Elevation Edit box used to set the current default elevation of objects being drawn. This elevation value is the distance in the Z axis from the XY plane of the current user coordinate system (UCS).

Thickness Edit box used to set the default thickness of objects being drawn. This value is a distance along the Z axis of the object.

 NOTES The default value for the color and linetype setting is Bylayer, which sets an object color or linetype to that of the layer in which it is placed.

See Also Change, Color, Elev, Layer, Linetype

DDGRIPS

Ddgrips displays the Grips dialog box for controlling selection methods, grip color, and size. Grips allows you to determine the selection-set sequence by first entering the objects or the command. The command line is **Ddgrips** (or **'Ddgrips**, to use transparently).

To Open the Grips dialog box

1. Choose Options ➤ Grips…

2. Provide information as needed in the dialog box(es).

OPTIONS

Select Settings Lets you *Enable Grips* to pick objects for editing using a grip box. *Enable Grips Within Blocks* determines whether one grip appears for the block or multiple grips appear for the entities in the block.

Grip Colors Opens the standard color dialog box to define a color for *Unselected* grips that are not filled in or for *Selected* solid grips.

Grip Size   Controls grip size using a slider bar and adjacent tile box.

📑 NOTES   Grips can be set with their specific system variables and are associated with specific AutoCAD commands, including **Stretch**, **Move** (multiple copy), **Rotate**, **Scale**, and **Mirror**.

👁 See Also   *System Variables:* Gripblock, Gripcolor, Griphot, Grips, GripsizeDD

DDIM

Ddim opens the Dimension Styles dialog box and allows you to set and visually control dimension and extension line settings, arrow type and size, text location and format, measurement units, dimension text appearance, and colors. Dimension styles can now have "families" of different settings. From a parent style, you can now specify different settings for each member of the family. The command line is **Ddim** (or **'Ddim**, to use transparently).

To Create and Modify Dimension Styles

1.   In **Windows,** choose Dimensioning toolbar ➤ Dimstyle flyout ➤ Dimstyle button. In **DOS,** choose Data ➤ Dimension Style.

2.   The Dimension Styles list box contains the names of all the dimension styles that were created for the current drawing. To activate a style, pick it from the list box with your cursor and the style will appear in the Name edit box. The Family settings allow you to specify variations in the style for each of the related dimension types: *Linear, Radial, Angular, Diameter, Ordinate,* or *Leader.*

3.   Once you have selected the appropriate dimension style, use the Geometry, Format, and Annotation subdialog boxes to make changes to the Dimension Style.

 **OPTIONS: GEOMETRY**

The Geometry sub-dialog box allows you to manipulate the appearance of the geometry and overall scale of the dimension. All Geometry settings are stored as *Dimension Variables*.

Dimension Line Controls the appearance of the dimension line. You can **Suppress** the display of dimension lines when they are outside the extension lines; option **1** suppresses the first dimension line and stores the value in the variable *Dimsd1*; option **2** suppresses the second dimension line and stores the value in the variable *Dimsd2*. When you are using oblique strokes (ticks) rather than arrows on the dimension line, the **Extension** option allows you to specify the distance that the dimension line is to extend beyond the extension line (*Dimdle* variable). The **Spacing** option allows you to enter a distance for the spacing between the dimension lines of a baseline dimension (*Dimdli* variable). The **Color** option allows you to set the color for a dimension line via the Select Color dialog box, or by entering a color value in the text box (*Dimclrd* variable).

Extension Line Controls the appearance of the extension lines. The **Suppress** option suppresses the display of extension lines; option **1** suppresses the first extension line and stores the value in the variable *Dimse1*; option **2** suppresses the second extension line and stores the value in the variable *Dimse2*. The **Extension** option allows you to specify a distance to extend the extension line above the dimension line (*Dimexe* variable). The **Origin Offset** allows you to specify a distance for the offset between the extension lines and the origin points (*Dimexo* variable). The **Color** option allows you to display and set the color for an extension line, via the Select Color dialog box or by entering a color value in the text box (*Dimclre* variable).

Arrowheads Controls the appearance of the arrowheads. By default the second arrowhead is set the same as the first selected and the value is stored in the *Dimblk* variable. You may also specify different arrowheads for the first and second arrowheads; in that case, the values are stored in the *Dimblk1* and *Dimblk2* variables. The **Size** option displays and sets the size of arrowheads (*Dimasz* variable). To change the size, enter a value in the text box. Selecting User Arrow... from the preset options shown in the 1st and 2nd

Arrowhead drop boxes, opens the User Arrow dialog box and allows you to load a user-defined arrowhead (*Dimsah* variable).

Center   Controls the appearance of center marks and lines for the diameter and radial dimensions used by the **Dimcenter**, **Dimdiameter,** and **Dimradius** commands. When you are using Dimdiameter or Dimradius, the center mark will be drawn only if you position the dimension line outside the circle or the arc. The Mark option creates a center mark; the Line option creates a center line; the None option creates no center mark or line; and the Size option displays and sets the size of the center mark or line. All of these values are stored in the *Dimcen* variable: a center mark is stored as a positive value; a center line is stored as a negative value; None is stored as a zero; and the size is stored as an actual value.

Overall Scale   Sets the overall scale factor of your drawing by specifying size, distances, or offsets and storing it in the *Dimscale* variable.

Scale to Paper Space   AutoCAD calculates the scale factor based on scaling between the current model-space viewport and paper space. Selecting Scale to Paper Space deactivates Feature Scaling and converts the *Dimscale* value to 0.0.

 OPTIONS: FORMAT...

The Format sub-dialog box allows you to set the location of dimension text, arrowheads, leader lines, and the dimension line. All Format settings are stored as *Dimension Variables*.

User Defined   Allows you to pick a location for dimension text by specifying a position at the Dimension line location prompt (*Dimupt* variable). If this option is not selected, AutoCAD determines the location of dimension text using the Horizontal Justification settings.

Force Line Inside   Draws dimension lines between extension lines even when arrowheads are placed outside the extension lines (*Dimtofl* variable).

Fit   Controls the placement of text, arrowheads, and leader lines inside or outside the extension lines based on the available space between the extension lines (*Dimfit* variable).

Horizontal Justification   Controls the horizontal justification of text along dimension and extension lines (*Dimjust* variable). The **Centered** option centers the text between the extension lines; **1st Extension Line** left-justifies the text along the dimension line, near the first extension line; **2nd Extension Line** right-justifies the text along the dimension line, near the second extension line; **Over 1st Extension Line** positions the text parallel to the first extension line; **Over 2nd Extension Line** positions the text parallel to the second extension line.

Text   Determines the position of dimension text inside and outside the extension lines. **Inside:** when this is selected, text inside the extension lines will always be horizontal, rather than aligned with the dimension line (*Dimtih* variable). **Outside:** when this is selected, text outside the extension lines will always be horizontal (*Dimtoh* variable).

Vertical Justification   Controls the vertical justification of dimension text along the dimension line (*Dimtad* variable). **Centered** centers the text between the extension lines; **Above** positions the text above the dimension line, at a distance determined by the *Annotation: Gap* option; **Outside** positions the text on the side of the dimension line farthest away from the defining points; and **JIS** sets the text position to conform to Japanese Industrial Standards.

OPTIONS: ANNOTATION...

The Annotation sub-dialog box allows you to specify the measurement units for dimensions, alternate measurement units, tolerances for dimension text, dimension text style variables, and linear and paper space scale factors. All Annotation settings are stored as *Dimension variables*.

Primary Units   Controls the display of primary measurement units and also lets you add a **Text Prefix** or **Text Suffix** to the default dimension text by entering labels in each edit box (*Dimpost variable*). The Units button opens the Primary Units dialog box and allows you to set all the measurement variables. The **Units** section lets you select the unit format, Decimal, Scientific, Engineering, Architectural, or Fractional (*Dimunit* variable). The **Angles** section lets you select the angle format, Decimal degrees, Degrees/Minutes/Seconds, Grads, Radians, and Surveyor. In the Dimension section you can specify the **Precision** or number of decimal places to be used in measurements (*Dimdec*) and also the **Zero Suppression** setting (*Dimzin*). The Zero Suppression setting contains check boxes for setting the appearance of **Feet** and **Inches** as well as suppressing **Leading** and **Trailing** zeros in dimension text. In the **Scale** section, the **Linear** option sets a length scale variable, which specifies a global scale factor for dimension length (*Dimlfac* variable). Checking the **Paper Space Only** box allows you to dimension accurately in paper space using model space units. AutoCAD stores the length scale for paper space as negative value in the Dimlfac variable.

Alternate Units   This option allows you to set alternate unit dimensioning. The variables are identical to those in the Primary Units, including labels for alternate dimension text **Prefix** and **Suffix**. The *Dimaltd, Dimaltf, Dimalttd, Dimalttz, Dimaltu, Dimaltz,* and *Dimaunit* variables are all manipulated in this option.

Tolerance   This option allows you to create tolerances for dimension text, with a choice of **None**, **Symmetrical** (a plus/minus expression of tolerance in one direction), **Deviation** (a plus/minus expression in both directions), **Limits** (a limit expression with the maximum value over the minimum value), and **Basic**. The Basic option creates dimension text with a box drawn to its full extents. Depending upon the choice selected, you will need to specify **Upper** and/or **Lower Value**, and **Text Justification** (Top/Middle/Bottom) and **Height** for the tolerance text. The variables *Dimtol, Dimlim, Dimtm, Dimtolj, Dimtp,* and *Dimtfac* are used to store the tolerance values.

Text   This option allows you to manipulate text style, height, text gap, and text color. The **Style** list box allows you to display and set the current style for dimension text (*Dimtxsty* variable). Use the Style command if you need to modify a style for dimension text. **Height** allows you to set the current dimension text height. If text style is set to 0, you can enter a dimension **Height**, which will be stored in the *Dimtxt* variable. The **Gap** option specifies the text gap (*Dimgap* variable), which determines a number of dimension text positioning variables: the distance around dimension text at the dimension line break; the distance of dimension text above a dimension line; and the position of the box drawn around tolerance text (*Tolerance Option: Basic Method*). The **Color** option allows you to set the color for dimension text (*Dimclrt* variable), via the Select Color Dialog box, or by entering a color value in the text box. The selected color is shown in the color box.

Round Off This option controls the rounding off of all dimension measurements (*Dimrnd* variable). A value of 0.25 will round all measurements to the nearest 0.25 unit; a value of 1.0 rounds all measurements to the nearest unit. The rounding value is not applied to angular dimensions.

 See Also   Ddunits, Dimensioning Commands, Units

DDINSERT

Ddinsert opens the Insert dialog box for inserting a block into your drawing. You can preset the block's insertion point, scale, and rotation angle, or insert the block as an exploded block. The equivalent command-line prompt is **Insert**. The command line is **Ddinsert**.

To Insert a Block

1. In **Windows**, choose Draw toolbar ➤ Block flyout ➤ Insert Block ... In **DOS**, choose Draw ➤ Insert... ➤ Block.

2. Provide information as needed in the dialog box(es).

 OPTIONS

Block...   Opens the Defined Blocks in this Drawing subdialog box offering an alphabetical list of the blocks that have been defined in your drawing. Select from this list for a block to insert. The *Pattern* edit box can be used as a query with wildcards to filter block names. Picking a block name from the list with your cursor duplicates the block name in the *Selection* edit box.

Files… Opens the Select Drawing File subdialog box showing a list of *Directories* and drawing *Files*. An image tile box displays a preview of selected drawings.

Specify Parameters on Screen Allows you to specify the block's insertion point from the command line or by picking a point on the screen. When enabled, you can avoid prompts by preselecting *Insertion Point*, *Scale*, and *Rotation* by recording that information in their appropriate edit boxes. When the *Attdia* variable value is 1, an Attribute Edit dialog box appears during block insertion.

Explode Inserts an exploded version of the block into your drawing. The equivalent command-line procedure requires an asterisk before the block name:

```
Insert
Block name (or ?): <*block name>
```

 **See Also** Base; Ddatte; Insert; *System Variables:* Attdia, Attreq, Insbase

DDLMODES

Ddlmodes displays the Layer Control dialog box for control of layers. The equivalent command-line prompt is **Layer**. The command line is **Ddlmodes** (or **'Ddlmodes**, to use transparently).

To Invoke Ddlmodes Layer Control

1. In **Windows**, choose Object Properties toolbar ➤ Layers…, or choose Data ➤ Layer… In **DOS**, choose Data ➤ Layers…

2. Provide information as needed in the dialog box(es).

60 Ddlmodes

 **OPTIONS**

Current Layer Identifies the current layer.

Layer Name/State/Color/Linetype Displays a list box with an alphabetized list of layer names, including their status, color, and linetype.

Select All Highlights all layers in the list box.

Clear All Deselects all layers in the list box.

New Enter new layer name or names (separating each with a comma) in the edit box below before picking New to add them to the list box.

Current Highlight the desired layer in the list box for display in the edit box before picking Current to change the current layer name at the top of the dialog box.

Rename First highlight the layer in the list box for editing in the edit box enter its new name, then pick Rename.

On Highlight layers in list box, then pick On to change the assignment adjacent to each layer name, turning selected layers on.

Off Highlight layers in list box, then pick Off to change the assignment adjacent to each layer name, turning selected layers off.

Thaw Highlight layers in list box, then pick Thaw to change the assignment adjacent to each layer name, thawing selected layers.

Freeze Highlight layers in list box, then pick Freeze to change the assignment adjacent to each layer name, freezing all selected layers.

Unlock Highlight layers in list box, then pick Unlock to change the assignment adjacent to each layer name, unlocking all selected layers.

Lock Highlight layers in list box, then pick Lock to change the assignment adjacent to each layer name. Locking selected layers preserves objects on that layer from editing. However, their color and linetype can be changed, turned on/off, and thawed/frozen.

📍 OTHER OPTIONS

When *Tilemode* is set to 0 (off) you are in paper space and can manipulate layers in model-space viewports or paper space as follows:

Cur VP: Thw Highlight layer with cursor in list box, then pick Thw to change the assignment with "." adjacent to the layer name in current active model-space viewport or paper space.

Cur VP: Frz Highlight layers with cursor in list box, then pick Frz to change the assignment with **C** adjacent to layer name in current active model-space viewport or paper space. Freezing or thawing layers from the *Cur VP:* boxes overrides global setting.

New VP: Thw Highlight layers with cursor in list box, then pick Thw to change the assignment with "." adjacent to the layer name, thawing layers in new viewports.

New VP: Frz Highlight layers with cursor in list box, then pick Frz for assignment of **N** adjacent to layer name, freezing layers in new viewports.

Set Color... Displays the Select Color subdialog box to choose color for selected layers. (See **Color/Colour** and **Ddcolor**.)

Set Ltype... Opens the Select Linetype subdialog box to choose linetype for selected layers. (See **Linetype** for loading layers.)

Filters Opens the Set Layer Filters subdialog box using a popup list to assist in grouping portions of common layer names to turn *On/Off*, *Freeze/Thaw*, *Lock/Unlock*, in *Current Vport* or *New Vports*. Wildcards can be used in edit boxes to search *Layer Names*, *Colors*, and *Ltypes*. *Reset* cancels the filtering process. Picking *On* toggles the visibility of the filtered layers in the list box.

👁 **See Also** Color; Layer; Linetype; Mspace; Mview; Pspace; Rename; *System Variables:* Tilemode, Viewports, Vplayer

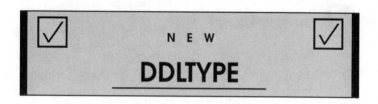

Ddltype opens the Select Linetype dialog box that allows you to view, select, and load linetypes. The command line is **Ddltype**.

To Change or Load the Linetype

1. In **Windows**, choose Object Properties toolbar ➤ Linetype button or Data ➤ Linetype… In **DOS**, choose Data ➤ Linetype…

2. Click on the desired linetype in the list box.

 **OPTIONS**

ISO pen width Allows you to view and edit an ISO pen width setting from the selected list box.

Linetype Scale Allows you to enter a scale factor that will affect both existing and newly created objects.

Load Opens the Load or Reload Linetypes subdialog box to view and select predefined linetypes stored in the *Acad.LIN* file or user-defined linetypes stored in alternate .LIN files.

NOTES The list box shows the linetypes that have already been loaded. If you do not see the linetype you require, click on the *Load* button to view and select from more standard linetypes.

See Also Linetype; Ltscale; *System Variables*: Celtscale, Psltscale

DDMODIFY

Ddmodify opens a dialog box specific to the object selected, including 3dfaces, arc, associative hatch, attribute, body, block, circle, definitions, dimension, ellipse, external reference, leader, line, mtext, point, polyline, ray, region, shape, solid, spline, trace, text, viewport or xline. The upper portion of each dialog box contains a Properties section to modify color, linetype, layer name, and thickness. The command line is **Ddmodify**.

To Modify an Object

1. In **Windows**, choose Object Properties toolbar ➤ Properties… In **DOS**, choose Modify ➤ Properties…

2. **Select object to modify:** Pick the object you wish to change. [Retain prompt above.]

3. Provide information as needed in the dialog box(es).

 OPTIONS

The following controls are common to all the Modify dialog boxes:

Color…   Picking this button or its adjacent color swatch displays the Select Color subdialog box to change a layer color. (See **Color/Colour, Ddcolor**.)

Layer…   Opens the Select Layer subdialog box to change an object's layer by highlighting it in the *Layer Name* list box or entering it in the *Set Layer Name* edit box.

Linetype…   Opens the Select Linetype subdialog box to change linetype for selected layers. (See **Linetype** for loading layers.)

Handle   Displays the AutoCAD "handle" or unique identifier associated with the object selected.

Thickness   An edit box to enter an object's thickness value.

LtScale/Linetype Scale An edit box to change an object's Ltscale value.

 **OTHER OPTIONS**

The control options presented vary depending upon the type of object selected. The following controls are found in one or more of the Modify dialog boxes:

X,Y,Z Edit boxes for relocating an object's initial coordinates.

Pick Point If you are using the current UCS (user coordinate system), you can temporarily exit the dialog box to pick a new point on the screen, using your cursor or entering coordinates from the command line.

Scale and Rotation Edit boxes to update the object's XYZ scale and rotation.

Justify Opens a popup list of text justifications.

Style Opens a popup list of text styles currently defined in your drawing by the **Style** command. Additional check boxes are included to toggle *Text* as Right Side Up/Upside Down or Forward/Backward, and to select *Mode* as Invisible, Constant, Verify, and/or Preset.

Radius and Angle Edit boxes to change an arc angle's *Radius, Start Angle,* and *End Angle* while displaying Total Angle and Arc Length.

Tag Edit box to change an attribute's tag value.

Prompt Edit box to modify an attribute's prompt label.

Default Edit box to alter an attribute's default assignment.

Height, Rotation, Width Factor, and Obliquing Edit boxes to change each property.

Size, Rotation, Width Factor and Obliquing Edit boxes to change each property using the current UCS to define angles and points.

Columns and Rows Edit boxes to create a rectangular array of a block.

Col Spacing and Row Spacing Edit boxes to set the columns and row spacing for a rectangular array of a block. This feature duplicates the **Minsert** command.

Radius Edit box lets you enter a new radius while displaying the Diameter, Circumference, and Area of a circle.

Columns and Rows Edit boxes to create a rectangular array of an external reference (xref).

Vertex Listing Lists successive vertices of coordinate X, Y, and Z values for polylines.

Fit/Smooth Offers option buttons for changing the type of line or surface curve fitting from None to Quadratic, Cubic, Bezier, or Curve Fit.

Mesh Provides toggles to set Closed or Open mesh in the M or N direction for polylines. Also provides boxes accepting a range between 2 and 200 to control the accuracy of surface approximation in the M and N directions when using surface fit for a 3D polyline mesh. The edit boxes store the system variables *Surfu* and *Surfv*.

Polyline Displays check boxes to confirm a Closed polyline and to establish an LT Gen (linetype generation) pattern.

Visibility Toggles to make a 3Dface's edges invisible. Assigning the system variable *Splframe* to 1 makes all edges visible regardless of the visibility settings.

👁 **See Also** Arc, Attdef, Block, Circle, Ddattdef, Dimensioning Commands, Dtext, Layer, Line, Pline, Point, Shape, Solid, Text, 3DFace, Trace, Viewports, Xrefs

DDOSNAP

Ddosnap displays the Running Object Snap dialog box allowing you to have multiple object snap modes active while picking specific geometric points on an object and to set the target box size for your graphic's cursor crosshairs. To override a running osnap, enter the specific osnap at the command line. The equivalent command-line commands are **Osnap** and **Aperture**. The command line is **Ddosnap** (or **'Ddosnap**, to use transparently).

To Set the Osnaps

1.   Choose Options ➤ Running Object Snap…

2.   Select settings as appropriate in the dialog box.

 **OPTIONS**

Select Settings   Activating one or more pick boxes in this section lets your pick location determine the osnap modes applied. For example, if both the Endpoint and Midpoint boxes are checked, AutoCAD automatically selects the mode based on which point is closer to the target box. Each mode can be overridden at the command line by entering the uppercase letters shown:

ENDpoint   Picks the end point of objects.

MIDpoint   Picks the midpoints of lines and arcs.

CENter   Picks the center of circles and arcs.

NODe   Picks a point object. (See **Ddptype**.)

QUAdrant   Picks a main point on an arc or circle.

INTersection   Picks the intersection of objects.

INSertion   Picks the insertion point of blocks and text.

PERpendicular   Picks the point on an object perpendicular to the last point.

TANgent   Picks a tangent point on a circle or arc.

NEArest   Picks the point on an object nearest to the cursor.

Apparent Intersection   Picks the apparent intersection of two dimensionally separated lines.

Quick   Shortens the time it takes AutoCAD to find an object snap point. Quick does not work in conjunction with INTersect.

Aperture Size   This section lets you adjust the aperture box size by moving the slider bar and viewing it in the adjacent tile box.

NOTES   Cancel all osnap modes from the dialog box by deselecting all pick boxes. Entering **Osnap** at the command line and pressing ↵ at the **Object snap modes:** prompt will also cancel all osnap modes.

See Also   Aperture; Osnap; Point Selection; *System Variables:* Aperture, Osmode

DDPTYPE

Ddptype opens the Point Style dialog box to select and control the appearances of points and to place point objects in your drawing, using the Node Osnap override. Points also appear as markers for the **Divide** and **Measure** commands. The command line is **Ddptype** (or **'Ddptype**, to use transparently).

To Set a Point Style

1.   Choose Options ➤ Display ➤ Point Style...

2.   Select a point style, and define the point size.

 OPTIONS

The dialog box offers 16-point mode image tiles. Pick the desired tile, then use the *Point Size* edit box to adjust point size.

Point Size   Edit box for setting point size. Selecting an option button changes the size specifications from Relative to Absolute as described below.

Set Size Relative to Screen   Option button to set point size as percentage of screen size.

Set Size in Absolute Units   Option button to set actual point size based on absolute units.

 **See Also**   Point; *System Variables:* Pdmode, Pdsize

DDRENAME

Ddrename opens the Rename dialog box to change the name of a block, dimension style, group, layer, linetype, text style, user coordinate system, named view, or viewport configuration. The command line is **Ddrename**.

To Activate the Rename Dialog Box

1.   Choose Data ➤ Rename…

2.   Select the appropriate object from the Named Objects list box.

 **OPTIONS**

Selecting the object from the *Named Objects* list box registers associated names in the *Items* list box. Pick the item to be renamed and it will appear in the *Old Name* edit box.

Old Name   Enter item to be renamed or pick from *Items* list box. Use wildcards for renaming groups of objects with common characters.

Rename To: Enter new name of item(s) shown in the *Old Name* edit box, using wildcards for groups of objects with common characters, then pick the *Rename To* box. The renamed objects will appear in the Items list box.

NOTES   Ddrename can also be used to find out which objects are in use in a current drawing.

 **See Also**   Rename, Wildcard characters

DDRMODES

Ddrmodes opens the Drawing Aids dialog box to change several mode settings by accessing the functions for **Ortho**, **Fill** (Solid·Fill), **Group**, **QText**, **Blipmode**, **Snap**, **Grid**, **Isoplane**, and the system variable *Highlight*. The command line is **Ddrmodes** (or '**Ddrmodes**, to use transparently).

To Open the Ddrmodes Dialog Box

1.   Choose Options ➤ Drawing Aids…

2.   Select the desired function from the dialog box.

 OPTIONS

When you issue Ddrmodes, the following options appear as checkboxes in which you can either select an option or enter a distance value.

Modes   Pick boxes to toggle *Ortho* mode, *Solid Fill*, *Quick Text*, *Blips*, *Highlight*, and *Groups*. Ortho mode forces lines to be drawn vertically or horizontally following the orientation of the crosshairs. The **Fill** command makes areas solid for solids, traces and polylines. Quick Text uses the **Qtext** command to temporarily replace text with rectangles to reduce drawing regeneration. Blips are toggled on or off with the **Blipmode** command, placing tiny crosses on the screen when you select points. The *Highlight* system variable controls the ghosting appearance of objects when selected. *Groups* toggles automatic group selection on or off.

Snap   Picking *On* sets the Snap mode, while the *X Spacing*, *Y Spacing*, and *Snap Angle* edit boxes let you adjust the spacing and angle of the X and Y axis. *X Base* and *Y Base* edit boxes let you enter a Snap basepoint's X and Y coordinates. The F9 function key or the Ctrl-B combination performs the same toggle function as the Snap pick box. *Snap Angle* values determine the orientation of crosshairs on the screen.

Grid   Picking *On* toggles Grid mode on and off, to display a series of reference dots on the screen. Edit boxes for *X Spacing* and *Y Spacing* allow you to set the same intervals for your Grid and Snap distances.

Isometric Snap/Grid   Picking *On* switches your drawing to an isometric view. Option buttons set the cursor orientation for *Left*, *Top*, and *Right* drawing planes.

 **See Also**   Blipmode; Dtext; Fill; Grid; Isoplane; Ortho; Qtext; Snap; *System Variables:* Gridmode, Gridunit, Orthomode, Pickstyle, Snapang, Snapbase, Snapisopair, Snapmode, Snapstyl, Snapunit

DDSELECT

Ddselect opens the Object Selection Settings dialog box to define your method for selecting objects. The command line is **Ddselect** (or **'Ddselect**, to use transparently).

To Set Object Modes

1. Choose Options ➤ Selection…

2. Provide information as needed in the dialog box(es).

OPTIONS

Selection Modes   Multiple settings can be configured from this section. **Noun/Verb Selection:** adds a target box to the graphics cursor for selecting objects prior to issuing specific commands, thus permitting the cursor to function as a pickbox. Table 3 shows the commands that support noun/verb selections.

Table 3: Commands Allowing You to Use the Cursor as a Pick Box

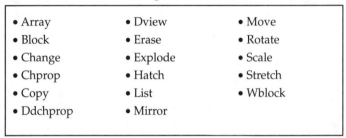

• Array	• Dview	• Move
• Block	• Erase	• Rotate
• Change	• Explode	• Scale
• Chprop	• Hatch	• Stretch
• Copy	• List	• Wblock
• Ddchprop	• Mirror	

The Selection Modes section also offers the following combinations for object selection methods: **Use Shift to Add:**, which allows you to select or deselect multiple objects for Noun/Verb Selection sets; **Press and Drag:**, which permits you to hold down the pick button, drag, then release, for creating a selection window; **Implied Windowing:**, which enables you to use a selection window by picking from left to right, or use a crossing window by picking from right to left at the **Select objects:** prompt; **Object Grouping**, which toggles object grouping on or off; **Default:**, which returns the Selection Mode settings to their original Noun/Verb Selection and Implied Windowing.

Pickbox Size This section furnishes a slider bar with an image tile to dynamically alter your pickbox size.

Object Sort Method This section opens the Object Sort Method subdialog box and lets you rearrange the following sort methods for objects in your database:

Object Selection

Object Snap

Redraws

Slide Creation

Regens

Plotting

PostScript Output

 See Also Ddgrips, Grips, SystemVariables: Noun/Verb Selection-Pickfirst, Use Shift to Add-Pickadd, Press and Drag-Pickdrag, Implied Windowing-Pickauto, Pickbox Size-Pickbox, Object Grouping-Pickstyle

DDUCS

Dducs opens the UCS Control dialog box to rename, restore, list, or delete any existing UCS (user coordinate system). The command line is **Dducs**.

To Restore an Existing UCS

1. In **Windows**, choose Standard toolbar ➤ UCS flyout Named UCS button or View ➤ Named UCS… In **DOS**, choose View ➤ Named UCS…

2. View or provide information as needed in the dialog box.

OPTIONS

Current Select the UCS to be made current from the UCS Names list box.

Delete Deletes a highlighted UCS from the list box.

List… Opens the UCS dialog box to display origin point and direction of X, Y, and Z axis relative to current UCS.

Rename To: Highlight *name* in list box for editing in the edit box, then pick *Rename To:* to confirm new UCS name in the list box.

NOTES   The list box always contains the *World* Coordinate System name. Entries for *Previous* and *No Name* may also appear.

See Also   Ddrename; Dview; Elev; Plan; Rename; UCS; Vpoint; *System Variables:* Thickness, Ucsfollow, Ucsicon, Ucsname, Ucsorg, Ucsxdir, Ucsydir, Worlducs

DDUCSP

Dducsp opens the UCS Orientation dialog box. It displays image tiles of preset UCS (User Coordinate System) views, and allows you select one and change the current UCS setting. The command line is **Dducsp**.

To Select a Preset UCS

1.   In **Windows**, choose Standard toolbar ➤ UCS flyout ➤ Preset UCS button or View ➤ Preset UCS. In **DOS**, choose View ➤ Preset UCS…

2.   Select preset image tile and set it *Relative to Current UCS* or *Absolute to WCS.*

OPTIONS

(Image tiles)   For the following UCS orientations: World, Top, Back, Left, Front, Right, Current View, Bottom, and Previous.

Relative to Current UCS   Option button to change current UCS based on an associated image tile.

Absolute to WCS   Option button to change UCS based on an associated image tile.

👁 **See Also**   Dducs; Dview; Plan; *UCS; System Variables:* Ucsfollow, Ucsicon, Ucsname, Ucsorg, Ucsxdir, Ucsydir, Worlducs

DDUNITS

Ddunits opens the Units Control dialog box to set up the drawing's units of measure, angle measurement and direction, and precision. The command line is **Ddunits** (or **'Ddunits**, to use transparently).

To Display the Ddunits Dialog Box

1. Choose Data ➤ Units…
2. Provide information as needed in the dialog box(es).

 OPTIONS

Units   This section includes the following option buttons for setting units of measure: Scientific, Decimal, Engineering, Architectural, and Fractional.

Angles   This section provides the following option buttons to set angle measurement: Decimal Degrees, Deg/Min/Sec, Grads, Radians, and Surveyor.

Precision   A list box displays default accuracy levels for measurement units and angles.

Direction…   This option opens a **Direction Control** subdialog box with option buttons to indicate the direction of angles: East, North, West, and South. An *Other* option button enables a *Pick* button and *Angle* edit box as options.

DDVIEW

Ddview opens the View Control dialog box to make, delete, and re-store views.

To Invoke the Ddviews Dialog Box

1. Choose View ➤ Named Views...

2. Provide information as needed in the dialog box(es).

 OPTIONS

Views   Displays view names with Pspace or Mspace.

Restore   Pick button to restore view by highlighting view name from the list box.

New...   Opens the Define New View subdialog box for saving a new view. Option buttons allow you to save the *Current Display* as a view or to *Define Window.* Assign a *New Name* in the edit box, then use the *Window* button to temporarily exit dialog box for creating the view. Pick the *Save View* button to exit. Display boxes identify X and Y coordinates for the *First Corner* and *Other Corner.*

Delete   Pick button to delete view by highlighting view name from the list box.

Description...   Opens the View Description subdialog box specifying data on the highlighted view.

 See Also   Mspace; Pspace; *System Variables:* Tilemode, View

DDVPOINT

Ddvpoint opens the Viewpoint Presets dialog box for establishing a 3D view by dynamically picking an angle from the X axis in the XY plane. The command line is **Ddvpoint**.

To Set a 3D View

1.   Choose View ➤ 3D Viewpoint ➤ Rotate...
2.   Provide information as needed in the dialog box.

 OPTIONS

The Viewpoint Presets dialog box provides pick buttons to *Set Viewing Angles* Absolute to WCS or Relative to UCS. An image tile box rotates a white arm to preset viewing angles with your cursor when picking outside the circle and to specific angles when picking within the circle. The designated angle then appears in the edit box for X Axis and XY Plane. Picking *Set to Plan View* shifts the view to plan view relative to the selected coordinate system.

 See Also   Plan, View, Vpoint

DELAY

Delay lets you set a designated time period for viewing a slide in a script file.

To Delay a Slide

1. At the command line enter **Delay** (or **'Delay**, to use transparently).

2 Delay time in milliseconds: Enter the desired number (maximum 32767 ms).

 See Also Mslide, Rscript, Script, Vslide

DIMENSIONING COMMANDS

Prior to Release 13, dimensioning was accomplished by first using the Dim command to put the command line in dimensioning mode (Dim: mode), then issuing a dimensioning subcommand. With Release 13, many of the dimensioning subcommands have been implemented as full commands and are available through the Windows toolbars, the DOS menus, and the command line.

Moreover, some sets of the previous dimensioning subcommands have been grouped into entirely new dimensioning commands. For example, the new **Dimlinear** command combines the previous **Dim: Horizontal**, **Dim: Vertical**, and **Dim: Rotate** subcommands; the new **Dimedit** command combines the **Dim: Hometext**, **Dim: Newtext**, and **Dim: Trotate** subcommands.

To maintain compatibility with previous versions of AutoCAD, all of the existing Dimensioning mode subcommands are still available and may be used in the same way.

In this section, the new Dimensioning commands are outlined first: **Dimaligned** to **Dimtedit**. Dimensioning mode subcommands that do not have a new corresponding command are then documented: **Dim: Exit** to **Dim: Variables**.

AutoCAD generally uses the same types of dimensions and dimension label components as standard drafting. Figure 2 gives examples of the five types of dimensions possible in AutoCAD drawings: linear, angular, diametric, radial, and ordinate. Dimension labels consist of the elements illustrated in Figure 3.

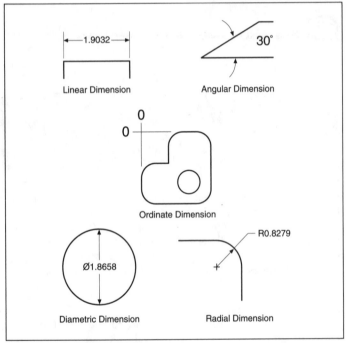

Figure 2: Types of dimensions

VARIABLES FOR CONTROLLING DIMENSIONS

Table 4 describes variables that control the way AutoCAD draws dimensions. These variables control extension line and text location, tolerance specifications, arrow styles and sizes, and other aspects of dimensioning.

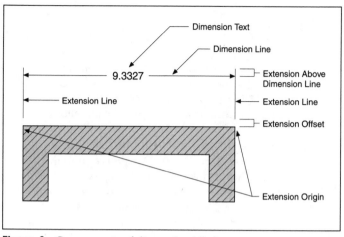

Figure 3: Components of dimension labels

Table 4: The Dimension Variables

Variable	Description
Dimalt	When on, dimension texts for two measurement systems are inserted simultaneously (**alt**ernate). Dimaltf and Dimaltd must also be set appropriately. The alternate dimension is placed within brackets. Angular dimensions are not affected. This variable is commonly used when inches and metric units must be displayed at the same time in a dimension. The default setting is off.
Dimaltd	When Dimalt is on, Dimaltd controls the number of decimal places the alternate dimension will have (**alt**ernate **d**ecimal places). The default value is 2.

Table 4: The Dimension Variables (continued)

Dimaltf	When Dimalt is on, Dimaltf controls the multiplication factor for the alternate dimension (**alt**ernate **f**actor). The value held by Dimaltf will be multiplied by the standard dimension value to determine the alternate dimension. The default value is 25.4, the number required to display metric units.
Dimalttd	When Dimalt is on, Dimalttd controls the alternate tolerance decimal places (**alt**ernate **t**olerance **d**ecimal). The default value is 2.
Dimalttz	When Dimalt is on, Dimalttz controls the alternate tolerance zero suppression (**alt**ernate **t**olerance **z**ero suppression). The default value is 0.
Dimaltu	When Dimalt is on, Dimaltu controls the the alternate units (**alt**ernate **u**nits). The default value is 2.
Dimaltz	When Dimalt is on, Dimaltz controls the alternate unit zero suppression (**alt**ernate unit **z**ero suppression). The default value is 0.
Dimapost	When Dimalt is on, you can use Dimapost to append text to the alternate dimension (**alt**ernate **post**). For example, if Dimapost is given the value *mm*, the alternate dimension will appear as valuemm instead of just value. The default value is nul. To change a previously set value to nul, enter a period for the Dimapost new value.
Dimaso	When on, dimensions will be associative (**asso**ciative). When off, dimensions will consist of separate drawing entities with none of the associative dimension properties. The default is on.
Dimasz	Sets the size of dimension arrows or Dimblks (**a**rrow **s**ize). If set to 0, a tick is drawn in place of an arrow (see Dimblk). The default value is .18 units.

Table 4: The Dimension Variables (continued)

Dimaunit	Sets the angle unit format. The default value is 0 = decimal degrees. Other settings are: 1=degrees/mins/secs/; 2=Gradians; 3=Radians; 4= Surveyor's Units.
Dimblk	You can replace the standard AutoCAD dimension arrow with one of your own design by creating a drawing of your symbol and making it a block. You then give Dimblk the name of your symbol block. This block must be drawn corresponding to a one-by-one unit area and must be oriented as the right-side arrow. The default value is nul.
Dimblk1	With Dimsah set to on, you can replace the standard AutoCAD dimension arrows with two different arrows using Dimblk1 and Dimblk2. Dimblk1 holds the name of the block defining the first dimension arrow, while Dimblk2 holds the name of the second dimension arrow block.
Dimblk2	See Dimblk1.
Dimcen	Sets the size of center marks used during the Center, Diameter, and Radius dimension subcommands. A negative value draws center lines instead of the center mark cross, while a 0 value draws nothing. The default value is 0.09 units.
Dimclrd	Lets you specify colors for dimensions lines, arrowheads, and dimension leader lines.
Dimclre	Sets color for dimension extension lines.
Dimclrt	Sets color for dimension text.
Dimdec	Sets the number of decimal places for tolerance values of a primary unit. The initial value is 4.
Dimdle	With Dimtsz given a value greater than 0, dimension lines can extend past the extension lines by the amount specified in Dimdle (dimension line extension). This amount is not adjusted by Dimscale. The default value is 0.

Table 4: The Dimension Variables (continued)

Dimdli	Sets the distance at which dimension lines are offset when you use the Baseline or Continue dimension subcommands (dimension line increment). The default is 0.38 units.
Dimexe	Sets the distance the extension lines are drawn past the dimension lines (extension line extension). The default value is 0.18 units.
Dimexo	Sets the distance between the beginning of the extension line and the actual point selected at the Extension line origin: prompt (extension line offset). The default value is 0.0625 units.
Dimfit	Controls the placement of text an arrowheads inside or outside of extension lines. The default value is 3.
Dimgap	Sets the distance between the text and the dimension line and lets you enclose text within a box by assigning it a negative value. The default value is 0.09.
Dimjust	Controls the position and justification of text on dimension lines. The default value is 0.
Dimlfac	Sets the global scale factor for dimension values (length factor). Linear distances will be multiplied by the value held by Dimlfac. This multiple will be entered as the dimension text. The default value is 1.0. This can be useful when drawings are not drawn to scale.
Dimlim	When set to on, dimension text is entered as two values representing a dimension range rather than a single value. The range is determined by the values given to Dimtp (plus tolerance) and Dimtm (minus tolerance). The default value is off.

Table 4: The Dimension Variables (continued)

Dimpost	Automatically appends text strings to dimension text. For example, if Dimpost is given the value "inches," dimension text will appear as value inches instead of just value. The default value is nul. To change a previously set value to nul, enter a period for the Dimpost new value. If you use Dimpost in conjunction with appended dimension text, the Dimpost value is included as part of the default dimension text.
Dimrnd	Sets the amount to which all dimensions are rounded. For example, if you set Dimrnd to 1, all dimensions will be integer values. The number of decimal places affected depends on the precision value set by the Units command. The default is 0.
Dimsah	When set to on, allows the separate arrow blocks Dimblk1 and Dimblk2 to replace the standard AutoCAD arrows (separate arrow heads). If Dimtsz is set to a value greater than 0, Dimsah has no effect.
Dimscale	Sets the scale factor for dimension variables that control dimension lines and arrows and text size (unless current text style has a fixed height). If your drawing is not full scale, you should set this variable to reflect the drawing scale. For example, for a drawing whose scale is ¼" equals 1', you should set Dimscale to 48. The default value is 1.0.
Dimsd1	When turned on, this suppresses the drawing of the first dimension line. The default value is off.
Dimsd2	When turned on, this suppresses the drawing of the second dimension line. The default value is off.
Dimse1	When set to on, the first dimension line extension is not drawn (suppress extension 1). The default is off.

Table 4: The Dimension Variables (continued)

Dimse2	When set to on, the second dimension line extension is not drawn (**s**uppress **e**xtension **2**). The default is off.
Dimsho	When set to on, dimension text in associative dimensions will dynamically change to reflect the location of a dimension point as it is being moved (**sho**w dimension). The default is off.
Dimsoxd	When set to on, dimension lines do not appear outside of the extension lines (**s**uppress **o**utside e**x**tension **d**imension lines). If Dimtix is also set to on and the space between the extension lines prohibits the display of a dimension line, no dimension line is drawn. The default is off.
Dimstyle	Identifies the current dimension style. Use the Save and Restore dimensioning commands for alternate Dimstyles. The default is *UNNAMED.
Dimtad	When set to on and Dimtih is off, dimension text in linear dimensions will be placed above the dimension line (**t**ext **a**bove **d**imension line). When off, the dimension line will be split in two and text will be placed in line with the dimension line. The default value is off.
Dimtfac	Sets the scale factor for text height of tolerance values based on Dimtxt, the dimension text height variable. Use Dimtfac to display the plus and minus characters when Dimtol is on and Dimtm does not equal Dimtp, or when Dimlim is on. The default is 1.0.
Dimtih	When set to on, dimension text placed between extension lines will always be horizontal (**t**ext **i**nside **h**orizontal). When set to off, text will be aligned with the dimension line. The default value is on.
Dimtix	When set to on, dimension text will always be placed between extension lines (**t**ext **i**nside e**x**tension). The default value is off.

Table 4: The Dimension Variables (continued)

Dimtm	When Dimtol or Dimlin is on, Dimtm determines the minus tolerance value of the dimension text (tolerance minus).
Dimtofl	With Dimtofl on, a dimension line is always drawn between extension lines even when text is drawn outside (text outside— forced line). The default is off.
Dimtoh	With Dimtoh on, dimension text placed outside extension lines will always be horizontal (text outside—horizontal). When set to off, text outside extension lines will be aligned with dimension line. The default is on.
Dimtol	With Dimtol on, tolerance values set by Dimtp and Dimtm are appended to the dimension text (tolerance). The default is off.
Dimtolj	Sets the vertical justification of tolerance values relative to the nominal dimension text. The default is 0 (=bottom).
Dimtp	When Dimtol or Dimlim is on, Dimtp determines the plus tolerance value of the dimension text (tolerance plus).
Dimtsz	Sets the size of tick marks drawn in place of the standard AutoCAD arrows (tick size). When set to 0, the standard arrow is drawn. When greater than 0, tick marks are drawn and take precedence over Dimblk1 and Dimblk2. The default value is 0.
Dimtvp	When Dimtad is off, Dimtvp allows you to specify the location of the dimension text in relation to the dimension line (text vertical position). A positive value places the text above the dimension line while a negative value places the text below the dimension line. The dimension line will split to accommodate the text unless the Dimtvp value is greater than 1.

Table 4: The Dimension Variables (continued)

Dimtxsty	Specifies the text style of the dimension. The default text style is standard.
Dimtxt	Sets the height of dimension text when the current text style height is set to 0. The default value is 0.18.
Dimtzin	Controls suppression of zeros for tolerance values.
Dimunit	Sets the unit format for all dimesion styles except angular dimensions. The default value is 2 (=Decimal). Other values are: 1=Scientific; 3=Engineering; 4=Architectural; 5=Fractional.
Dimupt	Controls how the cursor operates for User Positioned Text. The default is 0=off. Cursor controls only the location of the dimension line. The other toggle is 1=on. When Dimupt is on, you can use the cursor to position text as well as the dimension line.
Dimzin	Determines the display of inches when Architectural units are used. When set to 0, zero feet or zero inches will not be displayed. When set to 1, zero feet and zero inches will be displayed. When set to 2, zero inches will not be displayed. When set to 3, zero feet will not be displayed.

DIMENSIONING AND DRAWING SCALES

Take care when dimensioning drawings at a scale other than one-to one. If the *Dimscale* dimension variable is not set properly, arrows and text will appear too small or too large. In extreme cases, they may not appear at all. If you enter a dimension and arrows or text do not appear, check the Dimscale setting and make sure it is a value equal to the drawing scale.

STARTING THE DIMENSIONING PROCESS

Depending upon your system configuration or your preferences, you may access the dimensioning commands in a number of different ways.

- **Windows toolbar** From the Dimensioning toolbar, click on the appropriate Dimensioning button.

- **DOS Pull-down menu** From the Draw menu, select Dimensioning, then the appropriate option on the popup submenu.

- **Command line directly** Each dimensioning command can be invoked directly at the command prompt.

- **Command Line with Dim/Dim1** All of the dimensioning subcommands from previous releases of AutoCAD are still available in Release 13 for compatibility purposes. To use them, enter **Dim** or **Dim1** at the command prompt. At this point, the prompt changes to Dim: and you can enter any dimensioning subcommand. Use Dim1 if you want to enter a single dimension.

Dimaligned

Dimaligned aligns a dimension with two points or an object. The dimension text appears in the current style. Figure 4 illustrates the difference between aligned and rotated dimensions. Dimension settings are modified with the Ddim dialog box. On the command line, use Dimaligned.

To Align a Dimension

1. In **Windows**, choose Dimensioning toolbar ➤ Aligned Dimension button. In **Dos**, choose Draw ➤ Dimensioning ➤ Aligned.

2. First extension line origin or RETURN to select: Pick a first, then a Second point on the object you wish to dimension, or press ↵. If you press ↵, you will be prompted to select an object.

88 Dimensioning Commands

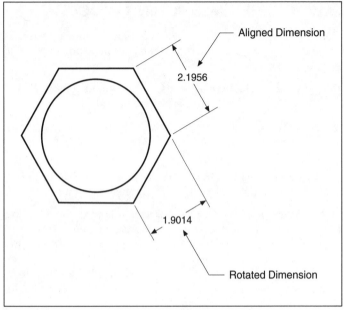

Figure 4: Aligned and rotated dimensions

3. Dimension line location (Text/Angle): If you wish to modify the text or text angle, enter an option (**T, A**). To position the dimension line dynamically, drag your cursor and pick a point; or enter a coordinate for the location of the dimension line.

 **OPTIONS**

Text This option (**T**) allows you to edit and customize the dimension text. In **DOS**, AutoCAD displays the dimension measurement at the command prompt Dimension Text<measured length>: and allows you to modify it. If you wish to enter a different value, enter it at the command prompt and press ⏎. If you wish to insert additional text before the dimension measurement, or append text after it, place angle bracket signs (<>) to represent the dimension value and add the desired text before or after. For example, if you wish to add "inches" *after* the value, type <> **inches** at the Dimension Text: prompt.

In **Windows**, when you select the Text option (**T**), AutoCAD opens the Edit Mtext dialog box, and allows you to change and customize the text. To change the measured dimension, enter a new value between the displayed angle brackets (<>). Enter text before or after the dimension value (<>) as desired. To add text above the dimension value, enter it before the <> and press ↵. To add text below the dimension value, press ↵ after the <> and then type the text.

Angle   This option (**A**) allows you to change the default angle of the text. Text will be placed horizontally (0 degrees) unless you specify a dimension text orientation at the Enter text angle: prompt.

Dimangular

Creates a dimension label showing the angle described by an arc, circle, or two lines, or by a set of three points. An arc with dimension arrows at each end is drawn and the angle value is placed using the current text style. Dimension settings can be modified with the Ddim dialog box. On the command line, use **Dimangular**.

To Create an Angular Dimension

1. In **Windows**, Choose Dimensioning toolbar ➤ Angular Dimension button. In **DOS**, choose Draw ➤ Dimensioning ➤ Angular.

2. Select arc, circle, line, or RETURN: Pick an object as indicated by the prompt or press ↵ to indicate angles using your cursor.

    • If you selected an arc or a circle, continue with step 3.

    • If you selected a line, you will be prompted Second line:. Select another line, and then continue with step 3.

    • If you pressed ↵, you may specify the desired angle by giving three points: the Angle vertex:, the First angle endpoint:, and the Second angle endpoint:. Then continue with step 3.

3.   Dimension arc line location (Text/Angle): If you wish to modify the text or text angle, enter an option (**T, A**). Otherwise, drag your cursor and pick a point, or enter a coordinate for the location of the dimension line as the extension line with text appears.

 **OPTIONS**

For a description of the *Text* and *Angle* options, see the **Dimaligned** command.

Dimbaseline

Dimbaseline draws a series of dimension strings using the baseline of the most recently inserted dimension as its first extension line. You are prompted only for the second extension line origin. Each dimension is placed above the last dimension and offset by an increment set in the *Dimdli* system variable. If the original dimension is linear, the new dimensions are drawn parallel to the first dimension. On the command line, enter **Dimbaseline**.

To Continue a Dimension from the Baseline

1.   In **Windows**, choose the Dimensioning toolbar ➤ Baseline Dimension button. In **DOS**, choose Draw ➤ Dimensioning ➤ Baseline.

2.   Second extension line origin: Pick a point or press ↵ to select a new base dimension.

3.   Select base dimension: Select a new base dimension and continue, or press ↵ to exit Dimbaseline.

Dimcenter

Dimcenter places a cross at the center point of a selected arc or circle. To choose center lines instead of a center cross, and to change the size of the center mark, use the *Dimcen* dimension variable, or reset them in the Geometry dialog box of the **Ddim** Command. On the command line use **Dimcenter**.

To Mark the Center of an Arc or Circle

1. In **Windows**, choose the Dimensioning toolbar ➤ Center Mark button. In **DOS**, choose Draw ➤ Dimensioning ➤ Center Mark.

2. Select arc or circle: Pick an arc or circle and the center mark will appear.

Dimcontinue

Draws a series, or "chain," of related dimensions by using the second extension line of the most recently inserted dimension as its first extension line. All of the "chained" dimension measurements add up to a total measurement of the object. You are prompted only for the second extension line origin. If the original dimension is linear, the related dimensions are placed in line with, and parallel to, this dimension. The *Dimfit* system variable controls the positioning of the dimension lines and text between the selected points. On the command line, use **Dimcontinue**.

To Continue a Dimension

1. In **Windows**, choose Dimensioning toolbar ➤ Continue Dimension button. In **DOS**, choose Draw ➤ Dimensioning ➤ Continue.

2. Second extension line origin or RETURN to select: Select as many points as you wish along the measured object. AutoCAD draws a series of dimensions, each starting from the second extension line of the last dimension in the chain. Press ↵ if you wish to pick a new dimension for the start point.

3. Select continued dimension: Pick a new dimension string and continue, or press ↵ to exit Dimcontinue.

Dimdiameter

Draws different types of diameter dimensions depending upon the size of the arc or circle, and upon the dimension settings created in

Ddim Format dialog box, and stored in the dimensioning system variables. On the command line, use **Dimdiameter**.

To Dimension an Arc or Circle Diameter

1. In **Windows**, choose the Dimensioning toolbar ➤ Radial Dimension Flyout ➤ Diameter Dimension button. In **DOS**, choose Draw ➤ Dimensioning ➤ Radial ➤ Diameter.

2. Select arc or circle: Pick the arc or circle as appropriate.

3. Dimension line location<Text/Angle>: If you wish to modify the text or text angle, enter an option (**T**, **A**). Or drag the cursor to position the text (and leader).

Unless you modify the text, the dimension value will be preceded by a diameter symbol. If a dimensioned circle or arc is large enough, the diameter dimension will be positioned within it. Otherwise it is positioned outside the circle or arc, with a leader line pointing to the center. A center mark is also placed at the center of the arc or circle.

 **OPTIONS**

For a description of the *Text* and *Angle* options, see the **Dimaligned** command.

NOTES The point at which you pick the arc or circle determines one end of the dimension arrow. If you want the dimension to be in a horizontal or vertical orientation, use the **Quadrant Osnap** override. Pick the left or right quadrant for a horizontal dimension; pick the top or bottom quadrant for a vertical dimension.

Dimedit

Dimedit is a new dimensioning command that allows you to change and manipulate selected text and extension lines. Dimedit can be used to change the same elements on several dimension objects at once. Using this command, you can Rotate text; shift it back to its original "home" position; and edit dimension text. The

Oblique option allows you to skew existing dimension extension lines to an angle other than 90 degrees to the dimension line.

To Edit Dimensions

1. At the command line, enter **Dimedit**.

2. DimensionEdit (Home/New/Rotate/Oblique) <Current>: Select an option or press ↵ to select the default.

3. Select Objects: Select as many dimension objects as desired.

 **OPTIONS**

Home   Repositions all selected dimension text objects in their default positions.

New   Allows you to replace dimension text on several dimensions at once. In **DOS**, at the prompt Dimension text < >: enter a new dimension string. All dimensions selected will be changed to the new text. In **Windows**, selecting New opens the Edit Mtext dialog box and allows you to change and customize the dimension text.

Rotate   Allows you to rotate all selected dimension text to a specified angle. At the prompt Enter text angle:, enter the required angle.

Oblique   Allows you to change all selected extension lines to a specified angle. At the prompt Enter obliquing angle (RETURN for none):, enter the required angle.

Dimlinear

Creates a linear dimension. Dimlinear allows you to position linear dimensions in either a horizontal or a vertical direction, as well as allowing you to rotate the dimension line and text to a specified angle. On the command line, use **Dimlinear**. This new command combines existing dimensioning subcommands Dim: Horizontal, Dim: Vertical, and Dim: Rotate.

To Create Linear Dimensions

1. In **Windows**, choose the Dimensioning toolbar ➤ Linear
Dimension. In **DOS**, choose Draw ➤ Dimensioning ➤
Linear.

2. First extension line origin or RETURN to select: Pick a
point on the object to be dimensioned or press ↵.

3. Second extension line origin: Pick a second point on the
object.

- If you pressed ↵, you will be prompted to **Select object to dimension:**. When you select an object, Auto-
CAD automatically locates the origin points for the
extension lines.

4. Dimension line location (Text/Angle/Horizontal/Verti-
cal/Rotated): Enter an option if you wish to modify the dimension text (T, A), specify horizontal or vertical
dimensioning (H, V), or rotate the dimension (R). Otherwise, drag your cursor and pick a location, or enter a coordinate for the location of the dimension line as the
extension line with text appears.

 **OPTIONS**

For a description of the *Text* and *Angle* options, see the **Dimaligned**
command.

Horizontal Allows you to specify a horizontal dimension. You
may also do this dynamically. If you drag your cursor up or down
the screen, the horizontal dimension will appear.

Vertical Allows you to specify a vertical dimension. You may also
do this dynamically. If you drag your cursor to the left or right
across the screen, the vertical dimension will appear.

Rotated allows you to create rotated dimensions. If you enter **R** to
select the Rotated option, you will be prompted Dimension line
angle <0>: Enter an angle of rotation for the dimension line.

Dimordinate

Creates an ordinate dimension string based on a datum or origin point. On the command line, use **Dimordinate**.

To Create Ordinate Dimensioning

1. In **Windows**, choose the Dimensioning toolbar ➤ Ordinate Flyout ➤ Automatic button. In **DOS**, choose Draw ➤ Dimensioning ➤ Ordinate ➤ Automatic.

2. Select Feature: Pick the location of the feature to be dimensioned.

3. Leader endpoint (Xdatum/Ydatum/Text): Specify an endpoint for the leader. AutoCAD will determine automatically whether to measure the X or Y coordinate. Alternatively, you may enter **X** or **Y** to specify the axis along which the dimension is to be taken. Enter **T** if you wish to modify the dimension text. Then press ↵.

4. Leader endpoint: Indicate the orientation of the dimension leader by picking a point.

 **OPTIONS**

For a description of the *Text* option, see the **Dimaligned** command.

NOTES If you pick a point at the first Leader endpoint: prompt, then AutoCAD selects the dimension axis based on the angle defined by the points you pick during the Select Feature: and Leader endpoint: prompts.

Dimoverride

Changes an individual dimension's properties, such as its arrow style, colors, scale, text orientation, etc. It allows you to override current Dimension Variable settings for selected objects only, without changing the current Dimension Style.

To Override Dimension Variable Settings

1. On the command line, type Dimoverride.

2. **Dimension variable to override: (or Clear to remove overrides):** Enter the name of a dimension variable, or type **C** to clear.

3. **Current value <current> New value:** Enter new value or setting for the dimension variable.

4. **Dimension variable to override:** Enter another dimension variable name and repeat the process, or press ⏎ to continue.

5. **Select objects:** Select dimension object(s) to change.

 **OPTIONS**

Clear Allows you to clear any dimension variable overrides. AutoCAD clears any overrides and the dimension object reverts to the setting defined by its dimension style.

Dimradius

Adds a radius dimension to arcs and circles in essentially the same way that Dimdiameter adds diameter dimensions. On the command line, enter **Dimradius**.

To Add a Radius Dimension

1. In **Windows**, choose the Dimensioning toolbar ➤ Radial Dimension flyout ➤ Radius. In **DOS**, choose Draw ➤ Dimensions ➤ Radial ➤ Radius.

2. **Select arc or circle:** Pick the arc or circle. The point at which you pick the arc or circle determines one end of the dimension arrow.

3. **Dimension line location<Text/Angle>:** If you wish to modify the text or text angle, enter an option (**T**, **A**). Or drag the cursor to position the text (and leader).

Unless you modify the text, the dimension value will be preceded by a radius symbol. If a dimensioned circle or arc is large enough, the radius dimension will be positioned within it. Otherwise it is positioned outside the circle or arc, with a leader line pointing to the center. A center mark is also placed at the center of the arc or circle.

Dimstyle

Allows you to create and modify dimension styles at the command line. The Ddim dialog boxes offer a more detailed and graphical approach to creating dimension styles, but Dimstyle allows a quick method of saving and creating dimension styles on the fly.

To Create/Modify a Dimension Style

1. At the command line, type **Dimstyle**.

2. Dimension Style Edit (Save/Restore/STatus/Variables/Apply/?): Type **?** to list the dimension styles in the current drawing, or select an option.

3. Depending upon the option chosen, the prompts will vary. Enter the required information.

 OPTIONS

Save Saves the current dimension variable settings as a dimension style that can later be restored using the Restore option. You can save multiple dimension styles.

Restore Makes an existing dimension style the current default style. You can either name a specific style or select an object that uses the style. *Restore* immediately changes the current dimension style to reflect any differences.

Status Displays the current dimension variable settings and descriptions. Once the dimension variables have been listed, Dimstyle ends.

Variables Lists the dimension variable settings of a dimension style. You can either name a specific style or select an object that uses the style. Once the dimension variables have been listed, Dim-style ends.

Apply Updates selected dimension objects to use the current dimension style, including any overrides.

? Lists the named dimension styles in the current drawing.

Dimtedit

Modifies the placement, justification, and rotation angle of a single dimension text object. At the command line, use **Dimtedit**.

To Move Dimension Text

1. In **Windows**, choose the Dimensioning toolbar ➤ Align Dimension Text flyout ➤ Left/Center/Right Buttons. In **DOS**, choose Draw ➤ Dimensioning ➤ Align Text ➤ Left/Center/Right options.

2. Select dimension: Pick a single dimension.

3. Enter text location (Left/Right/Home/Angle): Enter an option or pick a new location for the dimension text. You can drag the text to the next location with the cursor. If you move the text to a position in line with the dimension line, the dimension will automatically join to become a continuous line.

 **OPTIONS**

Left Justifies text to the left on linear, radial, and diameter dimensions.

Right Justifies text to the right on linear, radial, and diameter dimensions.

Home Moves dimension text back to its default position.

Angle Changes the angle for text. At the prompt **Text angle:**, enter an angle value, or indicate an angle by picking two points.

Dimensioning Mode Subcommands

Most of the new dimensioning commands are still available as sub-commands in Dimensioning mode (Dim: mode). Table 5 shows the correspondences between the Dim/Dim1 commands and the new AutoCAD dimensioning commands described above and elsewhere in this book. A number of dimensioning variables remain as Dim: subcommands only.

Table 5: The DIM Subcommands and the New Dimensioning
 Commands

DIM Subcommand	Dimensioning Commands
Dim: Aligned/AL	DIMALIGNED
Dim: Angular/AN	DIMANGULAR
Dim: Baseline/B	DIMBASELINE
Dim: Center/CE	DIMCENTER
Dim: Continue/CO	DIMCONTINUE
Dim: Diameter/D	DIMDIAMETER
Dim: Hometext/HOM	DIMEDIT Home
Dim: Horizontal/HOR	DIMLINEAR Horizontal
Dim: Leader/L	LEADER
Dim: Newtext/N	DIMEDIT New
Dim: Oblique/OB	DIMEDIT Oblique
Dim: Ordinate/OR	DIMORDINATE
Dim: Override/OV	DIMOVERRIDE
Dim: Radius/RA	DIMRADIUS
Dim: Restore/RES	DIMSTYLE Restore
Dim: Rotated/RO	DIMLINEAR Rotated
Dim: Save/SA	DIMSTYLE Save
Dim: Status/STA	DIMSTYLE Status
Dim: Tedit/TE	DIMTEDIT

Table 5: The DIM Subcommands and the New Dimensioning
Commands (continued)

DIM Subcommand	Dimensioning Commands
Dim: Trotate/TR	DIMEDIT Angle
Dim: Variables/VA	DIMSTYLE Variables
Dim: Vertical/VE	DIMLINEAR Vertical
Remaining Subcommands	
Dim: Exit/E	Exits Dim mode and returns to command mode
Dim: Redraw/RED	Redraws the display
Dim: Style/STY	Switches to a new text style
Dim: Undo/U	Erases the most recent dimesion objects
Dim: Update/UP	Redraws dimensions to match the current settings

 See Also   Edit, Ddim, Ddmodify

DIST

Dist gives the distance between two points in two- dimensional or three-dimensional space. It also gives the angle in the current XY plane, the angle *from* the current XY plane, and the distance in X, Y, and Z coordinate values. The command line is **Dist** (or **'Dist**, to use transparently).

To Find the Distance between Two Points

1.   In **Windows**, choose Object Properties toolbar ➤ Inquiry fly-out ➤ Distance button. In **DOS**, choose Assist ➤ Distance.

2.   First point: Pick the beginning point of the distance.

3.   Second point: Pick the end point of the distance.

DIVIDE

Divide marks an object into equal divisions. You specify the number of divisions, and AutoCAD marks the object into equal parts. The command line is **Divide**.

To Divide an Object

1.   In **Windows**, choose Draw toolbar ➤ Point flyout ➤ Divide button. In **DOS**, choose Draw ➤ Point ➤ Divide.

2.   Select object to divide: Pick a single object.

3.   <Number of segments>/Block: Enter the number of segments to be marked (2-32767) or enter **B**.

 OPTIONS

<Number of segments>   A marker or point is located at specified intervals using the *Pdmode* and *Pdsize* variables for point size and type.

Block   Allows you to use an existing block as a marking device. You receive the prompt **Block name to insert:** and are asked whether you want to align the block with the object. If you respond **Y** to the **Align block with object:** prompt, the block will be aligned either along the axis of a line or tangent to a selected polyline, circle, or arc. The Block option is useful for drawing a series of objects that are equally spaced along a curved path.

NOTES By default, Divide uses a point object as a marker. Often, a point is difficult to see when placed over a line or arc. You can set the *Pdmode* system variable using the **'Ddptype** command transparently to change the appearance of the points, or you can use the Block option. The point marker can be picked with the **Node** object snap mode.

See Also Block; Ddptype; Measure; Point; *System Variables:* Mode; Pdmode; Pdsize

DLGCOLOR

DlgColor opens the Dialog Colors dialog box to customize the dialog box colors. At the command line, enter **Dlgcolor**.

To Set Dialog Box Colors

Choose Options ➤ Dialog Box colors.

OPTIONS

Item A popup list describing portions of the dialog box for which colors can be assigned.

Color Enter color number or name in the edit box.

Show… Opens the Sample dialog box to display a preview of selected colors.

Defaults Restores default dialog box color settings.

Read File Opens the Select Dialog Color file box for saving and restoring color settings as ASCII files with a .DCC extension.

Write File Opens the Create Dialog Color file box for making new .DCC files or editing existing files.

DONUT/DOUGHNUT

Donut draws a circle whose line thickness you specify by entering its inside and outside diameters (see Figure 5). To create a solid dot, enter **0** at the **Inside diameter:** prompt. The most recent diameters entered are the default values for the inside and outside diameter. Once you issue the Donut command and answer the prompts, you can place as many donuts as you like. Press ↵ to terminate the command. The command line is **Donut** or **Doughnut**.

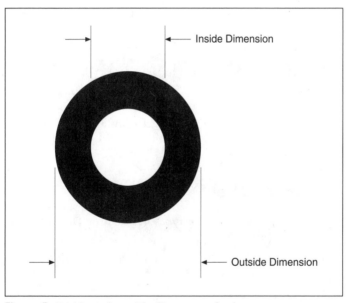

Inside Dimension

Outside Dimension

Figure 5: Inside and outside diameters of a donut

To Create a Donut

1.   In **Windows**, choose Draw toolbar ➤ Circle flyout ➤ Donut button. In **DOS**, choose Draw ➤ Circle ➤ Donut.

2. Inside diameter <current default>: Enter the inside diameter of the donut.

3. Outside diameter <current default>: Enter the outside
   diameter of the donut.

4. Center of donut: Pick a point for the center of the donut.

 NOTES Because donuts are actually polylines, you can
edit them with the **Pedit** command.

 See Also Fill; Pedit; *System Variables:* Fillmode

DRAGMODE

Dragmode controls when the Drag facility is used. The default,
Auto, lets you temporarily reposition selected objects by moving
them with your cursor.

To Drag an Object

1. On the command line, type **Dragmode** or **'Dragmode** to
   use transparently.

2. ON/OFF/Auto <current setting>: Enter the setting.

 OPTIONS

ON Enables the Drag mode, so that objects will be dragged whenever you issue the Drag command modifier.

OFF Disables the Drag mode, so that no dragging can occur.

Auto Causes all commands that allow dragging to automatically
drag objects, whether you issue the Drag command modifier or not.

NOTES When you are editing large sets of objects, the Drag function can slow you down. It takes time for AutoCAD to refresh a temporary image, especially a complex one. If you set Drag-mode ON, you can use the Drag function when appropriate by entering **DRAG** as a subcommand while performing a operation, and dispense with it when editing large groups of objects.

👁 **See Also** *System Variables:* Dragmode

DSVIEWER
Windows Only

The Dsviewer command lets you open the Aerial view window from the command line. You can also open Aerial view from the toolbar. Aerial view is a navigation tool that lets you see an entire drawing in a separate window, locate the area you want, and move to it quickly. The command line is **Dsviewer**.

To Open the Aerial View Window

Click the Aerial View button on the Standard toolbar. The entire drawing is displayed in the Aerial view window.

 NOTES The Aerial window is available for Windows only. To use it, your system must be configured for the Windows accelerated display driver with the display list option.

DTEXT/TEXT

Dtext allows you to enter several lines of text at once. This command also displays the text on the drawing area as you type. At the first prompt, you can set the justification or set the current text style. Using either the *Fit* or *Align* options, you can tell AutoCAD to fit the text between two points. The command line is **Dtext**.

To Enter Text Using Dtext

1.   In **Windows**, choose Draw toolbar ➤ Text flyout ➤ Dtext button. In **DOS**, choose Draw ➤ Text ➤ Dynamic Text.

2.   Justify/Style/<Start point>: Enter the desired options or pick a start point for your text.

3.   If you pick a point to indicate the beginning location of your text, you get the following prompts:

- Height <default height>: Enter the desired text height, or press ↵ to accept the default. This prompt only appears if the current style has its height set to 0.

- Rotation angle <default angle>: Enter a rotation angle, or press ↵ to accept the default.

- Text: Enter the desired text.

These prompts also appear after you have selected a style or set the justification option.

 OPTIONS

Start point   Lets you indicate the location of your text. The text is automatically left-justified.

Justify   Specifies the justification of text. The prompt is:

```
Align/Fit/Center/Middle/Right/TL/TC/TR/ML/MC/MR
/BL/BC/BR:
```

The two-letter options in this prompt set the justification based on the combination of top, middle, or bottom, and left, center, or right. For example, TL stands for "top left" and MC stands for "middle center." If you know the option, it can be entered directly at the Justify prompt.

Align Forces proportional resizing of text to fit between two points. You are prompted to select the two points. The text height is scaled in proportion to its width in the current text style.

Center Centers text on the start point, which also defines the baseline of the text.

Fit Forces text to fit between two points. Unlike *Align, Fit* keeps the default height and either stretches or compresses the text to fit.

Middle Centers text at the start point. The start point is in the middle of the text height.

Right Right-justifies the text. The start point is on the right side of the text.

Style Allows a new text style. The style you enter becomes the current style.

↵ If no option has been selected at the first prompt, pressing ↵ highlights the most recently entered line of text and displays the prompt Text:, allowing you to continue to add text just below that line. The current text style and angle are assumed, as is the justification setting of the most recently entered text.

NOTES   Each line of text created by Dtext is a separate object. Mtext allows you to add entire blocks of multiline text as a single object. If you use Dtext, a box appears showing the approximate size of the text. The text appears on your drawing as you type and the box moves along as a cursor. When you press ↵, the box moves down one line. You can also pick a point anywhere on the screen for the next line of text and still backspace all the way to the beginning line to make corrections. If you choose a justification option other than Left, the effects will not be seen until you finish entering the text.

The **Text** command works much like Dtext; however, it does not display the text on your drawing as you type. The text you enter appears only in the command-prompt area. Further, once you press ↵, the text appears on the drawing and you are returned to the command prompt. You must press ↵ twice to enter multiple lines of text. Dtext does not work with script files. Control codes such as %%d can be entered before or after your text to add diameter, underscores, tolerance symbols, and so on to your text.

👁 **See Also**   Change; Color; Ddedit; Ddrename; Ddstyle; Qtext; Rename; *System Variables:* Texteval, Textsize, Textstyle; Style

DVIEW

Dview displays your drawing in perspective and enables you to clip a portion of a view. Unlike the standard **Zoom** and **Pan** commands, Dview allows you to perform zooms and pans on perspective views. The command line is **Dview**.

To Display a Drawing with DView

1. Choose View ➤ 3D Dynamic View.

2. Select objects: Pick the objects that will help set up your perspective view.

3. CAmera/TArget/Distance/Points/PAn/Zoom/TWist/CLip/Hide/Off/Undo/< eXit>: Pick a point or select an option from the menu or enter the capitalized letter(s) of the desired option.

- If you pick a point you will be prompted to **Enter direction and magnitude angles:** BEFORE you select an option. enter the direction (+ or minus) and the desired angle, separated by a comma.

The prompts you receive next depend on the option selected in the preceding step.

 **OPTIONS**

CAmera   Allows you to move the camera location as if you were moving a camera around, while continually aiming at the target point. CAmera prompts you for the two angles of rotation: **Enter angle from XY plane:** and **Enter angle in XY plane from X-axis:**. At each prompt, you can either enter a value or select the view by using the cursor. If you enter a value, it will be interpreted in relation to the current UCS. See Figure 6.

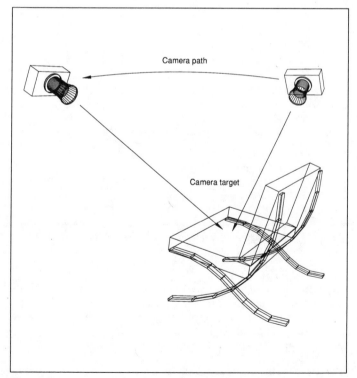

Camera path

Camera target

Figure 6:   The CAmera option controls the camera location relative to the target.

TArget Allows you to move the target location, as if you were pointing a camera in different directions while keeping the camera location the same. TArget prompts you for two angles of rotation, **Enter angle from XY plane:** and **Enter angle in XY plane from X-axis:** At each prompt, you can either enter a value or select the view by using the cursor. See Figure 7.

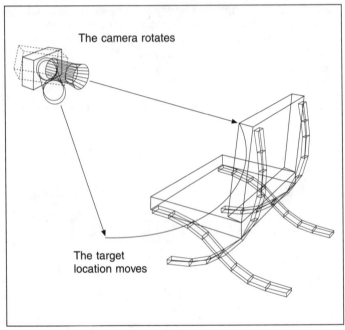

Figure 7: The TArget option controls the target location relative to the camera.

Distance Turns on the Perspective mode and allows you to set the distance from the target to the camera, as if you were moving a camera toward or away from the target point. At the prompt, enter a new distance or move the slide bar at the top of the screen to drag the three-dimensional image into the desired position.

POints Sets the target and camera points at X,Y, Z coordinates the same time. The points you pick are in relation to the current UCS.

At the prompt, pick a point for the target first, and then pick one for your camera location.

PAn Moves your camera and target point together, as if you were pointing a camera out the side window of a moving car. You cannot use the standard Pan command while viewing a drawing in perspective. See **Pan** for more information.

Zoom Zooms in and out when you are viewing a drawing in parallel projection. Provides the lens focal length when you are viewing a drawing in perspective. You cannot use the standard Zoom command while viewing a drawing in perspective.

If your three-dimensional view is a parallel projection, enter a new scale factor or use the slide bar at the top of the screen to visually adjust the scale factor at the **Dview/Zoom** prompt. If your three-dimensional view is a perspective, enter a new lens length value or use the slide bar at the top of the screen to determine the new lens length at the Dview/Zoom prompt. If you use the slide bar to adjust the focal length, the coordinate readout on the status line will dynamically display the focal length value.

Twist Rotates the camera about the camera's line of sight, as if you were rotating the view in a camera frame. At the *Dview/Twist* prompt, enter an angle or use the cursor to visually twist the camera view. If you use the cursor, the coordinate readout on the status line dynamically displays the camera twist angle.

CLip Hides portions of a three-dimensional view. For example, it removes foreground objects that may interfere with a view of the background (see Figure 8). CLip displays the prompt Back/Front/<Off>:. Enter **B** to set Back Clip Plane, **F** to set Front Clip Plane, or **O** or ↵ to turn off the Clip Plane function. If you select Back or Front, a prompt allows you to either turn the selected clip plane on or off or to set a distance to the clip plane. You can use the slide bar at the top of the screen to visually determine the location of the clip plane, or enter a distance value. A positive value places the clip plane in front of the target point; a negative number places it behind the target point.

Off Disables Front and Back clipping.

Hide Removes hidden lines from the objects displayed, turning a wire-frame view into a planar view.

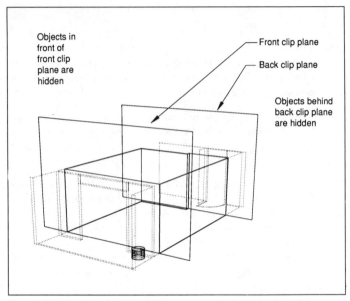

Objects in
front of
front clip
plane are
hidden

Front clip plane

Back clip plane

Objects behind
back clip plane
are hidden

Figure 8: The CLip option allows you to hide foreground or
background portions of your drawing.

eXit   Returns you to the AutoCAD command prompt. Any operation you performed while in the Dview command prompt will affect the entire drawing, not just the selected objects.

NOTES   Because a large drawing slows down the drag
function, you are prompted to select objects for dragging at the beginning of the Dview command. This limits the number of objects
to be dragged. You should select objects that give the general outline
of your drawing and sufficient detail to indicate the drawing's orientation. If you do not pick any objects, a default three-dimensional
house image appears to help you select a view. You can create your
own block image and use that as the default. The block should be
named *Dviewblock*.

See Also   *System Variables:* Backz, Frontz, Lenslength,
Target, Viewctr, Viewdir, Viewmode, Viewsize, Viewtwist; UCS

N E W

EDGE

The Edge command turns the visibility of three-dimensional face edges on or off. At the command line, enter **Edge**.

To Change the Visibility of a 3D Edge

1. In **Windows**, choose the Surfaces toolbar ➤ Edge button. In **DOS**, choose Draw ➤ Surfaces ➤ Edge.

2. Type **d** or select an edge to make invisible. The prompt is repeated, allowing you to select different edges until you press ↵.

- If you select the Display option by typing **d**, you will be prompted Select /<All>:. Select an edge, or type **a** to highlight all edges.

 **OPTIONS**

Select edge Allows you to select individual edges, and then hides the selected edges.

Display Highlights invisible edges, either selected edges or all invisible edges.

 See Also   Edgesurf; *System Variables:* Splframe, 3DFace

EDGESURF

Edgesurf draws a three-dimensional surface polygon mesh from four adjoining edges. These edges can be lines, arcs, polylines, or three-dimensional polylines, but they must join exactly end-to-end. On the command line, type **Edgesurf**.

To Create a 3D Surface Using Edgesurf

1. In **Windows**, choose the Surfaces toolbar ➤ Edge Surface button. In **DOS**, choose Draw ➤ Surfaces ➤ Edge Surface.

2. Select edge 1: Pick the first object defining an edge.

3. Select edge 2: Pick the second object defining an edge.

4. Select edge 3: Pick the third object defining an edge.

5. Select edge 4: Pick the fourth object defining an edge.

NOTES   The type of surface drawn by Edgesurf is called a *Coons surface patch* (see Figure 9). The first edge selected defines the M direction of the mesh, and the edges adjoining the first define the N direction. The endpoint closest to the point selected becomes the origin of the M and N directions.

The *Surftab1* and *Surftab2* system variables control the number of facets in the M and N directions, respectively. Increasing the number of facets gives a smoother mesh, but increases the file size of the drawing considerably. This increases file-opening, redrawing, and regeneration times. Increasing the values of *Surftab1* and *Surftab2* after creating the edgesurf will not smooth the 3D surface. Only edgesurfs created after, with the new values, will reflect the changes. See **Setvar** for details.

See Also   Pedit; Pface; *System Variables:* Splframe, Surftab1, Surftab2, 3DFace

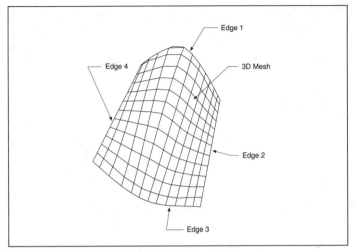

Figure 9: A Coons surface patch

ELEV

Elev allows you to set the default Z-axis elevation and thickness of objects being drawn. Normally, objects will be placed at a zero elevation. Once you enter an elevation or thickness with Elev, all objects drawn afterwards will be given the new Z-axis value; objects you drew before using the Elev command are not affected. You can also change the elevation of an existing object with the **Move** command. On the command line, use **Elev**.

To Set Elevation and Thickness

1. At the command line, type **Elev**.

2. New current elevation <current default>: Set a new default starting plane elevation in the Z-axis.

3. New current thickness <current default>: Set a new default extrusion thickness in the Z-axis.

NOTES   3D polylines, faces, and meshes, as well as view-ports and dimensions, ignore Elev settings. They do so because these entities cannot be extruded. Text and attribute definition entities are always given a zero thickness, regardless of the Elev values used during initial creation.

See Also   Ddemodes; Dducs; Move; *System Variables:* Elevation

ELLIPSE

Ellipse draws an ellipse for which you specify the major and minor axes, a center point, and two axis points; or the center point and the radius or diameter of an isometric circle. It also allows you to define a second projection of a three-dimensional circle by using the *Rotation* option. With Release 13 you may now draw a true ellipse rather than a polyline representation of an ellipse.

To Draw an Ellipse

1.   In **Windows**, choose the Draw toolbar ➤ Ellipse flyout ➤ button. In **DOS**, choose Draw ➤ Ellipse ➤ Center/Axis, End/Arc. The prompts which follow vary depending upon the preset options selected, and whether the isometric option under **Snap** is On or Off.

2.   If your isometric snap mode is active, the following prompt appears:

   • Arc/Center/Isocircle/<Axis endpoint 1>: Enter **I**, then pick a point defining one end of the ellipse, **A** for arc or **C** to enter a center point.

   If your **Isometric** Snap mode is not active, the prompt is:

- **Arc/Center/<Axis endpoint 1>:** Pick a point defining one end of the ellipse or type **C** to enter the center point.

3. For either of the above, the following prompts appear if you select the default option by picking a point:

- **Axis endpoint 2:** Pick a point defining the opposite end of the ellipse.

- **<Other axis distance>/Rotation:** Pick a point defining the other axis of the ellipse or enter **R** to enter a rotation value.

 **OPTIONS**

Axis endpoint   Allows you to enter the endpoint of one of the ellipse's axes (see Figure 10).

Center   Allows you to pick the ellipse center point.

Arc   Creates an elliptical arc. The angle of the first axis determines the angle of the arc.

Other axis distance   Appears after you have already defined one of the ellipse's axes. Enter the distance from the center of the ellipse to the second axis endpoint).

Isocircle   Appears when you set the Style option for the **Isometric** command to Isometric. This option creates an isometric circle in the current isometric drawing plane.

Rotation   Allows you to enter an ellipse rotation value between 0 and 89.4 degrees. Imagine the ellipse to be a two-dimensional projection of a three-dimensional circle rotated on an axis. As the circle is rotated, its projection turns into an ellipse. The rotation value determines the rotation angle of this circle. A 0-degree value displays a full circle; an 80-degree value displays a narrow ellipse.

NOTES   Release 13 introduces the true elliptical object. The next release of AutoCAD will not support a polyline representation of an ellipse. Set the *Pellipse* system variable to 1 for a

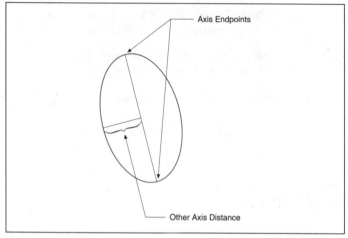

Axis Endpoints

Other Axis Distance

Figure 10: Axis endpoints and other axis distance

polyline ellipse or 0 for a true ellipse. If you create an ellipse which is actually a polyline, you can edit it using **Pedit**.

👁 See Also Isoplane; Snap; Spline; *System Variables:* Pellipse, Snapisopair

END

End simultaneously exits and saves the current drawing. Edits made prior to the End command are saved. The previous copy of the drawing is changed to a .BAK file.

📝 NOTES For unnamed drawings in which you opened a new drawing and never entered the **Save** command during your editing session, in Windows, the Create Drawing File dialog box appears; in DOS, the Save Drawing As dialog box appears. Enter the drawing name in the Files edit box.

When the *Filedia* system variable is set to 0, the command-line prompt requests a **File name:**. The End command will fail if the current drawing was set to read-only. In this case, you can use the **Saveas** command to save the drawing to another name before quitting.

 See Also   Files, Qsave, Quit, Save/Saveas

ENVIRONMENT SETTINGS

A variety of AutoCAD settings control its memory use and tell it where to find support files. In Windows, you may manipulate these settings via the Preferences command and dialog box (see **Preferences**). In **DOS**, use the DOS **Set** command to set the *DOS environment* (a small portion of memory which is used to store data). When AutoCAD starts up, it looks in the DOS environment for any information that is specifically set aside for AutoCAD.

To Set the DOS Environment

To set these variables in DOS, use the **DOS Set** command before starting Windows. For example, to direct AutoCAD to look in *Acad\Support* and *Acad\font* directories for support files, at the DOS prompt enter:

```
SET ACAD=C:\ACAD\SUPPORT;C:\ACAD\FONTS
```

To set the environment before you run AutoCAD, include this line in the batch file that starts AutoCAD.

 OPTIONS

Table 6 gives a listing of the environment settings and their uses. It also shows the command switches used to make some of the settings, and the names of the settings as they appear in the Windows Preferences dialog box.

Table 6: The AutoCAD Environment Settings

Environment Setting	Command Line Switch	Environment Dialog Name	Purpose
ACAD	/S	Support Dirs:	Indicates the directory or directories for support files
ACADCFG	/C	NA	Indicates where configuration files *Acad.cfg* and *Acad.ini* are found
ACADALTMNU	NA	Alt. Menu File:	Indicates where to find alternate tablet menu files, if you have a digitizing tablet
ACADDRV	/D	Drivers Dir:	Indicates where to find the Protected mode ADI drivers
ACADHELP	NA	Help File:	Indicates where to find the AutoCAD help files
ACADLOGFILE	NA	Log File:	Indicates where AutoCAD is to place the command prompt log file
ACADMAXMEM	/M	Max. Memory:	Indicates the maximum amount of memory in bytes that AutoCAD requests from the operating system
ACADMAXPAGE	NA	Max. Bytes in Page:	Indicates the maximum number of bytes to be sent to the first page file
ACADPAGEDIR	NA	Page File Dir:	Indicates the directory where page files are stored

Table 6: The AutoCAD Environment Settings (continued)

Environment Setting	Command Line Switch	Environment Dialog Name	Purpose
ACADPLCMD	NA	Plotting:	Indicates the shell command AutoCAD is to use for plot spooling
AVECFG	NA	Rendering Env… ➤ Config. File Dir:	Indicates where to store the renderer's configuration files
AVEDFILE	NA	Rendering Env… ➤ AVERDFILE:	Indicates where .RND rendering hard copy files are displayed
AVEFACEDIR	NA	Rendering Env… ➤ Face File Dir:	Indicates the location and name for storing the renderer's temporary files
AVEPAGEDIR	NA	Rendering Env… ➤ Page File Dir:	Indicates the location and name for the renderer's RAM page files
RDPADI	NA	NA	Indicates the location and name of the protected mode ADI rendering drive for the renderer
RHPADI	NA	NA	Indicates the location and name of the protected mode ADI hard copy rendering driver for the renderer

NOTES You may manipulate Environment settings in Windows via the command line switches in the Program Manager as well as via the Preferences command. To add command line switches in Windows, highlight the AutoCAD icon in the Program Manager, then select Properties in the File pull down menu to display the Program Item Properties dialog box.

AutoCAD looks for environment settings in the following order. First, it looks for the command switch settings made from the Program Manager. If no command switches are used, it looks for settings made from the Preferences command. If neither of these were used, AutoCAD uses settings made from the DOS Set command.

See Also Preferences

ERASE

Erase deletes one or several selected objects from a drawing. On the command line, use **Erase**.

To Erase Objects

1. In **Windows**, choose the Modify toolbar ➤ Erase button. In **DOS**, choose Modify ➤ Erase.

2. Select objects: Select the objects to be erased, by picking or using any selection method.

 **OPTIONS**

As well as the standard selection options, the following are useful with the Erase command:

Single Lets you pick a single object only. From the keyboard you can also enter **Si** at the **Select objects:** prompt.

Last Lets you erase the last entity drawn. From the keyboard you can enter **L** at the **Select objects:** prompt. You can also enter Previous or **P** from the keyboard to erase the previous selection set.

Oops Lets you unerase the last erase. (See **Oops**). (The Undo command will reverse the entire Erase sequence but not the last object erased.)

 NOTES To erase an object that is overlapped or superimposed by another, hold down the Ctrl key at the **Select object** prompt. Pick a point where two or more objects overlap, such that it is difficult to select the correct object. The prompt <Cycle on> appears at the command line. Continue clicking on the same point until the object you want to erase is highlighted, then press ⤶.

See Also Multiple, Oops, Select, Undo

EXIT

Exit ends the AutoCAD session and returns to the DOS prompt or Program Manager in Windows. **Quit** is the command-line equivalent of this selection.

To End an AutoCAD Session

Choose Files ➤ Exit AutoCAD.

NOTES If any work was done during the drawing session and the drawing was never saved or named, an AutoCAD message box displays Save Changes to (file name) so you can pick the Yes/Save Changes, No/Discard Changes, or Cancel Command button.

If no work was done to the drawing, the drawing session is terminated immediately without any warning message.

 See Also End, Quit

EXPLODE

Explode reduces a block, polyline, associative dimension, body, multiline, polyface and polygon mesh, region, group, or three-dimensional mesh or solid to its component objects. If a block is nested, Explode only "unblocks" the outermost block. In Release 13, Explode works with non-uniformly scaled blocks.

To Explode an Object

1. In **Windows**, choose the Modify toolbar ➤ Explode flyout Explode button. In **DOS**, choose Modify ➤ Explode.

2. <Select objects>: Select block, 2D, 3D, or wide polyline, multiline, 3D solid, Region, Polyface mesh, circle or arc to be exploded by picking or specifying any window selection set, including *window*, *wpolygon*, and *fence*.

 NOTES Blocks inserted with **Minsert** cannot be exploded. You can't explode Xrefs and their dependent blocks unless you bind them. Mirrored blocks cannot be exploded with the Explode command, but may be exploded using the new Xplode command. Wide polylines lose their width properties when exploded.

 See Also Select, Undo, Xplode, Xref

EXTEND

Extend lengthens an object to meet another object. Objects that can be extended include arcs, elliptical arcs, lines, open polylines, and rays. In Release 13, you may also extend objects to an "implied" as well as to an actual boundary.

To Extend an Object

1. In **Windows**, choose the Modify toolbar ➤ Trim flyout ➤ Extend button. In **DOS**, choose Modify ➤ Extend.

2. Select boundary edges: (projmode – <current value>, Edgemode – <current value> Select objects: Select the entity or use fence selection to designate the boundary objects.

3. <Select objects to extend>Project/Edge/Undo: Select objects to be extended by picking an object, using fence selection, or entering U to undo the last extend operation. You may also enter **P** or **E** to reset the Project or Edge settings.

- If you type P, you will be prompted None/Ucs/View/ <current value>:.

- If you type E, you will be prompted Extend/No extend <current value>:.

 OPTIONS

Project Specifies the projection mode for AutoCAD to use when extending objects: with None: only selected objects which actually intersect with the boundary are extended; UCS: specifies projection onto the XY plane of the current UCS; View: extends all selected objects that intersect with the boundary in the current view. This option is controlled by the system variable *Projmode*. *Projmode* settings are zero = "None"; 1 = "UCS"; 2 = "View".

Edge   Allows you to extend objects to implied as well as actual boundaries; boundary edges do not have to be exactly in the path of the objects to be extended. This option is controlled by the system variable *Edgemode*: a setting of 0 "No extend" will not extend objects to the implied boundary; a setting of 1 "Extend" will allow objects to extend to an implied boundary.

Undo   Restores the previously executed option.

NOTES   You cannot extend objects within blocks or use blocks as boundary edges.

See Also   Change; Lengthen; *System Variables:* Edgemode, Projmode; Trim

FILES

When the *Filedia* system variable is set to 0, Files allows you to manipulate files at the command line on your disk without having to exit AutoCAD. You can list all or specified files, as well as delete, rename, copy, or unlock them. At the command line, use **Files** (or '**Files** to use transparently).

To Access the File Utility Menu

1.   In **Windows**, choose File ➤ Management ➤ Unlock Files. In **DOS**, choose File ➤ Management ➤ Utilities.

2.   If you are in the Drawing editor and the *Filedia* system variable is set to 0, the screen switches to Text mode and the File Utility menu appears. Enter the number corresponding to the desired option:

```
0. Exit File Utility Menu
1. List Drawing files
```

```
2. List user-specified files
3. Delete files
4. Rename files
5. Copy file
6. Unlock files
Enter selection (0 to 6) <0>:
```

If the *Filedia* system variable is set to 1, the File Utilities dialog box appears with the following choices:

- **List files** Opens the File List subdialog box to display the directory you specify.

- **Copy file** Opens the Source File subdialog box to locate and assign the file you want to copy to the Destination File subdialog box so that you can name the new file.

- **Rename file** Opens an Old File Name subdialog box to reassign its directory or name to a New File Name subdialog box.

- **Delete file** Opens the File(s) to Delete subdialog box in order to rearrange files into other directories, accepting wildcard specifications. *Select All* and *Clear All* button boxes assist in deleting files.

- **Unlock files** Opens the File(s) to Unlock subdialog box to unlock files that have been locked due to another user's instructions or by an aborted AutoCAD session. A list is displayed showing which user locked the file and when it was locked. *Select All* and *Clear All* button boxes assist in unlocking groups of files.

- **Exit** Closes the File Utilities dialog box.

NOTES When entering file names, you must include the file extension. For the *Unlock Files* option, give the .DWG file name. The *File Utilities* option on the opening Main menu works in the same way as the **Files** command.

When deleting files, take care not to delete files AutoCAD needs for its internal operation. If you or someone on your network is currently editing a file, do not delete AutoCAD temporary files with the extension .$AC, .AC$, or .$A. Table 7 lists other AutoCAD file extensions and their purposes.

Table 7: AutoCAD File Extensions and their Meanings

File Description	Standard Extension	Lock File Extension
.3DS		3D Studio file
.ADS		ADS applications file
.ADT	.ADK	Audit report file
.AHP		AutoCAD Help file
.ARX		AutoCAD run-time extension file
.ASM		Sample ADS source code file
.BAK	.BKK	Drawing backup file
.BAT		DOS commands batch file
.BDF		Display font file
.BKn		Emergency backup file where n=sequential number
.C		ADS source code file
.CC		ADS source code file
.CFG	.CFK	AutoCAD configuration file
.CUS		Custom Dictionary file
.DBF		Database file
.DCC		Dialog box color control
.DCE		Dialog box error report
.DCL		Dialog Control Language definition file
.DCT		Dictionary file
.DEF		ADS source code file
.DFS		Default file settings file
.DLL		Dynamically linked library file
.DWG	.DWK, .DWL	Drawing file
.DXB	.DBK	Binary data exchange file
.DXF	.DFK	ASCII Drawing interchange file
.DXX	.DXK	Attribute data in DXF format

Table 7: AutoCAD File Extensions and their Meanings (continued)

File Description	Standard Extension	Lock File Extension
.EPS		Encapsulated PostScript file
.ERR		AutoCAD error report
.EXP		DOS driver file
.FLM	.FLK	AutoShade filmroll file
.FNT		DOS display font file
.GIF		Graphics Interchange format
.H		ADS include file
.HDX		Help index file
.HLP		Windows Help file
.LIB		ADS library file
.LIN	.LIK	Linetype definition file
.LSP		AutoLISP program file
.MID		Identification information file
.MLI		Render materials file
.MLN		Multiline library file
.MNC		Compiled menu file (Windows only)
.MND		Menu definition file
.MNL		AutoLISP functions related with a menu file
.MNR		Windows Menu resource file
.MNS		Windows Menu source file
.MNU	.MNK	Menu template file
.MNX	.MXK	Compiled menu file (DOS only)
.MPR	.MPK	Mass properties text output file
.OLD	.OLK	Backup of a file converted from an early version of AutoCAD
.PAT		Hatch-pattern library file
.PCP	.PCK	Plot-configuration settings file

Table 7: AutoCAD File Extensions and their Meanings (continued)

File Description	Standard Extension	Lock File Extension
.PCX		PCX raster-image file
.PFB		PostScript font file
.PFM		PostScript font metric file
.PS		PostScript file
.PSF		PostScript support file
.PLT	.PLK	Plot file
.SAB		ACIS solid binary file
.SAT		ACIS solid ASCII file
.SCR		Command Script file
.SHP		Shape/font source file
.SHX	.SHK	Shape or Font file
.SLB		Slide library file
.SLD	.SDK	Slide file
.STL		Stereolithography file
.TIF		TIFF raster-image file
.TTF		TrueType font file
.TXT	.TXK	Attribute extract or template file (CDF/SDF format)
.UNT		Units conversion file
.WMF		Windows metafile
.XLG	.XLK	External references log file
.XMX		External message file

FILL

Fill turns on or off the solid fills of solids, traces, and polylines. When Fill is off, solid filled areas are only outlined, both on the

screen and in prints. The dialog box option for solid fill is
Ddrmodes (Options ➤ Drawing Aids).

To Fill an Object

1. At the command line, type **Fill** (or **'Fill** to use
transparently).

2. Enter **On** or **Off** or press ↵.

👁 See Also Ddrmodes; Pline; Solid; *System Variables:* Fillmode, Trace

FILLET

Fillet uses an intermediate arc to join two nonparallel lines, a line
and an arc, or segments of a polyline.

To Use Fillet

1. In **Windows**, choose the Modify toolbar ➤ Feature flyout
➤ Fillet button. In **DOS**, choose Construct ➤ Fillet.

2. Polyline/Radius/Trim <Select first object>: Pick the first
object to fillet, P, R, or T. If you enter **P**, the prompt Select
2D polyline: appears; if you enter **R**, you are prompted to
Enter fillet radius. If you enter **T**, you are prompted:
Trim/No trim:.

3. Select second object: Pick the second object.

   • If you select multiple edges of a 3D solid, the following
   prompt appears: Enter radius<current>: Enter a distance or press Enter to display Chain/Radius <Select
   edge>: prompt. Select an edge, Enter **C** to pick adjacent edges, or enter **R** to set a new radius.

 **OPTIONS**

Polyline Fillets all line segments within a polyline. You are prompted to select a two-dimensional polyline. All joining polyline segments are then filleted.

Radius Allows you to specify the radius of the fillet arc.

Trim Allows you to toggle the trim option ON or OFF, and set it as a temporary default (using the system variable *Trimmode*). Turning trim OFF allows you to add a bevel while retaining the original line segments.

Chain Activates multiple adjacent edges selection.

Edge Activates single edge selection.

 NOTES Fillet joins the end points closest to the intersection. The location you use to pick objects determines which part of the fillet is retained. If the lines (or line and arc) already intersect, Fillet substitutes the specified arc for the existing corner. To connect two nonparallel lines with a corner rather than an arc, set the radius to **0**. You can also fillet just a corner of a polyline by picking its adjacent segments. Both segments, however, must be part of the same polyline. If you are not viewing the current UCS in plan, Fillet may give you the wrong result. Use the **Plan** command to view the current UCS in plan before issuing Fillet.

See Also Chamfer; *System Variables:* Filletrad, Trimmode

FILTER

Filter opens the Object Selection Filters dialog box to generate a selection-set filter based on combinations of object properties and to save them to a file name. At the command line, use **Filter** (or **'Filter** to use transparently).

To Filter Properties

1. In **Windows**, choose the Standard toolbar ➤ Select Objects flyout ➤ Selection Filters button. In **DOS**, choose Assist ➤ Selection Filters....

2. Apply coordinates, object type, color, layer, line type, block name, text style, or thickness to a filter.

 OPTIONS

List Box Displays a list box (in the upper portion of the dialog box) of the filtered objects in your current selection set.

Edit Item Pick box used to transfer the highlighted filter shown in the list box (at the upper portion of the dialog box) to the Select Filter area below. Pick Edit Item to transfer additional filters from the list box to the Select Filter area for editing. You can modify and Substitute the filters and their values displayed in the edit boxes below the Select Filter area.

Delete Pick box to remove the highlighted filter from the list box.

Clear List Pick box to remove all the filters from the list box.

Named Filters Area containing options to save, restore, and delete the current filter list.

Current Popup list displaying names of saved filters.

Save As Edit box for assigning a name and saving a filter list.

Delete Current Filter List Pick box for removing the saved filtered names from the Current popup list.

Apply Exits dialog box and executes the filtering procedure.

Select Filter Area containing X, Y, and Z coordinate edit boxes, and a Select subdialog box listing object types and relational operators as well as additional pick boxes. The Select subdialog box is specific to the entity type being filtered.

Add to List Appends an object in the *Select Filter* area to the filter list in upper portion of dialog box.

Substitute Pick box to replace highlighted filter criteria with the one in the Select Filter area.

Add Selected Object Pick box temporarily exits the dialog box allowing you to select objects from the drawing and add them to the filter list.

NOTES Entering Filter transparently ('**Filter**) at the command line allows you to apply the **P** (previous) selection set to access the filtered entities. The following operands must be paired and balanced for filters to operate correctly:

- Begin AND/End AND
- Begin Or/End Or
- Begin XOR/End XOR
- Begin NOT/End NOT

GRID

Grid turns on the grid and sets the grid spacing. At the command line, use **Grid**.

To Turn on the Grid

In **Windows**, choose Status Bar ➤ Grid. In **DOS**, type **Grid** at the command line.

To Change the Grid Settings

1. Choose Options ➤ Drawing Aids.

2. When the Drawing Aids dialog box appears, enter the desired grid spacing or other options.

 **OPTIONS**

Grid spacing(X)   Allows you to enter the desired grid spacing in drawing units. Enter **0** to make the grid spacing match the Snap setting.

ON   Turns on the grid display. (The F7 key performs the same function).

OFF   Turns off the grid display. (The F7 key performs the same function.)

Snap   Sets the grid spacing to match the Snap spacing. Once set, Grid spacing will dynamically follow every change in the Snap spacing.

Aspect   Specifies a grid spacing in the Y axis that is different from the spacing in the X axis.

NOTES   If you follow the grid spacing value with **X** at the prompt, AutoCAD interprets the value as a multiple of the **Snap** setting. For example, if you enter **2**, the grid points will be spaced two units apart, but if you enter **2X**, the grid points will be twice as far apart as the Snap settings.

At times, a grid setting may obscure the view of your drawing. If this happens, AutoCAD automatically turns off the grid mode and displays the message "Grid too dense to display." If you are using multiple viewports in Paperspace, you can set the grid differently for each viewport.

See Also   Ddrmodes; *System Variables:* Gridmode, Gridunit

GRIPS

Object grips allow you to make quick changes to objects in a drawing. With this feature turned on (using the **Ddgrips** command), you can grab endpoints, center points, and midpoints of objects, and stretch, move, copy, rotate, mirror, or scale them. To reveal the grip points, click on a single object, or select multiple objects at the command prompt. Click on a single grip to edit it, or Shift-click on more than one grip to select several points. If you select multiple grips, you must click on one of the selected grips to begin editing.

When you click on a grip, it becomes a solid color and is called a *hot grip*. The command prompt will change to tell you the current edit option. You can tell you are in a grips edit option by the asterisks that surround the option name, as in **STRETCH** or **MOVE**.

You may toggle grips ON or OFF at the command line as well as via the Ddgrips dialog box. On the command line, type **Grips**. At the New value for GRIPS: prompt, type **0** to turn off Grips, or **1** to turn Grips on.

 OPTIONS

Once you select a grip, you see the **STRETCH** prompt along with another prompt showing the options available under **STRETCH**. To switch to the **MOVE**, **ROTATE**, **SCALE**, and **MIRROR** options, press ↵ (the options repeat after **MIRROR**). The hot grip is assumed to be the base point of the edit for all of these options. To specify a new base point, enter **B** ↵ at any of the grips options. You can also copy the selected objects by entering **C** ↵, or undo the last grips option by entering ~**U**. To remove grips from an object, press the Esc key.

 See Also   Copy, Ddgrips, Mirror, Move, Rotate, Scale, Stretch

N E W

GROUP

Group opens the Object Grouping dialog box that allows you to group objects for editing purposes. At the command line, use **Group**.

To Select Object Groups

1. In **Windows**, choose the Standard Toolbar ➤ Object Group. In **DOS**, choose Assist ➤ Group Objects....

2. Enter information as appropriate in the dialog box.

 OPTIONS

Group Name This list box displays the names of existing groups.

Selectable Indicates whether a group is selectable. If a group is selectable, selecting just a single group member will select all group members, except those on locked layers. If a group is unselectable, selecting a single group member will select only that object.

Group Identification The group name, and optional description, are shown in this area when a group is selected from the Group Name list.

Create Group Allows you to create a *New* group and specify whether it is *Selectable*. Enter a name in the *Group Identification* text box, or use the *Unnamed* check box to create an unnamed group.

Change Group Allows you to make changes to an existing group. You may *Remove* or *Add Objects* to the group, *Rename*, or *Re-order* the group, change or add the *Description* and *Selectable* setting, or *Explode* the group.

NOTES Although a "group" has been created, you may edit individual objects within the group using **Grips**.

See Also Ddgrips; Grips; *System Variables:* Pickstyle

HATCH

Hatch fills an area defined by lines, arcs, circles, or polylines with either a predefined pattern, a user-defined pattern, or a simple hatch pattern. The equivalent dialog box command is **Bhatch**.

To Select a Hatch

1. At the command line, type **Hatch**.

2. Pattern (? or name/U,style) <default pattern>: Specify a predefined pattern name, enter U, or press ↵.

3. Scale for pattern <current default>: Specify a new value or press ↵.

4. Angle for pattern <current value>: Specify a new value or press ↵.

5. Select hatch boundaries or RETURN for direct hatch option: Select existing objects to hatch, or press ↵ and follow the prompts to define a new area for hatching. If you press ↵ to select the direct hatch option, you may choose whether to retain the hatching boundary with the **Retain polyline?** <Y/N>. prompt.

 **OPTIONS**

Pattern name You may enter any valid AutoCAD pattern name as defined in the *acad.pat* file. To list all of the patterns, use the *?* option. To fill the area with individual lines instead of a hatch block, you should precede the pattern name with an asterisk (*). In general, the pattern scale should be the same as the drawing scale. If a hatch area contains internal objects, the following hatch style codes control how the pattern is created. To use these codes, enter the pattern name at the Pattern prompt, followed by a comma and the code.

N Fills alternating areas (default option).

O Fills only the outermost area selected.

I Causes the entire area within the objects selected to be hatched, regardless of other enclosed areas within the selected area. Text is not hatched over.

? Lists the names of available hatch patterns.

U This option allows you to define a simple user-defined hatch pattern, including hatch angle, spacing between lines, and whether or not you want a single hatch or a cross-hatch. Cross-hatching occurs at 90 degrees to the first hatch lines. As with the predefined patterns, you may precede the **U** with an asterisk (*) to fill the area with single lines rather than hatch block, and you may append the hatch style codes (**N**, **O**, **I**) to control how the hatching is applied.

scaleXP When entered at the scale prompt, this modifier lets you specify a hatch scale relative to Paperspace. See **Zoom/XP**.

NOTES There are 67 predefined patterns, as illustrated in Figure 11. You can create your own hatch patterns by editing the *Acad.PAT* file. This file uses numeric codes to define the patterns.

Use the **List** command to identify the pattern name, spacing, and scale.

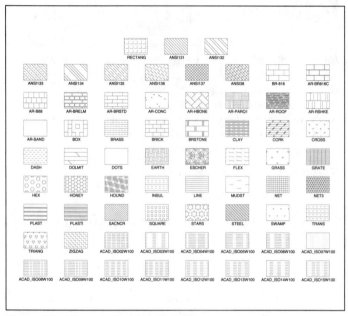

Figure 11: The standard hatch patterns

The objects that define the hatch area should be joined end-to-end and be closed. If you use lines and arcs, the end points of the objects must meet exactly end-to-end. Polylines should be closed.

To make the hatch pattern begin at a specific point, use the *Rotate* option under the **Snap** command to set the snap origin to the desired beginning point. Hatch uses the snap origin (*Snapbase* system variable) to determine where to start the hatch pattern.

⊚ See Also Bhatch; Explode; Hatchedit; Snap; *System Variables:* Hpang, Hpdouble, Hpname, Hpscale, Hpspace

N E W

HATCHEDIT

The Hatchedit command modifies an existing *associative* hatch block. The hatch pattern must have been associated with the hatched object, via the **Bhatch** command. If the original object is altered, you may resize the hatching to follow the object. At the command line, use **Hatchedit** to open the Hatchedit dialog box.

To Edit a Hatch Block

1. In **Windows**, choose the Modify toolbar ➤ Special Edit flyout ➤ Hatch Edit button. In **DOS**, choose Modify ➤ Edit Hatch.

2. <Select hatch object>: Select the hatch object you wish to modify.

3. In the Hatchedit dialog box, make the required modifications to the hatch pattern, and press **Apply**.

 **OPTIONS**

Pattern Type This drop box allows you to choose between predefined, user-defined, and custom hatch patterns.

Pattern Properties Allows you to manipulate specific properties of the chosen pattern type (see **Bhatch**).

Boundary Allows you to edit the boundary definition.

Inherit Properties Allows you to select a hatch object from your current drawing and apply its properties to the hatch object that you are currently editing.

Associative This check box allows you to disassociate the hatching from its boundary. (Only associative hatches may be edited.)

NOTES   If you prefer to use Hatchedit at the command line, rather than via the dialog box, type **-Hatchedit**. The command line version will prompt you through the appropriate options **Dis-associate/Pattern/Scale/Angle:**. The values of the hatching variables are saved as xdata in the hatch block reference.

See Also   Bhatch; Hatch; *System Variables*: Hpang, Hpdouble, Hpname, Hpscale, Hpspace, Snapbase

HELP/?

Help or ? opens up the Help dialog box to provide a brief description of how to use a particular command. You can use it on the fly by entering 'Help or '? at any prompt in the command. In Windows, you may press the F1 key to get context-sensitive Help on the current command.

- In **Windows**, choose the Standard toolbar ➤ ? or Help ➤ Contents... /Search for Help on .... In **DOS**, choose Help ➤ Help /Search for Help on....

 **OPTIONS**

Help Item   Edit box for locating specific commands. Enter the full name of help command or use an asterisk wildcard with portions of command name, then press ↵. Otherwise, use the Index... pick button for an alphabetical listing of all commands.

Index...   Pick button to access the Help Index subdialog box. Enter any command in the *Pattern* edit box or append it with an asterisk, then press ↵ to display available commands. Highlighting a specific command and picking OK will open its help subdialog box.

NOTES   When Help is used in the middle of a command, you receive information related to the specific prompt being displayed. Pick the slide bar along the right side of the dialog box or use Next and *Previous* to maneuver through the description.

HIDE

Hide removes hidden lines on an orthogonal or three-dimensional view when using Vpoint, Dview, or View. From the command line, use **Hide**.

- In **Windows**, choose Render toolbar ➤ Hide button. In **DOS**, choose Tools ➤ Hide.

 NOTES   For complex 3D views, you may want to use **Mslide** to save the view with hidden lines removed. In a perspective view, use the *Hide* option under **Dview**. You can also use **Shade** to get a quick rendering of a 3D model.

 See Also   Config, Dview, Mview, Shade, View

ID

Id displays the X, Y, and Z coordinate values of a point. At the command line, type **Id** (or **'Id** to use transparently).

To Display a Point's Coordinates

1. In **Windows**, choose Object Properties toolbar ➤ Inquiry
   flyout ➤ Locate Point button. In **DOS**, choose Assist ➤
   Inquiry ➤ Locate Point.

2. **Point:** Pick a point.

A point you select with Id becomes the last point in the current editing session (stored in the *Lastpoint* variable).

 See Also   Point; *System Variables:* Lastpoint

IMPORT/EXPORT

AutoCAD Release 13 offers several ways to transfer data to and
from other applications and file formats.

Import Functions

You can bring drawings or images from other applications into the
current AutoCAD drawing by using the Import functions. The program supports these file formats: .DXF/.DXB, .3DS, .SAT, .EPS,
.GIF/.PCX/.TIF, and (in Windows only) .WMF.

To Import Files Created in Other File Formats

1. In **Windows**, choose File ➤ Import to open the Import File
   dialog box. In **DOS**, choose File ➤ Import and then click
   on the required file format on the drop-down menu. (For
   most formats selected in DOS, the appropriate Select File
   dialog box will appear.)

2. In **Windows**, highlight the file type required in the List
   Files of Type selection box, then find and select the file

that you wish to import. In **DOS**, find and select the file
you wish to import.

3. When you have located the file you want to import,
choose OK.

In DOS, there are no dialog boxes for the raster import file formats
(.GIF/.PCX/.TIF). To import these file formats (or if *Filedia* is set to
0), enter the path and file name required at the command prompt.

Although the above steps outline the basic procedures for importing other file formats in Windows and DOS, there are a number of
variations and some additional prompts. Moreover, all of these file
import options have equivalent command-line versions. Table 8
lists the AutoCAD import options and their command equivalents,
as well as any procedural variations.

Table 8: AutoCAD File Import Functions

File Format	Command	Description/Comments
Drawing Exchange Format[1]		
.DXF	DXFIN	Imports ASCII format drawing exchange file. Used to transfer data from other CAD systems into AutoCAD.
.DXB	DXBIN	Imports binary coded drawing exchange format files created by programs such as AutoShade
3D StudioFiles		
.3DS	3DSIN	Imports selected 3D Studio geometry and rendering information. Prior to import, you must provide layer- and materials-handling information in the 3D Studio File Import Options dialog box.

Table 8: AutoCAD File Import Functions (continued)

File Format	Command	Description/Comments
Solid Models		
.SAT	ACISIN	Converts geometric objects stored in ASCII (.SAT) format into AutoCAD bodies, solids, and regions.
Postscript		
.EPS	PSIN	Inserts an Encapsulated PostScript image into the current drawing as an anonymous block. You need to specify the insertion point and scale factor for the block.
Raster Images[2]		
.GIF	GIFIN	Imports Graphics Interchange format.
.PCX	PCXIN	Imports standard Paint program format.
TIFF (.TIF)	TIFFIN	Imports Tagged Image format (scanned image format).
Windows Only		
.WMF	WMFIN	Imports Windows Metafile format files. You need to specify an insertion point and scale factor when importing the file.

1. In Windows, choose File ➤ Open (not File ➤ Import) to load .DXF and .DXB files.
2. Raster images are brought in as a block composed of 2D solid objects. You need to position the image (by dragging it) and scale it as you import it.

Export Functions

Using the AutoCAD export functions, you can convert AutoCAD drawings into several different formats. The formats can then be read by other applications: .DXF, .3DS, .SAT, .STL, .EPS, .BMP, and (in Windows only) .WMF and .PFB.

To Create Other File Formats

1. In **Windows**, choose File ➤ Export to open the Export Data dialog box, and highlight the required format in the List Files of Type selection box. In **DOS**, choose File ➤ Export and then click on the required file format on the drop-down menu.

For some file formats, such as .DXF or Postscript, the appropriate Create… File dialog box will appear immediately. For others, such as 3D Studio format, you will be prompted to **Select objects:** for export before the Create… File dialog box appears.

2. Enter the name of the file you wish to create in the File/File Name box, and choose OK. (If *Filedia* is set to 0, follow the command-line prompts.)

Table 9 lists the AutoCAD export options, their command equivalents, and any variations in the general procedure described above.

Table 9: AutoCAD File Export Functions

Format	Command	Description/Comments
Drawing Exchange Format		
.DXF	DXFOUT	Exports ASCII format drawing exchange file. Used to transfer data from AutoCAD to other CAD systems. In Windows, choose File ➤ Save As (not File ➤ Export) to create .DXF files. You will be prompted to specify the decimal-place accuracy of your .DXF file.

Table 9: AutoCAD File Export Functions (continued)

Format	Command	Description/Comments
3D Studio Files		
.3DS	3DSOUT	Converts selected AutoCAD geometry and rendering information into 3D Studio format. Prior to conversion, you must specify the division method and provide smoothing and welding information in the 3D Studio File Export Options dialog box.
Solid Models		
.SAT	ACISOUT	Converts AutoCAD objects, representing surfaces, solids and regions, to an ACIS file in ASCII format.
Stereolithography		
.STL	STLOUT	Outputs a single solid into an ASCII or binary format. The .STL format is compatible with Stereolithography Apparatus (SLA). The solid data is output as a triangulated mesh that represents the solid. After selecting the solid for output, you need to specify ASCII or binary format.
Windows Only		
.WMF	WMFOUT	Saves selected objects to Windows Metafile format, containing both vector and raster graphics.
.BMP	BMPOUT	Creates a bitmap image of selected objects in your drawing. There is no menu or dialog box option for creating bitmaps.

NOTES AutoCAD system variables and other options can be used to control the quality and precision of a number of these file conversions. Several system variables affect raster image quality. You can change the image aspect for .GIF and .TIFF files (*Riaspect*) and manipulate background color (*Ribackg*), edge detection (*Riedge*), number of colors (*Rigamut*), and brightness (*Rithresh*). When importing Windows Metafiles, you can control line width and solid fills using WMF Options (choose File ➤ Options ➤ WMF Options or type **Wmfopts**). When importing PostScript (.EPS) files, the *Psquality* system variable controls the rendering quality and whether they are drawn as filled objects or outlines. When exporting to .STL format, the *Facetres* system variable can be used to control the fineness of the triangulated mesh.

Besides importing and exporting, other options exist for transferring data between AutoCAD and other programs. AME models can be converted to AutoCAD solids using **Ameconvert**; using **Mslide**, slides of AutoCAD drawings can be made for inclusion in other graphics programs and desktop publishing programs; and in Release 13 for Windows, a variety of graphical and nongraphical objects can be shared between AutoCAD and other Windows applications by using Object Linking and Embedding (OLE).

See Also Cut and Paste; Insertobj; Mslide; OLE; Olelinks; Solid Modeling/Ameconvert; *System Variables:* Facetres, Psquality, Riaspect, Ribackg, Riedge, Rigamut, Rithresh

INSERT

This command inserts a named block or drawing into the current drawing. The equivalent dialog box command is **Ddinsert**.

To Insert Blocks

1. At the command prompt, type **Insert**.

2. Block name (or ?) <last block inserted>: Enter the block or drawing name or ~ (a tilde) to display the Select Drawing File dialog box.

3. Insertion point: Enter a coordinate value, pick a point with the cursor, or enter a preset option (see "Preset Options" below).

4. X scale factor <1> / Corner / XYZ: Enter an X scale factor; C for corner; **XYZ** to specify the individual X, Y, and Z scale factors; or ⏎ to accept the default X scale factor of 1.

If you press ⏎ without entering a value or option, the following prompt appears: Y scale factor (default=X):. Enter a Y scale factor or press ⏎ to use the scale factor for the Y axis as well.

5. Rotation angle <0>: Enter the rotation angle for the block or pick a point on the screen to indicate the angle. (This last prompt does not appear if you use the *Rotate* preset option.)

 **OPTIONS**

~ (tilde) Entered at the Block name... prompt, causes the Select Drawing File dialog box to appear. The dialog box lets you select external files for insertion.

= Replaces a block with an external file. (See "Notes" below.)

X scale factor Scales the block in the X axis. If you enter a value, you are then prompted for the Y scale factor.

Corner Allows you to enter the X and Y scale factors simultaneously. To scale the block by a factor of 1 in the X axis and 2 in the Y axis, enter **C** at the **X scale factor...** prompt and then enter **@1,2**.

Otherwise, enter a coordinate value or pick a point at the X scale factor... prompt to scale your block.

XYZ Gives individual X, Y, and Z scale factors. You will be prompted for the factors.

 PRESET OPTIONS

The following options are available at the Insertion point: prompt. They are called Insert "presets" because they allow you to preset the scale and rotation angle of a block before you select an insertion point. Once you select a preset option, the dragged image will conform to the setting used; you will not be prompted for a scale factor after you select the insertion point.

Scale Allows you to enter a single scale factor for the block. This factor governs X, Y, and Z axis scaling.

Xscale Sets the X scale factor.

Yscale Sets the Y scale factor.

Zscale Sets the Z scale factor.

Rotate Enters a rotation angle for the block.

PScale The same as *Scale,* but is used only while positioning the block for insertion to "preview" the scaled block. You are later prompted for a scale factor.

PXscale The same as *PScale,* but affects only the X scale factor.

PYscale The same as *PScale,* but affects only the Y scale factor.

PZscale The same as *PScale,* but affects only the Z scale factor.

PRotate The same as *Rotate,* but is used only while positioning the block for insertion. You are later prompted for a rotation factor.

NOTES If a block has previously been inserted, it becomes the default block for insertion (stored in the *Insname* system variable). Enter **?** to see a list of the blocks in the current file. Coordinate values are in relation to the current UCS.

To insert the individual objects in a block (rather than the block as a single object), type an asterisk before its name at the **Block name:** prompt. To bring the contents of an external file in as individual objects, insert the file in the normal way and use the **Explode** command to break it into its individual components. To insert a mirror image of a block, enter a negative value at either the **X** scale factor... or **Y** scale factor... prompt.

If the inserted block or file contains an attribute and the *Attreq* system variable is set to 1, you are prompted for the attribute information after you have entered the rotation angle. If the system variable *Attdia* is set to 1, a dialog box with the attribute prompts appears. (The default setting for *Attreq* is 1. *Attdia* is normally set to 0.)

You can also use Insert to replace or update a block with an external drawing file. For example, to replace a block named Chair1 with an external file named Chair2, enter **Chair1=Chair2** at the **Block name:** prompt. If the block and the external file names are the same (Chair1, for example), enter **Chair1=**. Note, however, that named objects in the current drawing have priority over those in an imported file.

When you attempt to replace blocks containing attributes, the old attributes will remain even though the block has been changed. To avoid them, you must delete the old block, insert the new (external) block, and reenter the attribute values. You can also use the **Attredef** command.

Finally, an external file will be inserted with its WCS (world coordinate system) aligned with the current UCS (user coordinate system). A block will be inserted with its UCS orientation aligned with the current UCS.

See Also   Attdef; Attredef; Base; Block; Ddattdef; Ddatte; Ddattext; Ddinsert; Explode; Files; *System Variables:* Attreq, Attdia, Filedia, Insname, Xplode, Xref

Insertobj allows you to insert a range of graphic and multimedia objects into an existing AutoCAD drawing. Objects include other AutoCAD drawings, sound clips, spreadsheets and media clips, clip art, paint files, word-processed documents, and presentation slides. Insertobj works with Windows' Object Linking and Embedding (OLE). It allows you to create objects for embedding into your current AutoCAD drawing. At the command line, type **Insertobj**.

To Insert an Object Into a Drawing

1.   Choose Edit ➤ Select Objects ➤ Insert Object.

2.   When the Insert New Object dialog box opens, double-click on the Object Type that you wish to embed in your drawing.

AutoCAD starts the native Windows application associated with the type of object that you have selected. For example, if you click on Powerpoint Slide, it will open Powerpoint and allow you to create a slide file (.PPT) for insertion into your drawing. If you click on Microsoft Clip Art, it will load the Clip Art gallery and allow you to select the item you require.

3.   Once you have created a new application object, choose Files ➤ Exit to simultaneously exit the application and insert the new object into your drawing.

The new object is inserted at the upper-left corner of the drawing. To reposition it, click on the object and drag it to a new position. When you click on an object, a frame and handles appear. You may use the handles to resize the object to the desired dimensions. If you need to edit an object that you have inserted, double-click on the object. The native application will be loaded again. Make the required changes, then choose File ➤ Update... to update the changes to your drawing.

 **OPTIONS**

Object Type   This list box is on the Insert New Object dialog box. It lists all of the applications on *your* system that support Object Linking and Embedding (OLE).

 **See Also**   Cut and Paste, Olelinks

Intersect allows you to create a composite solid or region that contains only the common volume of two or more overlapping solid objects or regions. In effect, it joins the objects, leaving only the area or volume where the objects intersect. At the command line, type **Intersect**.

To Create an Intersection Object

1. In **Windows**, choose the Modify toolbar ➤ Explode flyout ➤ Intersection button. In **DOS**, choose Construct ➤ Intersection.

2. Select objects: Click on the overlapping solids or regions for which you wish to derive the intersection.

AutoCAD removes all non-overlapping sections of the selected objects, leaving only the intersection objects created by their common areas and/or volumes.

NOTES Intersect can be used only for regions or solids. In step 2 above, you may select both regions and solids at the same time, and you may select objects from any number of planes. AutoCAD will group the selection set into subsets by region/solid and by plane before calculating the intersections and creating the intersection objects.

See Also Solid Modeling/Interference, Subtract

ISOPLANE

When the snap mode is set to the Isometric style, Isoplane lets you switch the cursor orientation between the left, top, and right isometric planes.

To Change the Cursor Orientation

1. At the command line, use **Isoplane** or **'Isoplane**.

2. Left/Top/Right/<Toggle>: Enter your choice or press ↵ to go to the next isoplane.

3. Current Isometric plane is: Lists the new isoplane.

NOTES Ctrl-E is a toggle control key that selects the next isometric plane in a cycle of isometric planes.

See Also Ddrmodes; Snap; *System Variables:* Snapisopair

LAYER

Layer creates new layers, assigns colors and line types to layers, sets the current layer, represses editing of layers, and allows you to control which layers are displayed. The dialog box equivalent is **Ddlmodes**.

To Create and Modify Layers

1. At the command line, type **Layer** or **'Layer**, to use transparently.

2. ?/Make/Set/New/ON/OFF/Color/Ltype/Freeze/Thaw/LOck/ Unlock: Enter an option.

 OPTIONS

? Displays the list of existing layers. Wildcards are accepted.

Make   Creates a new layer and makes it current.

Set   Makes an existing layer the current layer.

New   Creates a new layer.

On   Turns on layers.

Off   Turns off layers.

Color   Sets color of a layer.

Ltype   Sets line type of a layer.

Freeze   Freezes one or more layers.

Thaw   Unfreezes one or more layers.

Lock   Prevents editing of visible layers.

Unlock   Releases locked layers to allow editing.

NOTES   All Layer options except *Make*, *Set*, and *New* allow you to enter wildcard characters (question marks and asterisks) for input. For example, if you want to turn off all layers whose names begin with G, enter **G*** at the prompt.

The option pairs *Freeze/Thaw* and *On/Off* both control whether or not a layer is displayed. However, unlike *Off*, *Freeze* makes Auto-CAD ignore objects on frozen layers. This allows faster regenerations. *Freeze* also affects blocks differently than *Off*. Thawing layers requires a Regen if Regenauto if off.

Layer 0, the default layer when you open a new file, is white (number 7) and has the continuous line type. Layer 0 also has some unique properties. If you include objects on Layer 0 in a block, they take on the color and line type of the layer on which the block is inserted. The objects must be created with the *Byblock* option (see **Color**). The dimension layer Defpoints is also unique. When it is turned off, objects on this layer are still displayed, but will not appear on prints or plots. This makes the Defpoints layer suitable for layout lines.

See Also   Color; Ddlmodes; Linetype; Regen; Regenauto; *System Variables:* Clayer, Vplayer; Wildcard characters

N E W

LEADER

Leader creates a line connecting annotation to an object or feature. A leader line can be either a spline or made up of straight line segments. An arrowhead can be attached if desired. In some cases, a short horizontal line, called a *hook line,* connects the text or feature control frames to the leader line. Annotations placed at the end of a leader line become associated with the leader line. When you move, stretch, or copy the leader line, the annotation moves with it. At the command line, use **Leader**.

To Create a Leader Line

1. In **Windows**, choose the Dimensioning toolbar ➤ Leader button. In **DOS**, choose Draw ➤ Dimensioning ➤ Leader.

2. From point: Specify a point (or use Object Snap) to attach the leader to an object.

3. To point: Specify another point.

4. To point (Format/Annotation/ Undo) <current default>: Specify further point(s) as required, enter an option (**F**/**A**/**U**), or press ↵.

 OPTIONS

Format Allows you to specify the format of the leader line. Selecting *Spline* draws the leader line as a spline. *Straight* draws the leader as straight line segments. *Arrow* draws an arrowhead at the start point of the leader. *None* temporarily resets the arrow default to draw a leader with no arrowhead. *Exit* returns you to the **To point (Format/Annotation/Undo)** <Annotation>: prompt.

Annotation Inserts annotation at the end of the leader line. The annotation may be text, a block, an mtext object, or a feature control frame specifying geometric tolerances. If you wish to add text, enter it at this point. The *Mtext* option allows you to define a window in the drawing, then exits to a text editor—the Edit Mtext dialog box in Windows or the DOS Editor in DOS. You may then enter the desired multiline text (Mtext) and/or format strings. When you exit the editor, the text entered is inserted into the predefined window as an Mtext object in the drawing. The *Tolerance* option first opens the Symbol dialog box, then opens the Geometric Tolerance dialog box so you can create a feature control frame containing geometric tolerances. The feature control frame is attached to the end of the last vertex of the leader line. The *Copy* option allows you to copy any kind of annotation (text, block, feature control frame, or mtext) to the leader you are drawing. The copied annotation is associated with the leader line. The *Block* option allows you to insert a block at the end of the last vertex of the leader line. *None* ends the command without adding any annotation to the leader line.

Undo   Deletes the last line segment drawn.

NOTES   The Leader command creates complex leader lines, unlike Dimdiameter and Dimradius, which create simple automatic leaders for circles and arcs. How Mtext is displayed is determined by the prevailing measurement units and current text style in the drawing. The Mtext is vertically centered and is aligned horizontally with the last two segments of the leader line. Text and Mtext are inserted at a location determined by the current text gap (*Dimgap* system variable).

Leader lines are 2D objects similar to dimension objects. Like dimensions, they cannot have elevation or thickness. Although leader lines are not actually dimensions, their appearance is controlled by the same Ddim dimension variables: *Dimclrd* controls the leader color; *Dimclrt* controls the color of the annotation; *Dimblk/Dimblk1* controls the arrowheads; *Dimasz* controls the size of arrowheads; *Dimgap* controls the text gap between annotation and the hook line.

See Also   Ddim; Dimensioning Commands; Insert; Mtext; Spline; *System Variables:* Dimasz, Dimblk, Dimclrd, Dimclrt, Dimdiameter, Dimgap, Dimradius, Dimtad; Tolerance

LENGTHEN

Lengthen changes the length of selected objects and the included angle of arcs. Closed objects cannot be lengthened. At the command line, use **Lengthen**.

To Lengthen an Object

1. In **Windows**, choose the Modify toolbar ➤ Resize flyout ➤ Lengthen button. In **DOS**, choose Modify ➤ Lengthen.

2. DElta/Percent/Total/DYnamic/<Select object>: Select an object to display current length or enter an option.

 OPTIONS

Delta Allows you to specify an incremental length by which to lengthen a selected object. The length is incrementally increased from the endpoint closest to the pick point. If an arc is selected, the angle of the arc is changed by the specified increment. A positive value produces an extension; a negative value trims the object.

Percent Allows you to specify a percentage. The selected object is lengthened by that percentage. If an arc is selected, the included angle is increased by the specified percentage.

Total Allows you to specify an absolute value for the length (or included angle) for the selected object.

DYnamic Enters dynamic dragging mode. You may change the length or included angle by dragging one endpoint while the other remains fixed.

Undo Allows you to undo the last specification at any point while using the command options.

 See Also   Change, Extend, Grips, Trim

LIMITS

Limits determines the drawing boundaries. If you use a grid, it will appear only within the limits. At the command line, type **Limits** (or **'Limits** to use transparently).

To Establish Drawing Boundaries

1. Choose Data ➤ Drawing Limits.

AutoCAD will indicate which limits are being set with one of these prompts: Reset Model space limits: or Reset paper space limits:.

2. ON/OFF/<lower left corner> <0.0000,0.0000>: Enter the coordinate for the lower-left corner, or the *On/Off* option.

3. Upper right corner <12.0000,9.0000>: Enter the coordinate for the upper-right corner.

 **OPTIONS**

ON Turns on the limit-checking function. This keeps your drawing activity within the drawing limits.

OFF Turns off the limit-checking function. This allows you to draw objects without respect to the drawing limits.

NOTES To make the virtual screen conform to the limits of the drawing, turn on the limit-checking feature and then perform a Zoom/All operation. The **Mvsetup** command will set the limits of your drawing automatically according to the sheet size and drawing scale you select. The limits for paper space must be set independently of the Modelspace limits.

See Also Mspace; Mview; Pspace; Regen; *System Variables:* Limcheck, Limmin, Limmax, Viewres, Zoom

LINE

Line draws simple lines—either a single line or a series of line segments end-to-end. At the command line, use **Line**.

To Draw a Line

1. In **Windows**, choose the Draw toolbar ➤ Line flyout ➤ Line button. In **DOS**, choose Draw ➤ Line.

2. From point: Select a point to begin the line.

3. To point: Select the line endpoint.

4. To point: Continue to select points to draw consecutive lines or press ↵ to exit the Line command.

 **OPTIONS**

C Closes a series of lines, connecting the last start point and the last endpoint with a line.

↵ At the **From point:** prompt, lets you continue a series of lines from a previously entered line, arc, point, or polyline. If the last object drawn is an arc, the line is drawn at a tangent from the end of the arc.

U At the **To point:** prompt, deletes the last line segment.

 **NOTES**   You can convert lines to polylines using the **Pedit** command.

See Also   Mline, Osnap, Pedit, Pline, Ray, Xline

LINETYPE

Linetype enables you to control the type of line you can draw. The default line type is continuous or solid, but you can choose from several other types, such as a dotted or dashed line or a combination of the two (see Figure 12). Predefined line types are stored in a file called *Acad.LIN*. You can list these line types by entering a question mark at the Linetype prompt. **Ddltype** is the dialog box equivalent.

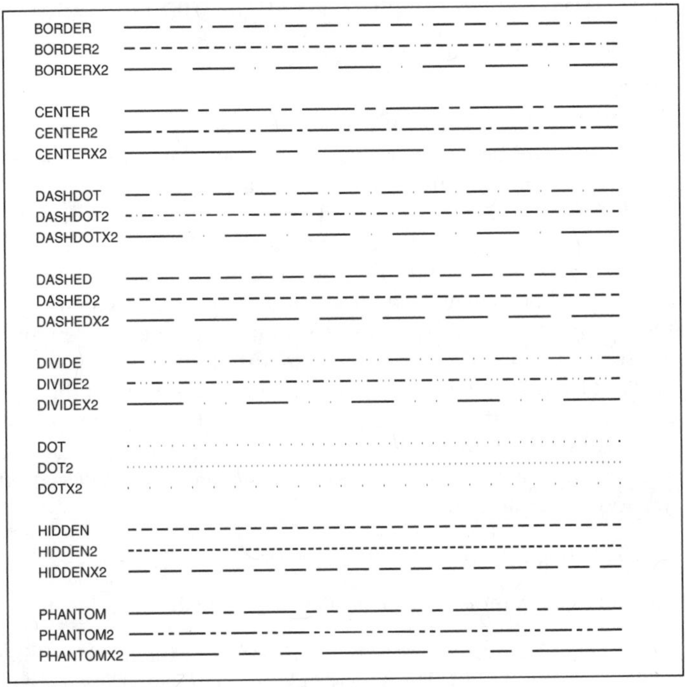

Figure 12: The Standard AutoCAD line types

To Change the Line Type

1.   At the command line, type **Linetype** or **'Linetype**, to use transparently.

2.   ?/Create/Load/Set: Enter the option name.

 **OPTIONS**

? Lists available line types in a specified external line type file.

Create Creates a new line type.

Load Loads a line type from a specified line type file.

Set Sets the current default line type.

NOTES   The *Create* option first prompts you for a line type name. This name can be any alphanumeric string of 31 characters or less (although the status line will display only the first eight characters). You are then prompted for the name of the file in which to store your line type. Next, you enter a description or graphic representation of the line type. Finally, you enter the line type pattern on the next line, where you will see an *A* followed by a comma and the cursor. Enter a string of numeric values separated by commas. These values should represent the lengths of lines as they will be plotted. Positive values represent the "drawn" portion of the line; negative values represent the "pen up," or blank, portion of the line; and a zero indicates a dot. The following below produces a line type segment with a dash .3 drawing units long and three dots spaced .05 drawing units apart:

```
.3,-.05,0,-.05,0,-.05,0,-.05
```

You can create complex line types only by editing the Acad.LIN file.

Several ISO 128 line types have been added to the standard line types with Release 13. The size of the line segments for each ISO line is defined for use with a 1 mm. pen-width. To use them with other ISO predefined pen widths, scale the line using the appropriate value. For a pen width of 0.5 mm., use an ltscale of 0.5.

You can assign line types to layers or to individual objects. Use the **Ltscale** command to make the scale of the line types correspond with the scale of your drawing.

A line type may appear continuous even though it is a noncontinuous type. Several things can affect the appearance of line types. For example, if the drawing scale is not 1:1, the **Ltscale** must be set to correspond with your drawing scale. If the drawing scale is ¼" equals 1', the Ltscale must be set to 48. A low *Viewres* value can also affect appearance, making line types appear continuous onscreen even though they plot as a noncontinuous line type. Regenerating exhibits the true appearance of line types. To display a list of line types currently loaded in your drawing, use **Ddltype**.

👁 **See Also**   Change; Ddemodes; Ddlmodes; Layer; Ltscale; *System Variables:* Plinegen, Psltscale; Viewres

LIST

List displays most of the properties of an object, including coordinate location, color, layer, and line type. List informs you if the object is a block or text. If the object is text, List gives its height, style, and width factor. If the object is a block, List gives its X, Y, and Z scale and insertion point. Attribute tags, defaults, and current values are also listed, if available. If the object is a polyline, the coordinate values for all its vertices are listed. You can also use List to identify hatch-pattern scale and angle. At the command line, use **List**.

To List Properties of an Object

1. In **Windows**, choose the Object Properties toolbar ➤ Inquiry flyout ➤ List button. In **DOS**, choose Assist ➤ Inquiry ➤ List.

2. Select objects: Pick the objects whose properties you wish to see.

NOTES   Listing objects causes AutoCAD to flip the
screen to text mode and pause when the response is lengthy. Pressing ↵ continues you through successive screens, then returns you to
the command line and the graphics mode.

See Also   Dblist

LOAD

Use Load to load a shape definition file (.SHP file) and convert it to
an .SHX file. Like text and blocks, shapes are single objects made
up of lines and arcs. At the command line, type **Load**.

To Load a Shape

1.   Choose Data ➤ Shape File to open the Select Shape File
     dialog box. If *Filedia* is set to zero, you will be prompted:
     Name of shape file to load (or ?):.

2.   Enter the name of the shape file (.SHP) at the prompt, or,
     if you are using the dialog box, use the *List Files of Type*
     box to select and load an .SHP file.

 NOTES   You can define shapes using Shape codes. Consult your *AutoCAD Customization Guide* for details. You can include
shape definitions in linetype patterns in the new complex line types.

See Also   Linetype; Shape; *System Variables:* Shpname

When Logfileon is on, AutoCAD records everything that appears
in the text window (both keystrokes and system prompts and responses) and writes it to an ASCII file. It continues to record until
you exit AutoCAD or use the Logfileoff command. At the command line, use **Logfileon** to turn on the log file option, and **Logfileoff** to turn it off.

To Turn On and Off the Log File

In **Windows**, choose Options ➤ Preferences ➤ Environment,
and then use the Log File check box to turn the log file on or
off. In **DOS**, choose Options ➤ Log Files, then clear the session log.

 NOTES   A new log session begins each time you open
AutoCAD. The log file grows with each session, and should be pe-
riodically edited or deleted. The default log file name is *acad.log*. In
Windows, you may change the name and location of the log file.
Choose Options ➤ Preferences ➤ Environment, then edit the listed
log file name and location as required.

See Also   Preferences

LTSCALE

Ltscale controls the scale of line types. Normally, line type definitions are created for a scale of 1:1. For larger scale drawings such
as 1:20, set Ltscale so that line types fit the drawing scale. Ltscale

globally adjusts all line type definitions to the value you give to Ltscale. At the command line, type **Ltscale** (or **'Ltscale** to use transparently).

To Set the Scale of Line Types

1. Choose Options ➤ Linetypes ➤ Global Linetype Scale.

2. New scale factor <current default>: Enter the desired scale factor.

NOTES Ltscale forces a drawing regeneration when *Regenauto* is on. If Regenauto is turned off, you won't see the effects of Ltscale until you issue **Regen**.

See Also Change; Linetype; *System Variables:* Ltscale, Psltscale

Makepreview allows you to create a preview image of any Auto-CAD Release 12 or earlier drawing without saving the drawing to Release 13 format. Release 13 AutoCAD automatically creates a pre-view image each time you save a drawing, whether it was created in Release 13 or not. Makepreview allows you to call an earlier draw-ing into Release 13, make a preview image, and exit without chang-ing the drawing format. The preview image(s) created will display in AutoCAD release 13 as well as third-party viewers. Once you have loaded the drawing, type **Makepreview**.

MEASURE

Measure marks an object into divisions of a specified length. Measurement begins at the end of the object closest to the pick point. If the object does not divide evenly by the specified length, the remaining portion will be located at the end farthest from the picked point. The command line is **Measure**.

To Measure an Object

1. In **Windows**, choose the Draw toolbar ➤ Point flyout ➤ Measure button. In **DOS**, choose Draw ➤ Point ➤ Measure.

2. Select object to measure: Pick a single object.

3. <Segment length>/Block: Enter the length of the segments to mark or **B** to insert a block.

 **OPTIONS**

Block   Establishes an existing, user-defined block as a marking device. You are prompted for a block name and asked if you want to align the block with the object.

NOTES   By default, Measure uses a point as a marker, but a point is often difficult to see when placed over a line or arc. Use **Ddptype** to set a point style or set the *Pdmode* and *Pdsize* system variables to change the appearance of the points, or select the *Block* option and use a block in place of the point.

The *Block* option is useful if you need to draw a series of objects a specified distance apart along a curved path. For example, to draw identical parking stalls for vehicles, create a block consisting of a line (or stripe) and identify the block name in step 3 above.

See Also   Block; Ddptype; Divide; Point; *System Variables:* Pdmode, Pdsize

170   Menu

MENU

Menu loads a custom menu file. Once you have loaded a menu into a drawing, that drawing file will include the menu file name. The next time you open the drawing file, AutoCAD will also attempt to load the last menu used with the file. At the command line, enter **Menu**.

To Load a Menu

In **Windows**, type **Menu**. In **DOS**, choose Tools ➤ Menus.

If the *Filedia* system variable is set to 1, the Select Menu File dialog list box appears. Use this box to select the menu file you want to use. If *Filedia* is not set to 1, respond to the following prompt at the command line:

Menu filename or . for none <acad>: Enter a menu file name.

NOTES   You can customize the *Acad.MNU* file using a text editor to make AutoCAD load a recompiled .MNX version of the same file name. When you load a menu file, AutoCAD looks for a corresponding .MNL file to load. You may place any custom AutoLISP file routines specified in this .MNL file. Locked menus create files of the same name with an .MKX extension.

See Also   Menuload/Menuunload; *System Variables:* Menuctl, Menuecho, Menuname

N E W

MENULOAD/ MENUUNLOAD

Windows Only

Menuload allows you to create custom menu groups or supplement existing menu groups with additional submenus. Both commands open the Menu Customization dialog box so you can customize, existing base menu files, and load and unload partial menu files.

To Customize and Load a New Menu Group

1. At the command line, enter **Menuload** to create and load a new menu.

2. When the Menu Customization dialog box appears, you may select a menu group.

3. To change an existing menu group or create a new group, click on the Menu Bar alternate dialog box. Then add or remove submenu groups as required from the selection presented.

4. Click on the Load button to load the new menu into your drawing.

Type **Menuunload** to unload a previously loaded menu. When the Menu Customization dialog box appears, select the *Unload* button.

 OPTIONS

Menu Group   Displays list box of all existing menu files. You may enter a menu name in the File Name edit box or select a menu from the Browse pick box. Menu groups can be individually loaded and unloaded from the list box. Check *Replace all* to remove all existing menu groups.

Menu bar   Contains a popup list of current menu groups. When you highlight a specific menu group, the Menu area shows the submenus that make up the highlighted menu group. You may customize menu groups by using the *Insert* and *Remove* options to insert and remove submenus in the displayed group.

 See Also   Menu

MINSERT

Minsert simultaneously inserts a block and creates a rectangular array of that block. You can rotate the array by specifying an angle other than 0 at the prompt. The command line is **Minsert.**

To Insert Multiple Objects

1.   In **Windows,** choose Miscellaneous toolbar ➤ Insert Multiple Blocks. In **DOS,** choose Draw ➤ Insert ➤ Multiple Blocks. The prompts for Minsert are similar to **Insert,** except for the following:

2.   Rotation Angle <0>: Enter the array angle.

3.   Number of rows ( ) <1>: Enter the number of rows in the block array. If the number of rows is greater than 1, the following prompts appear:

- Unit cell or distance between rows (---): Enter the distance between rows. Selecting *Unit cell* requires picking two points with your cursor; after picking the first corner, you are prompted for the Other corner:.

4. Number of columns (||||) <1>: Enter the number of columns in the block array. If the number of columns is greater than 1, the following prompt appears:

- **Distance between columns (||||):** Enter the distance or select the distance using your cursor.

A row-and-column array of the block will then appear at the specified angle.

NOTES The entire array acts like one block. Unlike **Insert**, Minsert does not permit you to explode a block or use an asterisk option. Listing the Minsert entities will provide such information as the number of columns, number of rows, and their spacing. Inserting a block with Minsert groups the entities into a single entity. See **Insert** for a description of the additional option prompts not described here.

 See Also Array, Insert

MIRROR/MIRROR3D

Mirror makes a mirror-image copy of an object or a group of objects. Mirror 3d mirrors objects about a plane. At the command line, type **Mirror** or **Mirror3D**.

To Mirror Objects

1. In **Windows**, choose the Modify toolbar ➤ Copy flyout ➤ Mirror or 3D Mirror button. In **DOS**, choose Construct ➤ Mirror or 3D Mirror.

2. Select objects: Pick the objects to be mirrored.

3. First point of mirror line: Pick one end of the mirror axis.

4. Second point: Pick the other end of the mirror axis.

5. Delete old objects? <N>: Enter **Y** to delete the originally selected objects or press ↵ to keep them.

If you selected Mirror 3D, in place of steps 3 and 4 above, you will be prompted: Plane by Object/Last/ZAxis/View/XY/YZ/ZX/<3 points>: Define a plane and axis for the mirror.

If you have enabled grips for mirroring, the sequence of steps is as follows (use the Select Settings area of the Grips dialog box to enable grips):

1. Select the object(s) to be mirrored and the grips will appear as the entities are highlighted.

2. Pick one of the grips as your "base" point. (A base, or selected, grip appears as a solid filled rectangle.) The Stretch mode prompt then appears at the command line.

3. Cycle through the grip mode commands by pressing ↵ or the spacebar, or by entering **mirror** or **mi** a sufficient number of times until the following prompt appears:

```
**MIRROR**
<Second point>/Base point/Copy/Undo/eXit:
```

4. To mirror the image *without* retaining the original object(s), using the selected grip as the base or first point of the mirror line, drag your cursor and pick the second point of the mirror-line axis. To mirror the image while *retaining* the original object(s), using the selected grip as the base point, enter **C** for *Copy* and pick the second point of the mirror-line axis. (You can hold the Shift key and drag your cursor to pick the second point instead of entering **C**.) Then press ↵ to exit.

- To select a new base point, enter **B** prior to picking the second point or before entering **C**.

 **OPTIONS**

B or ***Base point*** Disengages the cursor from the selected grip so you can assign a new base point for the first point of the mirror-line axis.

C, *Copy*, or ***Shift*** Makes a duplicate of original object(s).

U or ***Undo*** Allows you to undo the previous operation.

X, *eXit*, or ↵ Exits the command.

 NOTES Normally, text, attributes, and attribute definition entities are mirrored. To prevent this, set the *Mirrtext* system variable to 0. Mirroring occurs in a plane parallel to the current UCS (user coordinate system). Use the **Mirror3D** command to duplicate selected objects about an arbitrary plane.

See Also Ddgrips; Grips; *System Variables:* Mirrtext

MLEDIT

Mledit allows you to edit characteristics of a multiline object. Multilines consist of multiple parallel lines. Mledit allows you to control the way that multilines intersect in a drawing, to add and delete vertices, and to manipulate the display of corner joints. From the command line, use **Mledit**.

To Edit a Multiline

1. In **Windows**, choose the Modify toolbar ➤ Special Edit flyout ➤ Edit Multiline button. In **DOS**, choose Modify ➤ Edit Multiline…

2. When the Multiline Edit Tools dialog box appears, double-click on the desired option in the icon menu.

3. **Select first mline:** Select the multiline to be edited (or the vertex to be changed).

4. **Select second mline (or Undo):** Select next multiline, enter U to restore mutiline or enter to exit command.

 OPTIONS

The icon menu in the Multiline Edit Tools dialog box has four colums: the first column pertains to multilines which cross; the second to multilines that form a tee; the third to corner joints and vertices; and the fourth to cutting and welding multilines.

Cross Offers three cross-intersection options: *Closed Cross, Open Cross,* and Merged Cross. When you are prompted to **Select first mline:**, select the *foreground* multiline. At the next prompt **Select second mline:**, select the *intersecting* multiline.

Tee Tee offers three options: *Closed Tee, Open Tee,* and *Merged Tee.* When you are prompted to **Select first time:** select the multiline to trim or extend. At the next prompt, **Select second mline:**, select the intersecting multiline.

Corner Joint and Vertices *Corner Joint* creates a corner joint between multilines. AutoCAD trims or extends the first mline selected to its intersection with the second mline selected. Add/Delete vertex allows you to add a vertex to a multiline segment or delete an existing vertex.

Cut and Weld The *Cut Single* and *Cut All* options allow you to cut selected (or all) elements of a multiline at specified points.

Weld All Restores cut multiline segments. Select the break points on the multiline, and AutoCAD will weld the cut sections.

See Also Mline; Mlstyle; *System Variables:* Cmljust, Cmlscale, Cmlsytyle

N   E   W

MLINE

The Mline command draws multiple parallel lines. Multilines consist of between 1 and 16 parallel lines, or elements. Each element is offset from the origin of the multiline by an amount specified in the Multiline style invoked by Mlstyle. On the command line, type **Mline**.

To Draw a Multiline Object

1. In **Windows**, choose the Draw toolbar ➤ Polyline flyout ➤ Multiline button. In **DOS**, choose Draw ➤ Multiline.

2. Justification/Scale/Style <From point>: Specify the first point, or select an option.

3. Continue to pick points as required to create the multiline. When you pick a third point, you are offered the option to create a closed multiline object. Enter **C** to create a closed object, or press ↵ to exit the command.

💡 OPTIONS

Justification   Allows you to select between Top, Zero, and Bottom. Top positions the top line of the multiline object at the pick point(s); Bottom positions the bottom line of the multiline object at the pick points; Zero uses the pick point(s) as the center line.

Scale   Allows you to enter a different scale value for the multilines. Scale controls the overall width (or separation) of the multiline elements.

Style   Allows you to select a different multiline style from previously created styles.

Close Allows you to create a closed multiline by joining the last point picked to the origin point.

Undo Allows you to undo the previous multiline segment drawn.

 NOTES When you are drawing a multiline, you can use the current style. Or you can load a style from an external file or the symbol table. When the style has been loaded, you can use *Mlstyle* to edit it before you draw the multiline.

See Also Mledit, Mlstyle, Offset

N E W

MLSTYLE

You may use the Mlstyle command to create named styles for multilines which specify the number of lines (from two to sixteen), and the properties of each. You may also use Mlstyle to edit existing multiline styles. From the command line, use **Mlstyle**.

To Create or Edit a Multiline Style

1. In **Windows**, choose the Object Properties toolbar ➤ Multiline Style… or Data ➤ Multiline Style. In **DOS**, choose Data ➤ Multiline Style….

2. When the Multiline Styles dialog box appears, enter the required information. The dialog box displays a graphic representation of the current style and properties. As you define the new style or edit an existing style, the graphic displays the selected properties.

 **OPTIONS**

Current Popup menu for displaying and setting current multiline styles including those stored in external reference drawings.

Name Allows you to enter a new name for the new style or rename an existing style.

Description Allows you to enter an optional description.

Element Properties Displays all of the elements in the current multiline style. The *Add* and *Delete* options allow you to add or remove a line element in the style. *Offset* specifies the offset for line elements of the multiline. *Linetype* opens the Select Linetype dialog box, and allows you to select the element's line type. *Color* opens the Select Color dialog box to select the element's color.

Multiline Properties The *Display Joints* check box allows you to select or deselect the display of a line at the joints of the multiline. *Caps* allows you to select a line or arc for each end of the multiline, and also to specify an angle for the ends. *Fill* allows you to turn on fill for the multiline and to specify a fill *Color*.

Load Loads a style from the multiline library file (ACAD.MLN).

Save... Saves the style to the multiline library file (ACAD.MLN).

Add Allows you to append a multiline style in the Name text box to the current list.

Rename Renames an existing style after it has been edited.

 NOTES Once a multiline style has been created, all multilines drawn after that point will have the properties of that style.

See Also Color, Linetype, Mline, Offset

MOVE

Moves a single object or a set of objects in a specified direction. At the command line, type **Move**.

To Move Objects

1. In **Windows**, choose the Modify toolbar ➤ Move button. In **DOS**, choose Modify ➤ Move.

2. Select objects: Select the objects to be moved.

3. Base point or displacement: Pick the reference or "base" point for the move.

4. Second point of displacement: Pick the distance and direction in relation to the base point or enter the displacement value.

If you have enabled grips for moving, the prompts for Steps 1 and 2 and the options are the same as for **Mirror**, except for the following:

*   Cycle through the grip mode commands by pressing ↵ or the spacebar, or by entering **Move** or **M** a sufficient number of times until you see the following prompt:

    ```
    **MOVE**
    <Move to point>/Base point/Copy/Undo/eXit:
    ```

*   To move the object(s) with the selected grip as the base, drag your cursor and pick the second or displacement point. To move the object(s) using a new base point, enter **B** to pick your first reference point or enter coordinate values, then pick the second point of displacement.

NOTES AutoCAD assumes you want to move objects within the current UCS. However, you can move objects in three-dimensional space by entering XYZ coordinates or using the Osnap overrides to pick objects in three-dimensional space.

If you press ⏎ at the **Second point:** prompt without entering a point value, the objects selected may be moved to a position completely off your drawing area. Use the **U** or **Undo** command to recover.

To make multiple copies of the selected object(s), follow the steps above to define your base point, then hold the Shift key while picking the first copy point (to set copy mode on), and continue by picking additional points. (Entering **C** after selecting the base point will provide the same results.) Exit the command by pressing ⏎.

Pressing the Shift key in the last step to copy the first object from its source point to a destination point will set an automatic snap mode based on these two points. To apply *Multiple copy* using the snap mode, hold the Shift key down while copying additional objects.

See Also Ddgrips, Grips

MSLIDE

Mslide saves the current view as a raster image in a Slide file. (Slide files have .SLD extensions.) From the command line, use **Mslide**.

To Save as an .SLD File

Choose Tools ➤ Slide ➤ Save. When the *Filedia* system variable is set to 1, the Create Slide File dialog list box is displayed; when *Filedia* is set to zero, the following prompt appears: **Slide File :**, enter a file name.

 **See Also**   Delay, Script, Vslide

MSPACE

Mspace lets you switch from Paperspace to a Modelspace viewport. This command works only when you are in Paperspace
(**Tilemode** is set to 0). You move from Paperspace into Modelspace
via previously created viewports.

To Switch from Paperspace to a Modelspace Viewport

In **Windows**, choose the Status Bar ➤ Model, or View ➤ Floating Model Space. In **DOS**, choose View ➤ Floating Model
Space.

 **NOTES**   If the **Tilemode** system variable is set to 0 but no
viewports are available in Paperspace, you will receive the message
"There are no active Modelspace viewports."

 **See Also**   Mview, Pspace, Tilemode

N E W

MTEXT

Mtext allows you to create long, complex text entries, consisting of
any number of lines or paragraphs of text. Multiline or paragraph

text fits within a specified width in the drawing but may run to any length. On the command line, use **Mtext**.

To Create Multiline Text

1. In **Windows**, choose the Draw toolbar ➤ Text flyout ➤ Text button. In **DOS**, choose Draw ➤ Text ➤ Text.

2. Attach/Rotation/Style/Height/Direction/<Insertion point>: Specify the insertion point for the text.

3. Attach/Rotation/Style/Height/Direction/Width/2 points<Other corner>: Specify the size of the text boundary window by picking a diagonally opposite corner or entering **W** and defining the text width only.

4. If you are in **Windows**, the Edit Mtext dialog box opens and you may enter and format the multiline text. If you are in **DOS**, AutoCAD exits to the DOS Editor. You may use this ASCII editor to enter and format the multiline text.

When text entry is complete, AutoCAD inserts the text into the specified text boundary.

 OPTIONS

Attach Controls the alignment and positioning of the multiline text within the text window with the TL/TC/TR/ML/MC/MR/BL/BC/BR: prompt. The two-letter options set the justification based on the combination of top, middle, or bottom, and left, center, or right. For example, TL stands for "top-left" and MC stands for "middle-center."

Rotation Allows you to specify a rotation angle for the Mtext.

Style Allows you to select a different text style from the current style.

Height Allows you to enter a specific text height for the Mtext.

Direction Allows you to set the direction of the text as either Horizontal or Vertical.

Width Allows you to specify the width only of the text boundary window, rather than the both corners. If you enter a zero value, the text will not wrap but will extend horizontally until you press ↵.

Insertion point/Other corner Lets you define the text window into which the paragraph text will be placed.

NOTES In Windows, you can use the Edit Mtext dialog box to quickly set properties either for the entire object or just for selected portions. Paragraph or multiline text has more options for editing than line text. You may use underlining, overlining, and apply special fonts, color, and height to single words within a paragraph.

If you have created a paragraph that is too long to fit in the text window, the text will overflow in the direction specified by the Attach setting: top-aligned text will "spill" down, and bottom-aligned text will "flow up" from the specified boundary window; center-aligned text will spread both above and below the text window. Multiline text, no matter how many lines or paragraphs, forms a single object and can be moved, stretched, erased, copied, mirrored, or scaled.

You can use any standard text editor to create multiline text, both in Windows and in DOS. In Windows, you will need to specify your choice of editor in the Options ➤ Preferences Misc dialog box.

See Also Ddedit; Ddmodify; Dtext/Text; Mtprop, Preferences; Spell; Style; *System Variables:* Fontalt, Fontmap, Mtexted

Mtprop allows you to change Mtext properties. The command opens the Mtext Properties dialog box and allows you to modify the properties of paragraph text created using the Mtext command.

To Change Mtext Properties

1. At the command line, type **Mtprop**.

2. Select an Mtext object: Select a section of paragraph text.

3. In the Mtext Properties dialog box, modify the text properties as required.

 **OPTIONS**

The Mtext properties that may be changed are detailed more fully in the Mtext command option and "Notes."

Contents   This dialog box area allows you to modify the text characteristics of *Text Style*, *Text Height*, and *Direction*.

Object   This dialog box area allows you to modify the text-positioning variables of *Attachment*, *Width* of bounding box, and *Rotation*.

See Also   Ddedit; Ddmodify; Dtext/Text; Mtprop; Preferences; Spell; Style; *System Variables:* Fontalt, Fontmap, Mtexted

MULTIPLE

Multiple causes the next command to repeat until you cancel it. At the command line, enter **Multiple**, a space, and then the command.

The command repeats until you press Esc in **Windows**, or Ctrl-C in **DOS**. Because Multiple repeats only the command itself, any options or parameters must be specified each time.

MVIEW

Mview creates Paperspace viewports and controls the number, layout, and visibility of viewports. This command works in Paperspace only. At the command line, use **Mview**.

To Create a Paperspace Viewport

1. In **Windows**, choose the View toolbar ➤ Floating Viewports button or View ➤ Floating Viewports. In **DOS**, choose View ➤ Floating Viewports.

2. ON/OFF/Hideplot/Fit/2/3/4/Restore/<First point>: Pick a point indicating one corner of the new Paperspace viewport or enter an option. If you pick a point, you are prompted for the opposite corner. Mview then creates the viewport.

 **OPTIONS**

ON/OFF Turns the display of Modelspace on or off within the chosen viewport. When a viewport's Modelspace display is turned off, it no longer regenerates when it is moved or resized. This is helpful when you are rearranging a set of viewports.

Hideplot Controls hidden line removal for individual viewports at plot time. When you select this option, the **Select objects:** prompt appears. Pick the viewport you wish to have plotted with hidden lines removed. Selecting an entity inside the viewport will not select the viewport—you must pick the edge or border.

Fit Creates a single viewport that fills the screen.

2/3/4 Lets you create two, three, or four viewports simultaneously. Once you enter one of these options, different prompts appear, depending on the number of viewports requested. If you select **2**, you will be prompted Horizontal/<Vertical>:; if you select **3**, you will be prompted Horizontal/Vertical/Above/Below/Left/<Right>:. Then you will be prompted: Fit/<first point>:. Pick points to indicate the location of the viewports, or select the *Fit* option to force the viewports to fit in the display area.

Restore Translates viewport configurations created using the **Vport** command (Modelspace viewports) into paper-space viewport entities. You are prompted for the name of a viewport configuration.

NOTES The *Tilemode* system variable must be set to 0 to use Mview. If you are in Modelspace when you issue Mview, you receive the message "Command not allowed unless TILEMODE is set to zero."

Grid and snap modes, as well as layer visibility, can be set individually within each Paperspace viewport.

Viewports, like most other entities, can be moved, copied, stretched, or erased. You can hide viewport borders by changing their layer assignments, then turning off their layers. You can also align positions of objects in one viewport with those of another by using the **Mvsetup** utility. Viewport scale can be set using the *xp* option under the **Zoom** command.

See Also Mspace; Mvsetup; Pspace; Tilemode; *System Variables:* Psltscale, Vplayer, Vports; Zoom

MVSETUP

Mvsetup sets up the Paperspace specifications of a drawing, including viewports, drawing scale, and sheet title block. On the command line, use **Mvsetup**.

To Set Up a Paper Space

Choose View ➤ Floating Viewports ➤ Mvsetup.

On a new drawing with *Tilemode* set to 1 (On), the following prompt appears: Enable paper space?(No/<Yes>):.

- If you enter **N**, you will be prompted to specify measurement Units, a Scale factor, and a Paper Height and Width. Auto-CAD will then draw a bounding box and exit the command.

- If you press ↵ to accept the default **Y**, the *Tilemode* system variable is set to 0 (Off), and the following prompt appears: Align/Create/Scale viewports/Options/Title block/Undo:.

 **OPTIONS**

Align Aligns locations in one viewport with locations in another viewport. If you select Align (**A**), you will receive the following prompt: Angled/Horizontal/Vertical alignment/Rotate view/Undo?:. *Angled* aligns locations by indicating an angle and distance. You are prompted to pick a base point to which others can be aligned. Next, you are prompted to pick a point in another viewport that you want aligned with the base point. You are then prompted for a distance and angle. *Horizontal/Vertical alignment* aligns views either horizontally or vertically. You are prompted for a base point (the point to be aligned to) and the point to be aligned with the base point. *Rotate view* rotates the view in a viewport. You are prompted for a viewport and base point, and then for the angle of rotation.

Create viewports   Creates new viewports. If you select this option (**C**), you will receive the prompt **Delete objects/Undo/<Create viewpoints>:.** *Delete objects* deletes existing viewport entities. *<Create viewports>* displays a list of options for creating viewports, as follows:

> *0: None*   Creates no viewports.
>
> *1: Single*   Creates a single viewport for which you specify the area.
>
> *2: Std. Engineering*   Creates four viewports set up in quadrants. You can set up these views for top, front, right side, and isometric.
>
> *3: Array of Viewports*   Creates a matrix of viewports by specifying the number of viewports in the X and Y axes. The *Add/Delete* option on the prompt adds or deletes options from the list. *Add* provides a title block for the list.
>
> *Redisplay/<Number of entry to load>*   Lets you view the list again.

Scale viewports   Sets the scale between Paperspace and the viewport. For example, if your drawing in Modelspace is scaled to $\frac{1}{4}$″ = 1′, and your title block in Paperspace is scaled to 1″ = 1″, you will want the scale factor of your viewport to be 48. When you select this option (**S**), the prompt **Select the viewports to scale:** appears. Once you've selected more than one viewport, the prompt **Set zoom scale factors for viewports. Interactive/<Uniform>:** appears. The Interactive option sets the scale of each selected viewport individually with a request to enter the ratio of paperspace units to modelspace units. You are prompted for the **Number of paperspace units:**, then the **Number of modelspace units:**. In the $\frac{1}{4}$″ scale example, you would enter **1** for the paper-space units and **48** for the model-space units.

Options   Allows you to set the MVSETUP preferences before you change your drawing. If you type **O**, you will receive the following prompt: **Set Layer/Limits/Units/Xref:.** *Set Layer* allows you to specify a layer for the title block. *Limits* allows you to reset the drawing limits by prompting **Set drawing limits?<N>**, *Units* allows you to specify the Paperspace units as feet, inches, meters, or millimeters. *Xref* allows you to specify whether the title block is to be inserted or externally referenced.

Title block Produces the prompt **Delete objects/Origin/Undo/<In-sert title block>:**. *Delete objects* deletes objects from Paperspace. *Origin* sets a new origin point for Paperspace. *<Insert title block>* displays the following:

```
Available paper/output sizes:

0: None
1: ISO A4 Size (mm)
2: ISO A3 Size (mm)
3: ISO A2 Size (mm)
4: ISO A1 Size (mm)
5: ISO A0 Size (mm)
6: ANSI-V Size (in)
7: ANSI-A Size (in)
8: ANSI-B Size (in)
9: ANSI-C Size (in)
10: ANSI-D Size (in)
11: ANSI-E Size (in)
12: Arch/Engineering (24 X 36)
13: Generic D size Sheet (24 X 36in)
Add/Delete/Redisplay/<Number of entry to
  load>:
```

Enter the number corresponding to the title block you want to use. *Add* and *Delete* let you add or delete a title block to or from the list. Add prompts you for a title block description for inclusion in the above list, the name of the file to be used as the title block. It allows you to specify the default usable area within the title block. *Redisplay* lets you view the list again.

Undo Undoes an option without leaving the Mvsetup utility.

NOTES When adding a title block to the list in the title block option, you must already have a title block drawing ready and in the current DOS path. The *Xp* option under the **Zoom** command can also be used to set the scale of a viewport. Mvsetup saves the current configuration to a file called *Mvsetup.DFS*.

SEE ALSO Ltscale; Mspace; Mview; Pspace; *System Variables:* Psltscale; Tilemode; Zoom

NEW

The New command lets you start a new drawing from scratch or use an existing drawing as a template for a new drawing. The command line is **New**.

To Begin a New Drawing

1. In **Windows**, choose the Standard toolbar ➤ New. In **DOS**, choose File ➤ New...

If changes were made to your current drawing, the Drawing Modification dialog box in DOS appears and prompts you to **Save Changes, Discard Changes, or Cancel**. In Windows the Save Changes to (file name) message box appears with options for *Yes, No,* and *Cancel.* If you previously have not invoked **Save** or **Qsave**, select *Yes* to save any edited or unsaved drawings before opening a new drawing. If you wish to save your current drawing and have previously not named it, the Save Drawing As dialog box opens and you may enter a name in the File edit box.

2. When the Create New Drawing dialog box opens, enter the new drawing name in the Edit box or double-click on the New Drawing Name... button.

If the *Filedia* system variable is set to 0, follow the command line prompts instead of using the dialog box.

To Use the Current Drawing as a Template

You can also assign a template or prototype drawing name when opening a new drawing. In the New Drawing Name... edit box or at the **Enter name of drawing:** prompt, enter the new file name followed by an equals sign and the name of the file you wish to use as a template. For example, you could enter

```
new drawing name=prototype name
```

There should be no spaces between the equal sign and the file
names. Drive and directory specifications can be included. To specify no prototype, use the following format:

    new drawing name=

If you are using the dialog box, the template name can also be entered in the Prototype... edit box.

If you don't want to use a prototype drawing, pick the No Prototype check box. To retain a drawing as the prototype, pick the Retain as Default check box. To retain no prototype as the default,
pick both the No Prototype and Retain as Default check boxes.

NOTES AutoCAD uses a file called *Acad.DWG* as the
prototype file for all new drawings. If you want different default
settings for your new drawings, you can open *Acad.DWG* and set it
up the way you want. This file is in the \ACADR13\COM-
MON\SUPPORT directory.

If you have a nonstandard prototype *Acad.DWG* file and you want
to open a file using the standard AutoCAD defaults, type an equals
sign after the new file name.

See Also End; Open; Qsave; Quit; Save; *System Variables:* Filedia, Dwgname, Dwgprefix, Dwgtitled, Savename

OFFSET

Offset creates an object parallel to and at a specified distance from
its original. The command line is **Offset**.

To Offset a Line

1. In **Windows**, choose the Modify toolbar ➤ Copy flyout ➤
Offset. In **DOS**, choose Construct ➤ Offset.

2.   Offset distance or Through <Through>: Enter a distance
     value, or pick two points, or enter **T** to specify an offset
     through-point after each object selection.

     •   Entering a distance value gets the prompt Side to
         offset. Pick the side on which you want the offset to
         appear.

     •   Selecting Through by entering **T** or pressing ↵ prompts
         you for the Through point:. Pick a point to locate the
         offset line.

3.   Select object to offset: Pick one object.

 OPTIONS

Offset Distance   If you enter a value at the Distance prompt, all the
offsets performed in the current command will be at that distance.
The prompt will continue offsetting objects at the specified distance
until you press ↵.

Through   Identifies a point through which the offset object will pass
after you have selected the object to offset. The prompt will continue
prompting for the next point until you press ↵.

 NOTES   Offset will offset only a single object. If you have
multiple, sequential lines or arcs to offset, use the **Pedit** command
to join them into one polyline object before performing the offset.

Window, Crossing, Fence, WPolygon, CPolygon and *Last* are not valid
selections for Offset. The offset distance is stored in the system variable *Offsetdist* as the default. If the value is negative, it defaults to
Through mode.

👁 **See Also**   Copy; Grips; Pedit; *System Variables*: Offsetdist

OLE

OLE (Object Linking and Embedding) is a Windows feature that lets you link AutoCAD drawings with drawings in other applications that support OLE. With AutoCAD Release 12, an AutoCAD drawing could be linked into a word processor or other Windows application. With Release 13, AutoCAD can act as an OLE client as well as a server. Objects from other OLE applications can be linked or embedded into AutoCAD drawing files.

 NOTES Although the linking and the embedding processes both insert information into an AutoCAD drawing (or from an AutoCAD drawing into another application), the relationship with the source object is different. Embed and Link are comparable to the AutoCAD commands **Insert** and **Xref**, respectively. When you *embed* an object, you effectively insert a copy of it into the destination document, and no permanent connection with the source object remains. When you *link* an object, it remains connected to the original object. If the original object changes, you need only update the links and the information in the destination document will be updated. You can even set a linked object to update automatically by using **Olelinks**.

👁 **See Also** Cut and Paste, Insert, Insertobj, Olelinks, Xref

☑ N E W ☑

OLELINKS

Windows Only

Allows you to update, change, and cancel existing links. On the command line, use **Olelinks**.

To Update Object Links

1.   Choose Edit ➤ Links.

2.   Make the required changes in the Links dialog box to modify the link information.

 OPTIONS

Links   Provides a list of each linked object in the current drawing along with its file name, source application, and update status information.

Update: Automatic   Picking the Update: Automatic radio button provides an automatic update of a linked object whenever the original object is changed.

Update: Manual   If you select the Update: Manual radio button, you will be prompted to update the link when you open the document which contains it.

Update Now   Updates any selected links from the Links list box.

Cancel Link   Breaks the connection with the source object, but retains a copy of the object in your document.

Change Link   Allows you to specify a new source location or file name.

Done   Closes the Links dialog box.

The remaining two options in the Links dialog box vary depending upon the OLE object under review. They allow you to display and edit the selected OLE object.

OOPS

Oops restores objects that have been accidentally removed from a drawing. On the command line, use **Oops**.

To Restore an Erased Object

In **Windows**, choose Miscellaneous toolbar ➤ Oops. In **DOS**, choose Modify ➤ Oops!.

NOTES Oops retrieves all objects erased by the last **Erase** and after executing **Bmake**, **Block**, or **Wblock**.

See Also U, Undo

OPEN

The Open command lets you open an existing drawing. The command line is **Open**.

To Open an Existing Drawing

1. In **Windows**, choose the Standard toolbar ➤ Open button. In **DOS**, choose File ➤ Open....

2. The Open Drawing list box displays files and directories for selection. Click on the desired drawing name. A preview image is displayed in the dialog box; you may preview the drawing before loading it into the drawing area.

If the *Filedia* system variable is set to 0, Open displays the following command line prompt: Enter name of drawing <current default>: Enter the name of an existing drawing.

 **OPTIONS**

Options common to DOS and Windows are:

Type it   Enter drawing name at command line.

Default   Restore original settings.

Read Only Mode or Read Only   Check this box if you wish to open a drawing in Read Only mode. Drawings that are opened in Read Only mode can be edited and saved to a new name. You may not save changes to the drawing's original name.

Options in DOS are:

Select Initial View   To open a drawing to a saved view, pick from the Select Initial View dialog box and highlight a view name or the last view.

Options in Windows are:

Find File   Opens the Find File dialog box, which allows you to Search or Browse through your drives and directories.

Search   Allows you to include search criteria such as file creation date and time.

Browse   Displays thumbnail images of all of the drawings in a selected directory. Once you have located the drawing you want, double-click on the image to open the drawing.

See Also   End; Exit New; Qsave; Quit; Save; *System Variables:* Dwgname, Dwgwrite, Filedia, Savefile, Savename, Savetime

ORTHO

Ortho forces lines to be drawn in exactly perpendicular directions following the orientation of the crosshairs. The command line is **Ortho** (or **'Ortho**, to use transparently).

To Turn Ortho On or Off

In **Windows** double-click on ORTHO in the status bar. In **DOS**, choose Assist ➤ Ortho.

NOTES   If you enter Ortho through the keyboard, you are prompted to turn Ortho **ON** or **OFF**. Use the F8 function key or the Ctrl-O key combination to toggle between Ortho On and Ortho Off. If you pick Ortho from the pull-down menu, it retrieves the Ddrmodes dialog box.

To force lines to angles other than 90 degrees, rotate the cursor using the *Snapang* system variable or by setting the Rotate option under the **Snap** command.

 See Also   Ddrmodes, Snap, *System Variables:* Orthmode, Snapang

OSNAP

Sets the current default Object Snap mode, allowing you to pick specific geometric points on an object. You can have several Object Snap modes active at once if you separate their names by commas. For example, to be able to select endpoints and midpoints automatically, enter **END,MID** at the Osnap prompt. AutoCAD knows to select the correct point (MID, END, etc.) according to which point is closer to the target box. The command is **Osnap** (or '**Osnap**, to use transparently). The equivalent dialog box command is **Ddosnap**.

To Pick Specific Geometric Points

1. In **Windows**, choose Standard toolbar ➤ **Osnap** flyout. In **DOS**, choose Assist ➤ Object Snap.

2. Object snap modes: Enter or select the desired default Object snap mode(s).

 **OPTIONS**

Center (CEN) Picks the center of circles and arcs.

Endpoint (END) Picks the endpoint of objects.

Insertion (INS) Picks the insertion point of blocks and text.

Intersection (INT) Picks the intersection of objects.

Apparent Intersection (APPINT) Sanps to the apparent intersection of two objects, although they may not actually intersect in 3D space.

Midpoint (MID) Picks the midpoint of lines and arcs.

Nearest (NEA) Picks the point on an object nearest to the cursor.

Node (NOD) Picks a point object. (See **Point**.)

Perpend (PER) Picks the point on an object perpendicular to the last point.

Quadrant (QUA) Picks a cardinal point on an arc or circle.

Quick (QUI) Sanps to the first object snap found. It must be used along with other snap modes. *Quick* does not work in conjunction with Intersection.

Tangent (TAN) Picks a tangent point on a circle or arc.

NONE Disables the current default Object snap mode. Entering **Off** or pressing ↵ at the **Object snap modes:** prompt does the same.

NOTES   You can use the Osnap overrides whenever you are prompted to select a point or object. Unlike the Osnap mode settings, the overrides are active only at the time they are issued. Enter the first three letters of the name of the override, or pick the override from the popup Cursor menu.

The Cursor menu is activated in different ways depending on the pointing device that you are using: if you have a four-button device, press the *third* button (blue for some pucks); if you have a three-button device, press the *middle* button; if you have a two-button device, hold the Shift key down while pressing the Right button. The *Acad.MNU* file supplied with AutoCAD assigns these buttons to the Cursor menu. The Cursor menu lists point filters as well as snap modes.

See Also   Aperture; Ddosnap; Point Selection; *System Variables: Osmode*

PAN

Pan shifts the display to reveal parts of a drawing that are off the screen. Drawings retain the same magnification. On the command line, type **Pan** (or **'Pan** to use transparently).

To See Offscreen Drawing Areas

1. In **Windows**, choose Standard toolbar ➤ Pan flyout. In **DOS**, choose View ➤ Pan ➤ Point.

If you use the command line or pick *Point* on the drop-down menu or the Pan flyout, you may specify one or two precise points of displacement:

2. Displacement: Pick the first point of view displacement.

3. Second point: Pick the distance and direction of displacement.

The Pan flyout and the drop-down menu also offer a range of pre-set displacement options: *Left, Right, Up, Down* and *Up/Left, Up/Right, Down/Left, Down/Right*.

You cannot use Pan while viewing a drawing in perspective. Use the **Dview** command's *Pan* option instead.

 See Also   Dview, Pan, View, Zoom

PEDIT

Pedit edits two- or three-dimensional polylines and three-dimensional meshes, changes the location of individual vertices in a polyline or mesh, and converts a nonpolyline object into a polyline. The editing options available depend on the type of object you select. See the following sections for information about individual Pedit operations. The command line is **Pedit**.

Pedit for 2D and 3D Polylines

Pedit modifies the shape of 2D and 3D polylines. If the object you select is not a polyline, respond to the Do you want to turn it into one? <Y>: prompt with **Y**.

To Edit Polylines

1. In **Windows**, choose the Modify toolbar ➤ Special Edit fly-out ➤ Edit Polyline button. In **DOS**, choose Modify ➤ Edit Polyline.

2. Select polyline: Select the object you want to edit as a polyline.

If the object selected is a 2D polyline, the following prompt appears:

```
Close/Join/Width/Edit vertex/Fit/Spline/Decurve/
  Ltype gen Undo/eXit <X>:
```

If the object is a 3D polyline, the following prompt appears:

```
Close/Edit vertex/Spline curve/Decurve/Undo/
  eXit <X>:
```

(If the polyline is closed, Open appears instead of Close in the prompt above.)

If the object is a standard line or arc, the following prompt appears:

```
Object selected is not a polyline
Do you want it to turn into one: <Y> Enter
  Y or N.
```

 **OPTIONS**

Close Joins the endpoints of a polyline. If the selected polyline is already closed, this option is replaced by Open in the prompt.

Open Deletes the last line segment in a closed polyline.

Join Joins polylines, lines, and arcs. The objects to be joined must meet exactly end-to-end.

Width Sets the width of the entire polyline.

Edit vertex Performs various edits on polyline vertices. See the section below on Pedit/Edit vertex.

Fit curve Changes a polyline made up of straight line segments into a smooth curve.

Spline curve Changes a polyline made up of straight line segments into a spline-fit curve.

Decurve Changes a smoothed polyline into one made up of straight line segments.

Ltype gen Causes the line type to continue uniformly around the vertices of the polyline when turned on.

Undo Cancels the last Pedit function issued.

eXit Exits the Pedit command.

NOTES The *Spline curve* option adjusts the "pull" of the vertex points on the curve by changing the *Splinetype* system variable. The default for *Splinetype* is 6. With *Splinetype* set to 5, the pull is greater. See **System Variables** for more details.

You can view both the curve and the defining vertex points of a spline-fit curve by setting the *Splframe* system variable to 1. The *Splinesegs* system variable determines the number of line segments used to draw the curve. A higher value generates more line segments for a smoother curve, but also a larger drawing file. The curve created by this process corresponds to a B-spline, but is not actually a true spline curve. You may convert a spline-fit polyline into a true B-spline (NURBS) curve by using the *Object* option on the **Spline** command.

See Also Pedit/Edit Vertex; Pedit/3D mesh; Pline; *System Variables*: Splframe, Splinesegs, Splintype

Pedit/Edit Vertex

Relocates, removes, moves, or inserts vertices in a polyline. Modifies a polyline's width at a particular vertex and alters the tangent direction of a curved polyline through a vertex.

To Edit a Polyline Vertex

Start the **Pedit** command, then select the polyline object you want to edit.

1. Close/Join/Width/Edit vertex/Fit/Spline/Decurve/Ltype gen/Undo/eXit <X>: Enter **E** for Edit vertex. An *X* appears on the first vertex of the selected polyline indicating · the vertex currently editable.

2. Next/Previous/Break/Insert/Move/Regen/Straighten/ Tangent/Width/eXit <N>: Enter the capitalized letter of the function to be used.

 **OPTIONS**

Next   Moves the X marker to the next vertex.

Previous   Moves the X marker to the previous vertex.

Break   Breaks polyline from the marked vertex. Move the X into the position where you want the break to begin and type **B** for Break. The prompt changes to **Next/Previous/Go/eXit <N>:**. Move the marker to another vertex to select the other end of the break. Once the X marker is in position, enter **G** to initiate the break.

Insert   Inserts a new vertex. A rubber-banding line stretches from the vertex being edited to the cursor. Enter points either using the cursor or by keying in coordinates.

Move   Allows relocation of a vertex. A rubber-banding line stretches from the vertex being edited to the cursor. You can specify points either using the cursor or by keying in coordinates. To move a vertex, you may alternatively use the Grip editor. See "Notes" below.

Regen   Regenerates a polyline. This may be required to see effects of some edits.

Straighten   Straightens a polyline between two vertices. Move the cursor to the position where you want the straightening to begin and enter **S**. The prompt changes to **Next/Previous/Go/eXit <N>:**. This allows you to move in either direction along the polyline. Once the X marker (see "Notes" below) is in position, type **G** to straighten the polyline. This removes all vertices between the two markers and creates one segment instead.

Tangent   Allows you to attach a tangent direction to a vertex for later use in curve fitting. A rubber-banding line stretches from the vertex to the cursor, indicating the new tangent direction. Indicate the new tangent angle by picking the direction using the cursor or by keying in an angle value. Tangent only affects curve-fitted or spline polylines.

Width   Varies the width of a polyline segment. When you have entered this function, the prompt changes to **Enter starting width <current default width>:**. This allows you to enter a new width for the currently marked vertex. When you have entered a value, the prompt changes to Enter ending width <last value entered>:. This allows you to enter a width for the next vertex.

eXit Exits from vertex editing.

NOTES When you invoke the *Edit vertex* option, an X appears on the polyline, indicating that the vertex is being edited. Press ⏎ to issue the default N for *Next vertex* and move the X to the next vertex. Type **P** to reverse the direction of the X. When inserting a new vertex or using the Width function, pay special attention to the direction the X moves when you select the Next function. This is the direction along the polyline in which the new vertex or the new ending width will be inserted.

You may use the Edit Vertex option to move a vertex. It is generally faster to move a vertex using the object grips. With the Grips on, click on the polyline to highlight the vertices. Click on the grip of the vertex you wish to move, and move it to the desired position.

If you select a 3D polyline, all the edit options except *Tangent* and *Width* are available. Also, point input accepts 3D points.

Pedit for 3D Meshes

Pedit smooths a 3D mesh or moves vertex points in the mesh.

To Edit a 3D Mesh

Start the Pedit command, then select a mesh. You will be prompted to choose one of the options described below.

```
Edit vetext/Smooth
  surface/Desmooth/Mclose/Nclose/Undo/eXit/<X>:
```

OPTIONS

Edit vertex Relocates vertices of a selected 3D mesh. When you select this option, you get the prompt:

```
Vertex (m,n)
```

```
Next/Previous/Left/Right/Up/Down/Move/REgen/
  eXit <N>: <option>
```

An X appears on the first vertex of the mesh, marking the vertex to be moved.

Next Rapidly moves the Edit vertex marker to the next vertex.

Previous Rapidly moves the Edit vertex marker to the previous vertex.

Left Moves the Edit vertex marker along the N direction of the mesh.

Right Moves the Edit vertex marker along the N direction of the mesh opposite to the Left option.

Up Moves the Edit vertex marker along the M direction of the mesh.

Down Moves the Edit vertex marker along the M direction of the mesh opposite to the Up direction.

Move Moves the location of the currently marked vertex.

REgen Redisplays the mesh after a vertex has been moved.

Smooth surface Generates a B-spline or Bezier surface based on the mesh's vertex points. The type of surface generated depends on the *Surftype* system variable.

Desmooth Returns a smoothed surface back to regular mesh.

Mclose Closes a mesh in the M direction.

Nclose Closes a mesh in the N direction.

Mopen Appears when a mesh is closed to open a mesh in the M direction.

Nopen Appears when a mesh is closed to open a mesh in the N direction.

Undo Cancels the last Pedit option issued.

eXit Exits the Edit vertex option or the Pedit command.

NOTES   You can use several system variables (see **Setvar**) to modify a 3D mesh. To determine the type of smooth surface generated, use the *Surftype* variable with the Smooth option. A value of 5 gives you a quadratic B-spline surface; a value of 6 gives a cubic B-spline surface; and 8 gives a Bezier surface. The default value for *Surftype* is 6.

The *Surfu* and *Surfv* system variables control the accuracy of the generated surface. *Surfu* controls the surface density in the M direction of the mesh, and *Surfv* controls density in the N direction. The default value for these variables is 6.

The *Splframe* system variable determines whether the control mesh of a smoothed mesh is displayed. If it is set to 0, only the smoothed mesh is displayed. If it is set to 1, only the defining mesh is displayed.

See **Boundary** for automatically grouping lines together into a single object by picking the internal region.

See Also   Boundary; Grips Pline; Spline; *System Variables:* Setvar, Splframe, Surftype, Surfu, Surfv; 3Dmesh, 3Dpoly

PFACE

Draws a polygon mesh by first defining the vertices of the mesh and then assigning 3dfaces to the vertex locations.

To Draw a Polygon Mesh

1. At the command line, type **Pface**.

2. Vertex 1: Pick a point for the first vertex to be used in defining the mesh. The vertex prompt repeats after each point is selected. The vertex number increases by 1 each time you pick a point. Remember the location of each vertex; you will need to know the number for the next step. When you have finished selecting points, press ↵.

3. Face 1, Vertex 1: Enter the number of the vertex from Step 1 that you want to correspond to the first vertex of the first face. When you enter a number, the same prompt appears with the vertex number increased by 1. You can define one face with as many of the points as you indicated in step 2. When you have defined the first face, press ↵.

4. Face 2, Vertex 1: Enter the number of the vertex that you want to correspond to the first vertex of the second face. When you have finished, press ↵.

 **OPTIONS**

–(**number**) Makes a face edge invisible when entered at the Face *n*, Vertex *n*: prompt. You must use a negative value for each overlapping edge.

Layer Specifies the layer for the face you are currently defining. Enter Layer at the Face *n*, Vertex *n*: prompt.

Color Specifies the color of the face you are currently defining. You can enter Color at the Face *n*, Vertex *n*: prompt.

NOTES Pface was designed for programmers who need an object type that can easily create 3D surfaces with special properties. Pfaces cannot be edited using Pedit. However, you can use **Array**, **Chprop**, **Copy**, **Erase**, **List**, **Mirror**, **Move**, **Rotate**, **Scale**, **Stretch**, and **Explode** on Pfaces.

See Also Edgesurf; Revsurf; Rulesurf; *System Variables:* Pfacemax; Tabsurf; 3DMesh

PLAN

Plan displays a user coordinate system "in plan"—that is, a view perpendicular to the UCS. This allows you to create and manipulate objects in 2D more easily. Plan affects only the active viewport. You can set the *Ucsfollow* system variable so that whenever you change to a different UCS, you get a plan view of it. The command line is **Plan**.

To View in Plan

Choose View ➤ 3D Viewpoint Presets ➤ Plan View ➤ Current/World/Named.

If you are using the command line, you will be prompted

<Current UCS>/Ucs/World:. Enter the capitalized letter of the desired option or press ↵ for the current UCS.

 **OPTIONS**

↵ Gives you a plan view of the current UCS. This is the default option.

U Gives you a plan view of a previously saved UCS. You are prompted for the name of the UCS you wish to see in plan. Enter a question mark to get a list of saved UCS's:

• **?/Name of UCS:** Enter ? for a list or the name of your saved UCS.

• **UCS name(s) to list <*>:** Press ↵ to view names.

W Gives you a plan view of the world coordinate system. This option is automatically issued when you pick PlanView (world) from the Display pull-down menu.

 See Also   *System Variables:* Ucsfollow, UCS

PLINE

Pline creates lines having properties such as thickness and curvature. Unlike standard lines, polylines can be grouped together to act as a single object. For example, a box you draw using a polyline will act as one object instead of four discrete lines. The command line is **Pline**.

To Create a Polyline

1. In **Windows**, choose the Draw toolbar ➤ Polyline flyout ➤ Polyline button. In **DOS**, choose Draw ➤ Polyline.

2. From point: Pick the start point of the polyline.

3. Arc/Close/Halfwidth/Length/Undo/Width/<Endpoint of line>: Enter the desired option or pick the next point of pline.

 OPTIONS

Arc   Changes Pline to **Arc** mode. The Arc options are then listed in the prompt:

Angle/CEnter/CLose/Direction/Halfwidth/Line/Radius/Second pt/Undo/Width/<Endpoint of arc>:

You can enter either the second point, angle, center, direction, radius, or endpoint of the arc. See the **Arc** command for the use of the Arc options.

Close   Draws a line from the current polyline end point back to its beginning, forming a closed polyline.

Halfwidth   Specifies half the polyline width at the current point. You are first prompted for the starting half width, which is half the width of the polyline at the last fixed point. Next, you are prompted for the ending half width—half the width of the polyline at the next point you pick.

Length   Draws a polyline in the same direction as the last line segment drawn. You are prompted for the line segment length. If an arc was drawn last, the direction will be tangent to the end direction of that arc.

Undo   Allows you to step backward along the current string of polyline or polyarc segments.

Width   Determines the whole width of the polyline. Subsequent polylines will be of this width unless you specify otherwise.

NOTES   To give a polyline a smooth curve shape, you must use the **Pedit** command after you create the polyline. The **Explode** command reduces a polyline to its line and arc components. Polylines with a width value lose their width once exploded. To control the uniformity of a line type that is not continuous around the vertices, set the *Plinegen* system variable to 1 or use the *Ltgen* option of Pedit.

See Also   Boundary; Explode; Offset; Pedit; *System Variables:* Plinegen, Plinewid

PLOT

Plot opens up the Plot Configuration dialog box for sending your drawing to a plotter. You can control the plotter pen selection and speed as well as where to preview the drawing on the plotter media. Plot also allows AutoCAD to reduce a scale drawing to fit on the media. Once you change any of the plotter settings, they become the default settings. Several plot configurations can be saved and recalled from the dialog box. The command line is **Plot**.

To Plot a Drawing Using the Dialog Box

In **Windows**, choose the Standard toolbar ➤ Print button. In **DOS** or **Windows**, choose File ➤ Print.

When the *Cmddia* system variable is nonzero, the Plot Configuration dialog box opens to display various plotting default parameters and conditions.

 **OPTIONS**

Device and Default Information The *Device and Default Selection...* pick box opens a subdialog list box with descriptions of current plot devices assigned during configuration. Additional pick boxes allow you to *Save Defaults To File...*, *Get Defaults From File...*, *Show Device Requirements...*, and *Change Device Requirements....* Plotting information can be saved to and retrieved from an ASCII .PCP file.

Pen Parameters... The *Pen Assignment...* pick box opens a subdialog list box for specifying color, pen, line type, speed, and pen width. Highlighting one or more entries in the list box allows you to edit their values in the *Modify Values* edit boxes. The *Feature Legend...* pick box opens a subdialog box displaying line types available for your selected plotting device.

Optimization... This pick box opens the Optimizing Pen Motion subdialog box for fine-tuning plot performance.

Additional Parameters This section of the dialog box contains radio buttons for selecting different area configurations: plotting your current Display screen, the drawing Extents, and Limits. You can also save a View or create a Window to define the drawing area to plot. The *View...* and *Window...* pick buttons allow you to retrieve saved images or pick points from the screen. A *Hide Lines* check box removes hidden lines from objects drawn in Paperspace assigned with the **Mview** command. A *File Name...* pick box lets you specify a specific name or type of file if you instead opt to check *Plot to File*.

Paper Size and Orientation Button boxes let you specify plotted units by Inches or MM (Millimeters). Use the *Size...* pick box to open the Paper Size subdialog box in order to select from predefined measurements or set user-defined proportions.

Scale, Rotation, and Origin A *Rotation and Origin...* pick box opens the Plot Rotation and Origin subdialog box to set the Plot Rotation angle and Plot Origin. Enter Plotted Inches = Drawing

Units in the edit boxes when you are working with an explicit scale or pick Scale to fit your drawing sheet.

Plot Preview Select the Preview… button after picking the *Partial* option button to preview the placement and paper size (in red) with the effective plotting area in blue, or select the *Full* option button to see the drawing on screen as it would appear on the paper. Full preview lets you zoom and pan for closer plot inspection.

To Plot a Drawing at the Command Line

1. In **Windows**, choose the Standard toolbar ➤ Print button. In **DOS** or **Windows**, choose File ➤ Print.

When the *Cmddia* system variable is zero, the Plot command prompts are as follows:

2. What to plot—Display, Extents, Limits, View or Window <default>: Enter the desired option. If View is chosen, you are prompted for a view name. Selecting the *Window* option prompts you to pick lower-left as **First corner:** and upper-right as the **Other corner:**. You can also simply enter the corresponding coordinates.

A description similar to the following list will appear on the text screen identifying your current plot settings:

```
Plotter port time-out = 30seconds
Plot device is Hewlett-Packard (HP-GL) ADI
 4.2 - by Autodesk
Description: HP Draftmaster I
Plot optimization level = 4
Plot will NOT be written to a selected file
Sizes are in Inches and the style is
 landscape
Plot origin is at (0.00, 0.00)
Plotting area is 43.20 wide by 33.81 high
 (MAX size)
Plot is NOT rotated
Area fill will NOT be adjusted for pen width
Hidden lines will NOT be removed
Scale is 1=1
```

```
Do you want to change anything?
(No/Yes/File/Save) <N>:
```

> Enter **Y** if you want to change the default plotter settings
> shown above, then proceed to Step 3. If you enter **N**,
> prompts similar to those in Step 16 appear.

3. Do you want to change plotters? <N>: To change the
plotter, enter **Y** and AutoCAD identifies the configured
plotters, similar to the following example:

```
1. Hewlett-Packard (HP-GL) ADI 4.2 — by
Autodesk:
Description: HP Draftmaster
2. PostScript device ADI 4.2 — by
Autodesk
Description: LaserWriter II
Enter selection (number or description)
<1>:
```

> Enter the number of the plotter you want.

4. AutoCAD returns you to the What to plot: Display, Extents, Limits, View or Window <E>: prompt, displaying
the changes. You can assign any description label to your
specific plotting device during configuration.

5. Prompts vary depending on the output device selected. If
your plotter supports multiple pens, hardware line types,
line-widths or software-controlled pen speeds, then Auto-
CAD displays a list of Object colors, Pen Number, Line
Type, Pen Speed, and Pen Width when you enter **Y** to the
following prompt:

```
Do you want to change any of the above
parameters? <N>:
```

> Changes can be entered globally by preceding each with
> an asterisk, or individually as prompts appear for Pen
> number <1>:, Line type <0>:, Pen speed <36>:, and Pen
> width: <0.010>:.

Pressing ⏎ advances through list; entering **C** with the specific color number moves you directly to that assignment; **S** shows the updated colors; and **X** exits the procedure.

6. Write the plot to a file? <N>: Enter **Y** to create a plot file or press ⏎ to plot the drawing. The Create Plot File dialog list box opens when the *Filedia* system variable is nonzero or the Enter file name for plot <default>: prompt appears just prior to processing the plot.

7. Size units (Inches or Millimeters) <I>: Enter the unit equivalent of your drawing.

8. Plot origin in Inches <0.00,0.00>: Enter the location of the drawing origin in relation to the plotter origin in X and Y coordinates. The coordinate values should be in final plot size, not in drawing scale sizes.

9. Enter the Size or Width, Height (in Inches) <MAX>: Enter the desired sheet size. You can specify and save up to five nonstandard user-defined sizes by entering them in X and Y coordinates.

10. Rotate plot clockwise 0/90/180/270 degrees <0>: Enter the orientation of the plot if other than 0 degrees rotation.

11. Pen width <0.010>: Enter the pen width used for solid fills.

12. Adjust area fill boundaries for pen width? <N>: Enter **Y** if you want the plotter to compensate for pen width on solid filled areas. If you respond **Y** to this prompt, AutoCAD will offset the border of a filled area by half the pen width so that the area will accurately plot.

13. Remove hidden lines? <N>: Enter **Y** if you want a 3D view to be plotted with hidden lines removed.

14. Specify scale by entering: Plotted Inches=Drawing Units or Fit or ? <F>: Enter a scale factor for plot or **F** to force drawing to fit entirely on the selected sheet size.

15. Effective plotting area: A value appears showing you the width and height of the final plotted image:

```
Specified plot size (44.70, 35.31)
exceeds actual paper size (43.20,
33.81). Proceed with plot anyway? <N>:
```

The size of the image will depend on the sheet size entered at the **Standard values for plotting size:** prompt, plus the scale factor. Entering **Y** accepts the current information and begins processing the plot output.

16. Enter file name for plot <>: If this prompt appears, as mentioned in Step 6, enter the desired plot file name.

17. A percentage value for Regeneration done will appear as AutoCAD sends information to the plotter.

18. Autocad responds with "Plot complete" when the output commences. Then the following prompt appears: **Press RE-TURN to continue:.** Press ↵ to return to the drawing editor.

NOTES Since some plotters do not have built-in line types, the *Select linetype* option may not appear on your plotter. The **Pen width** prompt works with the **Adjust fill** prompt, allowing your plotter to compensate for the pen width during area fills. If you respond with a **Y** at the Adjust fill prompt, AutoCAD uses the Pen width value to offset the outline of any filled areas to half the pen width. This causes the edge of filled areas to be drawn to the center line of the fill outline. If you are using a laser printer, the Pen width value determines the thickness of a typical line.

At times, even though all of your plotter settings are correct, your plot may not appear in the proper location on your sheet, or the drawing may not be plotted at all. This often occurs when you are plotting the extents of a drawing. AutoCAD often does not recognize changes to the extents of the drawing when major portions of a drawing have been removed or edited. If you have this problem with a plot, open the file to be plotted and issue **Zoom** *Extents*. Let the drawing complete the regeneration process (it will probably regenerate twice), and try plotting again. If the problem persists, double-check your size units, plot origin, plot size, and plot scale settings.

If you have problems rotating a plot, use the **UCS** command to create a UCS that is rotated the way you want, and the **View** command to save a view of your drawing in the new UCS. Then use the View option under the prompt. When plotting from Paperspace, such plots include all viewports and layer settings.

 **See Also**   ACAD.PGP; Config; *System Variables:* Cmddia, Filedia, Plotid, Plotter

POINT

Point creates a point object. Points can be used as unobtrusive markers that you can snap to using the **Node** Osnap override. The command line is **Point**. You may also use the Ddptype dialog box to select a point type.

To Draw a Point Object

1. In **Windows**, choose the Draw toolbar ➤ Point button. In **DOS**, choose Draw ➤ Point.

2. Point: Enter the point location.

OPTIONS

You can set the *Pdmode* system variable to change the appearance of points. You must set Pdmode before drawing points. Zero is the default setting. When Pdmode is changed, all existing points are updated to reflect the new setting. The setting values are as follows:

Pdmode Value	Object
0	A dot
1	Nothing

2	A cross
3	An *x*
4	A vertical line upward from the point selected

Adding 32, 64, or 96 to the values above selects a shape to draw *around* the point in addition to the figure drawn through it:

Pdmode Value	Object
32	A circle
64	A square
96	A circle inside a square

NOTES   You can combine the different *Pdmode* variables to create 20 different types of points. For example, to combine a cross (2) within a circle (32), set Pdmode to 34 (2 + 32).

See Also   Ddptype, Divide, Measure, *System Variables:* Pdmode, Pdsize

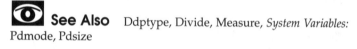

POINT SELECTION

You can enter a point by picking it with your cursor, keying in an absolute or relative coordinate value, or keying in a relative polar coordinate. You can also use modifiers called filters to align points in an X, Y, or Z axis. On the command line, whenever a point selection is required, type **.x**, **.y**, or **.z**, or a combination of these modifiers (e.g., **.xy**).

OPTIONS

Absolute coordinate   Specifies points by giving the X, Y, and Z coordinate values separated by commas, as follows:

Select point: 6,3,1

The X value is 6, the Y is 3, and the Z is 1. If you omit the Z value, AutoCAD assumes the current default Z value (see the **Elev** command to set the current Z default value). Absolute coordinates use the current UCS's origin as the point of reference.

Relative coordinates   Entered like absolute coordinates, except that an at sign (@) precedes the coordinate values, as follows:

Select point: @6,3,1

If you omit the Z value, AutoCAD assumes the current default Z value (see the **Elev** command for setting the current Z default value). Relative coordinates use the last point entered as the point of reference. To tell AutoCAD to use the last point selected, simply enter the at sign by itself at a point selection prompt.

Relative polar coordinates   Specify points by giving the distance from the last point entered, preceded by an at sign and followed by a less-than sign and the angle of direction, as follows:

Select point: @6<45

This entry calls for a relative distance of 6 units at a 45-degree angle from the last point entered.

Filters   Align a point along an X, Y, or Z axis by first specifying the axis on which to align, then selecting an existing point on which to align, and then entering the new point's remaining coordinate values. The following example aligns a point vertically on a specific X location:

To Use Point Filters

1.   In **Windows**, choose the Standard toolbar ➤ Point Filters flyout. In **Windows** or **DOS**, access the popup Cursor menu using your pointing device.

2. Point: Enter **.x** or select a known point to which you want to align vertically. For precision, use the Osnap overrides.

3. (need yz): Select a Y-Z coordinate. Again, you can use Os-nap overrides to align to other geometries.

The popup cursor menu provides the .X, .Y, .Z, .XY, .XZ, and .YZ filters. The cursor menu is activated in different ways depending on the pointing device that you are using: If you have a four-button device, press the *third* button (blue for some pucks); if you have a three-button device, press the *middle* button; if you have a two-button device, hold the Shift key down while pressing the *right* button. The *Acad.MNU* file supplied with AutoCAD assigns these buttons to the cursor menu. The cursor menu lists snap modes as well as point filters.

You can also enter **.xy**, **.yz**, or **.xz** at the prompt. For example, you can first pick an X-Y location and then enter a Z value for height.

NOTES To override the current angle units, base, and direction settings (set using the **Units** command), use double or triple lesser-than signs (<):

<<   Enters angles in degrees, default angle base (east), and direction (counterclockwise), regardless of the current settings.

<<<   Enters angles based on the current angle format (degrees, radians, grads, etc.), default angle base (east), and direction (counterclockwise), regardless of the base and direction settings.

You can enter fractional units regardless of the unit style setting. This means you can enter **5.5″** as well as **5′6″** when using the architectural format.

 **See Also**   Filter, Osnap, Units

POLYGON

Polygon allows you to draw a regular polygon of up to 1,024 sides.
To define the polygon, you can specify the outside or inside radius,
or the length of one side. The polygon is actually a polyline that can
be exploded into its individual component lines. The command
line is Polygon. Use the Pedit command to edit a polygon's width.

To Draw a Polygon

1. In **Windows**, choose the Draw toolbar ➤ Polygon flyout
   ➤ Polygon button. In **DOS**, choose Draw ➤ Polygon ➤
   Polygon.

2. **Number of sides:** Enter the number of sides.

3. **Edge/<Center of polygon>:** Enter **E** to select Edge option or
   pick a point to select the polygon center. If you select the default center of a polygon, the following prompts appear: **Inscribed in circle/Circumscribed about circle (I/C):** Enter
   the desired option. **Radius of circle:** Enter the radius of
   circle defining polygon size.

 OPTIONS

Edge   Determines the length of one face of the polygon. You are
prompted to select the first and second endpoint of the edge. Auto-
CAD then draws a polygon by creating a circular array of the edge
you specify.

Inscribed   Forces the polygon to fit inside a circle of the specified
radius; the endpoints of each line lie along the circumference.

Circumscribed   Forces the polygon to fit outside a circle of the specified radius; the midpoint of each line lies along the circumference.

Radius of circle Sets the length of the defining radius of the polygon. The radius will be the distance from the center to either an endpoint or a midpoint, depending on the *Inscribed/Circumscribed* choice.

 See Also Pedit; Pline; *System Variables:* Polysides

PREFERENCES

Preferences allows you to set a range of variables that control AutoCAD's appearance and functioning. In Windows, this command opens a series of tabbed dialog boxes to allow modification of an extensive set of controls. In DOS, only a limited set of Environment controls are accessed through this command. To manipulate a fuller set of DOS environment settings, use the DOS Set command. See **Environment Settings** for more information. The command line option is **Preferences**.

To Set AutoCAD Preferences

Choose Options ➤ Preferences.

 DOS OPTIONS

Only two variables may be controlled by the DOS Preferences command:

Measurement Allows you to select either Standard or Metric measurement systems.

Environment Allows you to specify a prototype drawing and identify a current drawing that uses the named prototype.

WINDOWS OPTIONS

In Windows, the Preferences command opens a tabbed set of sub-dialog boxes that allow you to specify preferences for the Auto-CAD graphics window, digitizer and keyboard input, location of drivers, support files, and rendering files, measurement units, as well as a range of miscellaneous preferences.

 SYSTEM PREFERENCES

Use this tabbed subdialog box to set variables that control the appearance of the graphics window, the automatic save feature, and digitizer and keyboard input.

AutoCAD Graphics Window Lets you control the various parts of the AutoCAD window. Two check boxes, *Screen menu* and *Scroll bars,* turn these features on and off. Scroll bars are only active when you install the nonaccelerated display driver.

Window Repair Lets you set the way the window image is repaired. Bitmap is best for super-high resolution displays (1280 × 1024 or greater). Fastdraw is best for VGA and Super VGA resolutions. Experiment with these settings to see which offers the fastest redraw times for your system.

Automatic Save Checking the *Every* box activates the automatic save feature. The save interval is specified in the *Minutes* edit box.

Digitizer Input These option buttons let you control the way AutoCAD works with your digitizer (if you have one installed). When *Digitizer* is selected, AutoCAD will respond to the configured digitizer. If you have no digitizer configured, AutoCAD will accept mouse input. When you select *Digitizer/Mouse,* AutoCAD will respond to both the digitizer and the mouse, depending upon whichever pointing device was last moved.

Keystrokes Controls how AutoCAD interprets keystrokes. Selecting the *AutoCAD Classic* radio button allows mode toggle keys to function, without regard to the definitions specified by the accelerator. Selecting the *Menu File* button allows the accelerator definitions to take precedence.

Fonts... This button opens the Font dialog box and allows you to set the font, font style, and size of the text in the command prompt, screen menu, and text window.

Color... This button opens the Color dialog box and allows you to set the color for the different parts of the AutoCAD graphics and text windows. Click on the graphic on the left to select the part of the screen to set, then use the RGB sliders or the basic color samples to set the color. The System Colors button will set the windows to the settings found in the Windows Control Panel.

 ENVIRONMENT PREFERENCES

Use this tabbed subdialog box to specify where AutoCAD should look for or place various resource files.

Directories Allows you to specify the search paths for Drivers (ADI), Support files (text fonts, menus, AutoLISP files, line types, and hatch patterns), and Page File information.

Files Specifies the search paths for Help files, the Alternate Menu file for use with digitizers, and the Log File. *Max Bytes in Page* sets the maximum number of bytes in the first page file.

Memory Sets memory paging. *Maximum* sets the amount of memory allocated by Windows to the AutoCAD pager. Use this option to reduce memory allocation.

 RENDER PREFERENCES

Use this tabbed subdialog box to make changes to the AutoCAD Rendering Environment:

Files Area The top area allows you to designate a directory other than the current one in which to place, the rendering Configuration, Face, Page, and Map files.

Raster Preview Options Allows you to select between Windows Metafile format and Bitmap format for the render preview image.

INTERNATIONAL PREFERENCES

Use this tabbed subdialog box lets you set measurement units and specify the prototype drawing:

Measurement Allows you to select either Standard or Metric measurement systems.

Prototype Drawing Allows you to specify a prototype drawing and identify a current drawing that uses the named prototype.

 MISC PREFERENCES

This tabbed subdialog box lets you specify the text editor and font mapping file for the Mtext command. The Misc tab also allows you to set the drawing and start up application window size, and configure the command line window.

Text Editor Allows you to name a specific text editor for the Mtext command to use. The name specified must reside in one of the directories listed in the *Environment* Preferences: Support text box.

Font Mapping Allows you to specify the search path for the font mapping file (.MAP) for Mtext.

Maximize Application on Start Up Checking this box will "maximize" any application started from within AutoCAD.

Maximize Drawing by Default Checking this box will "maximize" the size of the AutoCAD drawing window.

Plot Spooling Allows you to set the ACADPLCMD environment variable to allow use of a plot spooler.

History Lines Specifies the number of lines showing in the command window above the command prompt.

Docked Visible Lines Sets the number of lines visible at any one time when the command line is docked.

 See Also ACAD.INI, Environment Settings

PSDRAG

Psdrag controls the appearance of the PostScript image as you drag it into position using the **Import/Export** command **Psin**. At the command line, use **Psdrag**.

To Display the PostScript Image

1. In **Windows**, choose File ➤ Options ➤ PostScript Display.
   In **DOS**, choose File ➤ Import ➤ PostScript ➤ Display.

2. PSIN drag mode <0>: Enter 0 or 1, or press ↵.

 **OPTIONS**

0 Displays only the image's bounding box and file name while the image is being dragged.

1 Displays the rendered PostScript image while the image is being dragged into place. If the *Psquality* system variable is set to 0, this drag mode option has no effect. Only the bounding box is shown.

👁 **See Also** *Import/Export:* Psin, Psfill; *System Variables:* Psquality

PSFILL

Psfill fills two-dimensional polyline outlines with any PostScript pattern defined in the *Acad.PSF* PostScript support file. The pattern is not visible on the screen but is output with the **Psout** command. At the command line, use **Psfill**.

To Use a PostScript Fill Pattern

1. In **Windows**, choose the Draw toolbar ➤ Hatch flyout ➤ PostScript Fill. In **DOS**, choose Draw ➤ Hatch ➤ Post-Script Fill.

2. Select polyline: Pick the two dimensional polyline outline.

3. PostScript fill pattern (.=none)<.>/?: Enter a pattern name.

Entering **?** displays the following list of available patterns: Grayscale RGBcolor Allogo Lineargray Radialgray Square Waffle Zigzag Stars Brick Speck. The prompt is then repeated with the pattern name displayed in the brackets.

The appearance of fill patterns is controlled by a range of parameters. Depending upon the pattern you select, you will be prompted to specify the relevant parameters.

 See Also Import/Export: Psin/Psout, Psdrag

PSPACE

When you are working from Paperspace through a floating viewport into Modelspace, Pspace lets you move from Modelspace back to Paperspace. Paperspace must be enabled before you use Pspace. At the command line, use **Pspace**.

To Switch from a Floating Viewport to Paperspace

Choose View ➤ Paperspace. In **Windows**, you may also toggle between Modelspace viewports and Paperspace by double-clicking on MODEL/PAPER on the Status bar.

NOTES You use "Modelspace" in AutoCAD to do drafting and design work. "Paperspace" is an alternative work space that lets you arrange views of your Modelspace drawing and scale or size them for plotting. You can create floating viewports in Paperspace that are like windows into Modelspace. Layers, Snap, and Grid modes can be set independently for each viewport. You can also accurately control the scale of a viewport for plotting purposes. Use the **Mview** command.

See Also Mspace, Mview, Mvsetup, Tilemode, Vplayer, Vports, Zoom

PURGE

A drawing may accumulate unneeded blocks, layers, line types, dimension styles, shape files, or text styles. These objects and settings can increase the size of the drawing file, making the drawing slow to load and difficult to transport. Purge allows you to eliminate these elements. With Release 13, you may purge at any time, not just when you open a drawing.The command line is **Purge**.

To Purge Elements from the Drawing File

1. Choose Data ➤ Purge

2. Select the type of variable you wish to purge from the drop-down menu options.

When you select the variable type, AutoCAD displays each variable name of the type specified. Enter a **Y** to purge the variable or **N** to keep it. The All option purges all variables regardless of type.

NOTES The layer 0, the continuous line type, the standard text style, UCS, views, and viewport configurations cannot be purged. Nested blocks are removed only by repetitious purging and exiting of the drawing. The **Wblock** command describes an alternative and more effective method for purging.

 See Also   Wblock

QSAVE

Quickly saves a named drawing without asking for a file name. If saving an unnamed drawing, Qsave works like **Saveas**, enabling you to name the drawing before saving it. At the command line, use **Qsave**.

To Save a Drawing

In **Windows**, choose the Standard toolbar ➤ Save button. In **Windows** or **DOS**, choose File ➤ Save.

 See Also   Save/Saveas; *System Variables:* Dwgtitled, Savename

QTEXT

Qtext helps reduce drawing regeneration and redraw times by making text appear as a rectangular box instead of readable text. The rectangle approximates the height and length of the text. At the command line, enter **Qtext**.

To Display Text as a Rectangular Box

1. Choose Options ➤ Drawing Aids.

2. Click on the QuickText check box, or enter **ON** at the ON/OFF prompt on the command line.

 NOTES You do not see the effects of Qtext until you issue a **Regen** command.

👁 See Also Dtext; Regen; *System Variables:* Qtextmode; Text

QUIT

Quit exits a drawing without saving the most recent edits. On the command line, use **Quit**. The file reverts to the condition it was in following the last **Save** or **End** command.

To Exit without Saving

Choose File ➤ Exit.

If no changes were made to the current drawing, AutoCAD exits the program. If changes were made and not saved, a dialog box opens to Save Changes…, Discard Changes, or Cancel. If the drawing is un-named and you pick Save Changes…, the Save Drawing As list dialog box will open, giving you an opportunity to name the drawing.

👁 See Also End, Qsave; Save/Saveas; *System Variables:* Dbmod

N E W

RAY

Ray creates the "semi-infinite" lines that are generally used as construction lines in a drawing. The ray extends from a selected point to infinity. On the command line, use **Ray**.

To Create a Ray

1. In **Windows**, choose the Draw toolbar ➤ Line Flyout ➤ Ray button. In **DOS**, choose Draw ➤ Ray.

2. From Point: Specify a start point for the ray.

3. Through Point: Specify the point through which you want the ray to pass.

4. Continue to specify points to create multiple rays, if required, and then press ↵.

 **See Also** Xline

RECOVER

A drawing may become corrupted because of problems with your hard disk drive or floppy disk. Corrupted files cannot be opened by AutoCAD. Recover salvages as much of a file as possible and allows AutoCAD to read the file. The command line is **Recover**.

To Recover Corrupted Files

Choose File ➤ Management ➤ Recover...

If the *Filedia* system variable is set to 1, the Recover Drawing File list box is displayed so you can enter the drawing name that you wish to recover. Otherwise, the following command-line prompt appears:

```
Recover<current filename>: Enter file name
  to recover.
```

A series of messages appears indicating the action AutoCAD is taking to recover the file. An AutoCAD Alert dialog box opens after recovery to report whether the audit detected any errors in the recovered database. If so, the recovery is processed and reported to the screen.

AutoCAD Release 12 will not recover damaged files from earlier releases of AutoCAD.

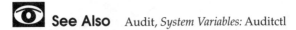 **See Also**   Audit, *System Variables:* Auditctl

N E W

RECTANG

Rectang allows you to draw a rectangular polyline. On the command line, use **Rectang**.

To Draw a Rectangle

1. In **Windows**, choose the Draw toolbar – Polygon flyout ➤ Rectangle button. In **DOS**, choose Draw ➤ Polygon Rectangle.

2. First corner: Specify a point.

3. Other corner: Specify the opposing corner.

 **See Also** Pline, *System Variables:* Plinewid

REDEFINE/UNDEFINE

Undefine suppresses any standard AutoCAD command. For example, if you load an AutoLISP Copy command you have written and then enter **Copy** at the command prompt, you will still get the standard Copy command. However, if you use Undefine to suppress the standard Copy command, you can use the AutoLISP Copy program. Redefine reinstates a standard command that has been suppressed.

To Suppress or Reinstate a Standard Command

1. At the command line, enter **Undefine** or **Redefine** as appropriate.

2. Command name: Enter the command name.

NOTES To enter the standard AutoCAD **Copy** command when an AutoLISP version might already be defined, precede the command with a period at the command prompt, as follows:

Command: .Copy↵
Select objects:

This is the only way to use an undefined command with the AutoLISP Command function.

REDO

Redo reverses the effect of the previous **U** or **Undo**. Redo must immediately follow the U or Undo. You are allowed only one Redo per command. If you enter a series of three *U*s (that is, three Undo 1's), only the last U can be restored.

To Undo Your Undo

In **Windows**, choose the Standard toolbar ➤ Redo, or Edit ➤ Redo. In **DOS**, choose Assist ➤ Redo.

Here is the most effective approach for restoring undo's:

undo 6

If this undoes too much, then try **redo**. If this undoes too much, then try **undo 4**. Otherwise, enter **u**.

 See Also   U, Undo, *System Variables:* Undoctl

REDRAW and REDRAWALL

During the drawing and editing process, an operation may cause an object to partially disappear. Often, the object was previously behind other objects that have since been removed. Redraw and Redrawall refresh the screen and restore such obscured objects. These commands also clear the screen of blips that may clutter your view. On the command line, use **Redraw/Redrawall** or (**'Redraw/'Redrawall** to use transparently).

To Redraw the Display

In **Windows**, choose the Standard toolbar ➤ Redraw flyout ➤
Redraw View or Redraw All button. In **Windows** or **DOS**,
choose View ➤ Redraw View or Redraw All.

 NOTES   Redraw will act only on the currently active
viewport. Redrawall, on the other hand, refreshes all viewports on
the screen at once. These commands affect only the virtual screen,
not the actual drawing database.

See Also   Regen, Viewres

REGEN and REGENALL

These two commands update the drawing editor screen to reflect
the most recent changes in the drawing database. On the command
line, use **Regen** or **Regenall**.

 NOTES   If you make a global change in the drawing database and Regenauto is turned on, a regeneration occurs automatically. If you have Regenauto turned off, regeneration will not occur
automatically, so changes to the drawing database are not immediately reflected in the drawing you see. If you need to see those
changes, use Regen to update the display. If you are using multiple
viewports, Regen affects only the active viewport. To regenerate
all viewports at once, use Regenall.

See Also   Regenauto, Viewres

REGENAUTO

Regenauto automatically regenerates the screen display to reflect the most recent drawing changes. For complex drawings, regeneration can be very time-consuming. Regenauto enables you to turn off automatic regeneration. Regenauto is on by default.

To Control Regeneration

1.   At the command line, type **Regenauto** or ('**Regenauto** to use transparently).

2.   ON/OFF/ <current status>: Enter ON or OFF as required.

 OPTIONS

On   Causes the display to be automatically regenerated when required to reflect global changes in the drawing database. Your display will reflect all the most recent drawing changes.

Off   Suppresses the automatic regeneration of the display. This can save time when you are editing complex drawings. When a command needs to regenerate the drawing, a prompt allows you to decide whether or not to regenerate the display.

 See Also   Regen; *System Variables:* Regenmode; Viewres

REGION

The Region command allows you to create 2D enclosed areas from existing overlapping closed shapes (called *loops*). The loops can be combinations of lines, polylines, circles, arcs, ellipses, elliptical arcs, and splines. They must be closed or form closed areas. On the command line, use **Region**.

To Create Regions

1. In **Windows**, choose the Draw toolbar ➤ Polygon flyout ➤ Region button. In **DOS**, choose Construct ➤ Region.

2. Select objects: Select the objects you wish to combine into a region.

3. Press ↵ to end the command. The command line shows how many loops were detected and how many regions were created.

You can create composite regions by subtracting, combining, or finding the intersection of regions.

To Create Composite Regions

1. In **Windows**, choose the Modify toolbar ➤ Explode flyout ➤ Union/Subtract/ Intersection button. In **DOS**, choose Draw ➤ Solids ➤ Union/Subtract/Intersection.

2. Select objects: Select the regions you wish to combine into a composite region.

3. Press ↵ to end the command.

You may select objects in any order to unite them with the **Union** command or to find the intersection with the **Intersect** command. When you wish to subtract one region from the other, you must first select the region from which you want to subtract.

NOTES   Regions may not be created from open objects that intersect to form a closed area, such as intersecting arcs or self-intersecting curves. (The related **Boundary** command allows you to create polyline boundaries from any intersecting objects.) Objects in a region must be in the same plane.

Regions are useful for calculating area properties for facilities management purposes (**Area** command). You can also hatch and shade regions, using the **Bhatch** or **Shade** commands, and analyze other properties.

See Also   Bhatch, Intersect, Subtract

REINIT

Reinit opens the Re-initialization dialog box to re-initialize the Input/Output ports, digitizer, display, and *Acad.PGP* file. At the command line, use **Reinit**, or choose Tools ➤ Reinitialize....

OPTIONS

I/O Port Initialization   This section contains check boxes for re-setting the I/O port for your digitizer and plotter.

Device & File Initialization   This section contains check boxes to reinitalize your digitizer, display, and *PGP* file.

 NOTES   If you edit your *Acad.PGP* file with the **Shell** command, check the PGP File box to activate those changes in your current drawing. If your cursor does not appear on the screen to permit you to select the check boxes, you can use the *Re-init* system variable and specify the sum of several reinitialization values. For example, enter **Re-init** and enter a value of **5** (1 = Digitizer + 4 = Digitizer reinitialization) for a digitizer analog failure. See system variables for additive values.

 **See Also**   ACAD.PGP, Re-init

RENAME

Rename renames any namable drawing element, such as a block, dimstyle, layer, line type, text style, etc. The dialog box equivalent command is **Ddrename**.

To Assign a New Object Name

1. At the command line, type **Rename**.

2. Block/Dimstyle/LAyer/LType/Style/Ucs/VIew/VPort: Enter the type of drawing element to be renamed.

3. Old (object) name: Enter old name of object.

4. New (object) name: Enter new name of object.

RENDER

Render uses light sources and surface settings to render a 3D model. Surfaces can be adjusted for reflectance, shininess, and smoothness. Multiple light sources can be added to the drawing to enhance the rendering, and the intensity of these light sources is adjustable. Render produces an image using information from a named scene, the current selection set, or the current view. On the command line, use **Render**.

To Render a Scene, Objects, or View

1. In **Windows**, choose the Render toolbar ➤ Render button. In **DOS**, choose Tools ➤ Render ➤ Render (on the drop-down Render menu).

2. In the Render dialog box, you may set the Rendering Type as required; select a Scene to Render; set Screen Palette options (shading, materials, and smoothing variables); and choose the Destination for the rendered output (Viewport, Render Window, or File).

3. Click on either the Render Scene or Render Objects button.

If you choose the Render Objects button, you will be prompted to **Select objects:** before the rendering can begin. If no scene or selection set is specified, Render will use the current view. If there are no lights in the drawing, Render will use a standard "over-the-shoulder" light source with an intensity of 1.

 PRESET OPTIONS

The following options are available on the Render toolbar (in Windows) and the Render drop-down menu (in DOS). Their command-line equivalents are shown in parentheses.

Lights...   Brings up a dialog box that lets you adjust, delete, or create a light source. You can set the intensity of the Ambient light and set the lighting drop-off to be inverse linear or inverse square (**Light** command).

Scenes...   Brings up a dialog box that lets you set up a scene you can later recall (**Scene** command).

Materials...   Brings up a dialog box that lets you create a new finish, or import, delete, export, or modify an existing finish. A preview sphere gives you a sample view of what your finish looks like (**Rmat** command).

Materials Library   Brings up a dialog box that shows a list of all the materials finishes available. You may select materials subsets and store them as named materials library (.MLI) files (**Matlib** command).

Preferences... Brings up a dialog box that lets you set the rendering preferences for the following: Rendering Procedures defaults; Screen Palette or color mapping techniques; Icon scale for Lights; Rendering (display) options; Render Quality and Face controls (**Rpref** command).

Preferences... Reconfigure This option on the Rendering Preferences dialog box lets you reconfigure the rendering display options (**Rconfig** command).

Statistics ... Provides information about the last scene rendered (**Stats** command).

 ADDITIONAL OPTIONS

Additional rendering options are available for images saved to a viewport.

Tools ➤ *Image* ➤ *Save* Lets you save a rendered image as an RND, GIF, TGA, or TIFF file. In the Save Image dialog box, select a file format and specify the size and offsets for the image (**Saveimg** command).

Tools ➤ *Image* ➤ *View* Lets you redisplay (or replay) a previously rendered image that was saved as an RND, GIF, TGA, or TIFF file. Enter a file name in the Replay dialog box. Choosing OK opens the Image Specifications dialog box and allows you to specify the image display size and offsets (**Replay** command).

RESUME

See **Script**.

REVSURF

Revsurf draws an extruded curved surface that is rotated about an axis, like a bell, globe, or drinking glass, as shown in Figure 13. Before you can use Revsurf, you must define both the shape of the extrusion and an axis of rotation. Use arcs, lines, circles, or two- or three-dimensional polylines to define this shape. The axis of rotation can be a line. The command line is **Revsurf**.

To Draw an Extruded Surface

1. In **Windows**, choose the Surfaces toolbar ➤ Revolved Surface button. In **DOS**, choose Draw ➤ Surfaces ➤ Revolved Surface.

2. Select path curve: Pick an arc line, arc, circle, two- dimensional polyline, or three-dimensional polyline defining the shape to be swept.

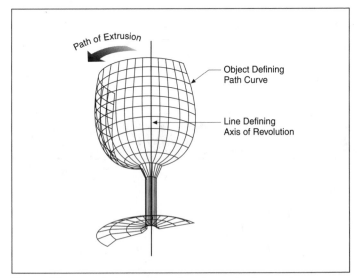

Figure 13: Extruded curved surface drawn by Revsurf

3. Select Axis of revolution: Pick a line representing the axis of rotation.

4. Starting Angle <0>: Enter the angle from the object selected as the start point of the sweep.

5. Included angle (+=ccw, -=cw) <Full circle>: Enter the angle of the sweep.

NOTES The point you pick on the object in step 3 determines the positive and negative directions of the rotation. You can use the "right-hand rule" illustrated in Figure 14 to determine the positive direction of the rotation. Imagine placing your thumb on the axis line, pointing away from the end closest to the pick point. The rest of your fingers will point in the positive rotation direction. The rotation direction determines the N direction of the surface while the axis of rotation defines the M direction.

You can control the number of facets used to create the Revsurf by setting the *Surftab1* and *Surftab2* system variables. *Surftab1* controls the number of facets in the M direction, while *Surftab2* controls the facets in the N direction. You can set these variables through the **Setvar** command or by entering the system variable from the command prompt. Resetting a higher value in *Surftab1* or *Surftab2* will not affect already drawn surfaces.

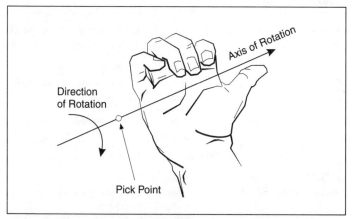

Figure 14: Determining the positive direction of rotation

 **See Also** Pedit; *System Variables:* Splframe, Surftab1, Surftab2; 3Dmesh

ROTATE

Rotate rotates an object or group of objects to a specified angle. On the command line, use **Rotate**.

To Rotate Objects

1. In **Windows**, choose the Modify toolbar ➤ Rotate flyout ➤ Rotate button. In **DOS**, choose Modify ➤ Rotate.

2. Select objects: Select as many objects as you like.

3. Base point: Pick the point about which objects are to be rotated.

4. <Rotation angle>/Reference: Enter the angle of rotation or **R** to specify a reference angle.

 **OPTIONS**

Reference Allows you to specify the rotation angle in reference to the object's current angle. If you enter this option, you get the prompts:

- **Reference angle <0>:** Enter the current angle of the object or pick two points representing a base angle.

- **New angle:** Enter a new angle or pick an angle with the cursor.

Rotate is also a grips option.

 **See Also** Ddgrips, Grips

ROTATE3D

Rotate 3D rotates an object or group of objects about an arbitrary 3D axis. On the command line, use **Rotate3D**.

To Rotate Objects

1. In **Windows**, choose the Modify toolbar ➤ Rotate flyout ➤ Rotate 3D button. In **DOS**, choose Construct ➤ 3D Rotate.

2. Select objects: Select as many objects as you like.

3. Axis by object/Last/View/Xaxis/Yaxis/Zaxis/<2points>: Specify a point or select an option.

4. <Rotation angle>/Reference: Enter the angle of rotation or **R** to specify a reference angle.

 OPTIONS

Axis by Object   Allows you to align the axis of rotation with an existing object (line, circle, arc, or 2D polyline).

Last   Uses the last axis of rotation.

View   Aligns the axis of rotation with the viewing direction of the current viewport that passes through a selected point. You will be prompted as follows: Point on view direction axis <0,0,0>: Select a point.

X\Y\Zaxis   Aligns the axis of rotation with one of the axes (X, Y, or Z) that pass through the selected point. You will be prompted as follows: Point on (X, Y, or Z) axis <0,0,0>:. Select a point.

2Points   Allows you to specify two points to define the axis of rotation. You will be prompted 1st point on axis: and 2nd point on axis:. Select two points.

RSCRIPT

See **Script**.

RULESURF

Rulesurf generates a polyon mesh "surface" between two curves. Before you can use Rulesurf, you must draw two curves defining opposite ends of the desired surface (see Figure 15). The defining curves can be points, lines, arcs, circles, two-dimensional polylines, or three-dimensional polylines. On the command line, use **Rulesurf**.

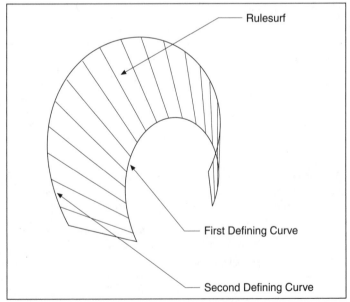

Figure 15: Defining the opposite ends of a surface for Rulesurf

To Use Curves to Define a Surface

1. In **Windows**, choose the Surfaces toolbar ➤ Ruled Surface button. In **DOS**, choose Draw ➤ Surfaces ➤ Ruled Surface.

2. Select first defining curve: Pick the first curve.

3. Select second defining curve: Pick the second curve.

 NOTES   The location of your pick points on the defining curves affects the way the surface is gnereated. If you want the furface to be drawn straight between the two defining curves, pick points near the same position on each curve. If you want the surface to cross between the two defining curves in a corkscrew fashion, pick points at opposite positions on the curves.

The *Surftab 1* system variable controls the number of faces used to generate the surface.

👁 **See Also**   pedit; *System Variables:* surftab 1

SAVE/SAVEAS

This command stores your currently open file to disk. At the command line, use **Save** to save changes to your drawing under the same name, or **Saveas** to save an unnamed drawing with a file name or rename a current drawing.

If the *Filedia* system variable is set to 1 and your drawing has not yet been named, the Save Drawing As dialog list box opens. Enter a drawing name in the File edit box. The next time you enter Save, the drawing is saved and no prompt appears.

If the *Filedia* system variable is set to 0, the following command line prompt appears: **Save Drawing As:**. Enter the file name or press ↵ to accept the default current file name.

NOTES During system configuration, AutoCAD lets you set a time interval for automatically saving your drawing. In **Windows**, you may set or change the automatic save option using the Options ➤ Preferences ➤ System option. In **DOS**, choose Options ➤ Auto Save Time to set a new time interval. The current drawing is saved to the default file name *Auto.sv$*. See the automatic-save feature of the **Config** command.

See Also Config; Preferences; Qsave; *System Variables:* Savefile, Savename, Savetime

NEW

SAVEASR12

This command allows you to save a current AutoCAD Release 13 drawing in Release 12 format.

To Save a Drawing in Release 12 Format

1. In **Windows**, type **SaveasR12**. In **DOS**, choose File ➤ Export... ➤ Release 12 DWG...

2. At the command prompt Save Release 12 drawing as: or in the Save Release 12 Drawing As dialog box, enter a file name to save the drawing in Release 12 format.

NOTES AutoCAD will save the original Release 13 drawing to a .BAK file of the same name. Exporting a drawing to Release 12 format may lose some AutoCAD Release 13-specific information. AutoCAD creates a drawing log, displayed in the text window, which lists any information that is lost or changed.

 **See Also** Save

SCALE

Changes the size of objects in a drawing. You can also scale an object by reference. At the command line, use **Scale**.

To Resize Objects

1. In **Windows**, choose the Modify toolbar ➤ Resize flyout ➤ Scale button. In **DOS**, choose Modify ➤ Scale.

2. Select objects: Pick the objects to be scaled.

3. Base point: Pick a point of reference for scaling.

4. <Scale factor>/Reference: Enter the scale factor, move the cursor to visually select new scale, or enter **R** to select the *Reference* option.

OPTIONS

Reference Allows you to scale the selected objects based on a reference length and a specified new length. When using the Reference option, at the **Reference length <1>:** prompt specify a distance. At the **Newlength:** prompt, specify a new distance. If the new length is longer than the reference length, the object(s) will be enlarged, and vice versa.

NOTES
As with **Mirror** and **Stretch**, you can work with grips by selecting an object before issuing the Scale command. AutoCAD will display the object with grips and, after you issue the command, will show the following prompt:

```
**SCALE**
```

```
<Scale factor>/Base point/Copy/Undo/Reference/
eXit:
```

Except for *Reference* (discussed above), the options here are similar to those available when working with the **Mirror** command. You can cycle through the options shown by pressing the spacebar.

See Also Change, Lengthen, Mirror, Select, Stretch

SCRIPT

Script "plays back" a set of AutoCAD commands and responses recorded in a script file. Script files, like DOS batch files, are lists of commands and responses entered exactly as you would enter them while in AutoCAD.

To Start a Script File

At the command line, enter **Script** or (**'Script** to use transparently). If the *Filedia* system variable is set to 1, the Select Script File dialog list box opens. Enter a script file name in the File edit box. If the *Filedia* system variable is set to 0, the following command-line prompt appears: Script file <current file name>:. Enter the script file name.

 **OPTIONS**

Delay **<milliseconds>** When included in a script file, makes AutoCAD pause for the number of milliseconds indicated.

Rscript When included at the end of a script file, repeats the script continuously.

Resume Restarts a script file that has been interrupted using the Backspace or Ctrl-C key.

Backspace   Interrupts the processing of a script file (you can also press Ctrl-C to do this).

 Notes   You can use Script files to set up frequently used macros to save lengthy keyboard entries or to automate a presentation. Another common use for scripts is to automate plotter and printer setup.

SELECT

Provides a variety of options for selecting objects and returns you to the command prompt once you have made your selection. The objects selected become the most recent selection in AutoCAD's memory. At the command line, use **Select**.

To Select Objects

1.   In **Windows**, choose the Select Objects toolbar. In **DOS**, choose Assist ➤ Select Objects.

2.   Choose an object selection method.

OPTIONS

Window   Selects objects completely enclosed by a rectangular window by prompting for **First corner:** and **Other corner:**. Enter **W** at the **Select objects:** prompt, or pick two points from left to right to automatically create a window selection set.

Crossing   elects objects that cross through a rectangular window. Enter **C** at the **Select objects:** prompt, or pick two points from right to left and automatically create a window selection set.

Group   Prompts to **Enter group name:**. Select all objects within a named group.

Previous Selects last set of objects selected for editing. You can use *Previous* to pick the objects you have picked with Select when a later command prompts you to select objects. The *Previous* option is useful when you want several commands to process the same set of objects, as in a menu macro.

Last Selects last object drawn or inserted.

All Selects all objects on thawed layers.

Remove Removes objects from the current selection of objects and displays the prompt **Remove object:**. Entering **A** returns to Add mode and restores the **Select object:** prompt.

Add Adds objects to the current selection of objects. You will usually use this option after you have issued the *R* option. The Remove and Add modes will remain in effect only during the specific command's execution and can be interchanged as often as necessary.

Multiple Allows you to pick several objects at one time before highlighting them and adding them to the current selection of objects.

Undo Removes the most recently added object from the current selection of objects.

BOX Allows you to use either a crossing or a standard window, depending on the orientation of your window pick points. If you pick points from right to left, you will get a crossing window. If you pick points from left to right, you will get a standard window.

AUto Allows you to select objects by picking them or by using a window, as you would with the *BOX* option. After you issue the *AUto* option, you can pick objects individually, as usual. If no object is picked, AutoCAD assumes you want to use the *BOX* option, and a window appears that allows you to use either a crossing or standard window to select objects.

SIngle Selects only the first picked object or the first group of windowed objects.

WPolygon Selects objects that are contained within any shape you define. The shape assumes a closed polyline. There are certain restrictions. For example, you cannot include intersecting rubberband lines, and you cannot place a vertex on an existing polygon segment.

CPolygon Similar to *WPolygon,* except it selects objects that cross or enclose any shape you define. The shape assumes a closed polyline. There are certain restrictions. For example, you cannot include intersecting rubber-band lines, and you cannot place a vertex on an existing polygon segment.

Fence Similar to *CPolygon,* except it selects intersecting or crossing objects with one or more rubber-band lines you define, including lines that intersect themselves.

NOTES The Select command maintains a selection set only until you pick a different group of objects at another **Select object:** prompt. Entering the AutoLISP command **(setq set1 (ssget))** at the command prompt allows you to create a selection set that you can return to again and again during the course of the current editing session. Whenever you want to select this group of objects again, enter **!set1** at the **Select objects:** prompt.

See Also Aperture, Ddselect, *System Variables:* Pickadd, Pickauto

SHADE

Produces a quick "Z buffer" shaded view of a 3D model by removing hidden lines. This command should not be confused with **AutoShade,** which is a separate program from AutoCAD. At the command line, use **Shade.**

To Shade a 3D Object

In **Windows,** choose the Render toolbar ➤ Shade button. In **DOS,** choose Tools ➤ Shade.

The *Shadedge* and *Shadedif* system variables give you some control over the way a model is shaded.

NOTES You can't directly plot images that were created using Shade. However, you can output a shaded image to a slide using the **Mslide** command. On systems that support fewer than 256 colors, Shade produces an image with hidden lines removed and 3dfaces in their original color. However, Shade can produce an image faster than the **Hide** command, and might be used where speed is a consideration. On systems with 256 colors or more, Shade produces a shaded image for which the light source and viewer location are the same.

See Also *System Variables:* Shadedge, Shadedif

SHAPE

Shape allows you to insert custom shapes, such as text font characters, into your drawing. Before you use Shape, you must load the file containing the shape(s). Use the **Load** command to load the Select Shape file dialog box, and select and load the desired file. Shapes act like blocks, but you can't explode them or attach attributes to them. The command line is **Shape**.

To Insert Custom Shapes

1. In **Windows**, choose the Miscellaneous toolbar ➤ Shape button. In **DOS**, choose Draw ➤ Insert ➤ Shape.

2. Shape name (or ?) <default>: Enter the name of the shape or a question mark to list available shapes.

3. Starting point: Pick the insertion point.

4. Height <1.0>: Enter the height value or select a height using the cursor.

5. Rotation angle <0.0>: Enter or visually select the angle.

NOTES Because shapes take up less file space than blocks, you may want to use shapes in drawings that do not require the features offered by blocks.

See Also Compile; Load; *System Variables:* Shpname; Wildcard characters

SHELL/SH

Shell and Sh allow you to use any DOS command and run other programs with low memory requirements without exiting AutoCAD.

To Open a DOS Shell

1. At the command prompt, type **Shell**.

2. OS Command: Enter a standard DOS command or press ⏎ to shell out to DOS.

NOTES If you want to use external DOS commands or programs, you must, *before* starting AutoCAD, either specify or set a path to the drive and directory where the commands or programs are located. If you press ⏎ at the OS Command: prompt, the DOS prompt appears and you can enter any number of external commands. Type **Exit** and press ⏎ whenever you are ready to return to the AutoCAD command prompt.

SKETCH

Allows you to draw freehand. (It actually draws short line segments end-to-end to achieve this effect.) The lines Sketch draws are only temporary lines that show the path of the cursor. To save the line, you must use the *Record* and *eXit* options. The command line is **sketch**.

To Draw Freehand

1. In **Windows**, choose the Miscellaneous toolbar ➤ Sketch button. In **DOS**, choose Draw ➤ Sketch.

2. **Record increment:** Enter a value representing the distance the cursor must travel before a line segment is generated along the sketch path.

3. **Pen eXit Quit Record Erase Connect:** Start your sketch line or enter an option.

 **OPTIONS**

Pen As an alternative to the pick button on your pointing device, you can press **P** from the keyboard to toggle between the pen-up and pen-down modes. With the pen down, the short temporary line segments are drawn as you move the cursor. With the pen up, no lines are drawn.

eXit Saves any temporary sketch lines and then exits the Sketch command.

Quit Exits the Sketch command without saving temporary lines.

Record Saves temporary sketched lines during the time you are using the Sketch command.

Erase Erases temporary sketched lines.

Connect Allows you to continue from the end of a sketch line.

.(period) Allows you to draw a long line segment while using the Sketch command. With the pen up, place the cursor at the location of the long line segment, then type a period.

NOTES   To draw using polylines with Sketch instead of standard lines, use the **Setvar** command to set the *Skpoly* system variable to 1.

The easiest way to use Sketch is with a digitizer equipped with a stylus. You can trace over other drawings or photographs and re-fine them later. The stylus gives a natural feel to your tracing.

The **Record increment:** prompt allows you to set the distance the cursor travels before AutoCAD places a line. The Record increment value can greatly affect the size of your drawing. If this value is too high, the sketch line segments are too apparent and your sketched lines will appear "boxy." If the increment is set too low, your draw-ing file becomes quite large, and regeneration and redrawing times increase dramatically.

Turn the **Snap** and **Ortho** modes off before starting a sketch. Other-wise, the sketch lines will be forced to the snap points, or drawn vertically or horizontally. The results of having the Ortho mode on may not be apparent until you zoom in on a sketch line. If you pre-fer, you can sketch an object and then use the **Pedit** or **Fit** command to smooth the sketch lines.

See Also   Pedit; Pline; *System Variables:* Sketchinc, Skpoly

SLIDELIB.EXE

Slidelib.EXE is an external AutoCAD program that runs inde-pendently from AutoCAD. Use it to combine several slide files into a slide library file. You use slide libraries to create icon menus and to help organize slide files.

To Build a Slide Library

At the DOS prompt, enter the following:

```
Slidelib slide-library-name < ascii-list ↵
```

 NOTES Before you can create a slide library, you must create an ASCII file containing a list of slide-file names to include in the library. Do not include the .SLD extension in the list of names. You can give the list any name and extension. You can then issue the Slidelib program from the DOS prompt.

👁 **See Also** Mslide, Vslide

SNAP

Controls the settings for the Snap mode. The Snap mode allows you to accurately place the cursor by forcing it to move in specified increments.

To Set Snap Mode

1. At the command prompt, type **Snap**.

2. Snap spacing or ON/OFF/Aspect/Rotate/Style <default spacing>: Enter the desired snap spacing, or select an option.

💡 **OPTIONS**

Snap spacing Allows you to enter the desired snap spacing. The Snap mode is turned on and the new snap settings take effect.

ON Turns on the Snap mode. Has the same effect as pressing the F9 key or Ctrl-B.

OFF Turns off the Snap mode. Has the same effect as pressing F9 or Ctrl-B.

Aspect Enters a Y-axis snap spacing different from the X-axis snap spacing.

Rotate Rotates the snap points and the AutoCAD cursor to an angle other than 0 and 90 degrees.

Style Allows you to choose between the standard orthogonal snap style and an isometric snap style.

NOTES You can use the *Rotate* option to rotate the cursor; the Ortho mode will conform to the new cursor angle. This option also allows you to specify a snap origin, allowing you to accurately place hatch patterns. The *Snapang* system variable also lets you rotate the cursor.

If you use the **Isometric** *Style* option, you can use the **Isoplane** command to control the cursor orientation. Also, the **Ellipse** command allows you to draw isometric ellipses. You can set many of the settings available in the Snap command using the **Ddrmodes** dialog box.

See Also Ddrmodes; Ellipse; Hatch; Isoplane; *System Variables:* Snapang, Snapbase, Snapisopair, Snapmode, Snapunit

SOLID

Solid creates solid-filled polygons. You determine the area by picking points in a crosswise, or "bow tie" fashion. Solid is best suited to filling rectilinear areas. Polylines are better for filling curved areas. Solids are filled only when the *Fillmode* system variable is set to On, and the view is set to Plan.

To Fill an Area

1. In **Windows**, choose the Draw toolbar ➤ Polygon flyout ➤ Solid button. In **DOS**, choose Draw ➤ Polygon ➤ 2D Solid.

2. First point: Pick one corner of the area to be filled.

3. Second point: Pick the next, adjacent corner of the area.

4. Third point: Pick the corner diagonal to the last point selected.

5. Fourth point: Pick the next, adjacent corner of the area or press ⏎ to create a filled triangle.

AutoCAD repeats Third point: and Fourth point: prompts to create further connected triangles and four-sided polygons as a single solid object. Continue to pick points until you have defined the area to be filled.

 NOTES In large drawings that contain many solids, you can reduce regeneration and redrawing times by setting the Fill command to *Off* until you are ready to plot the final drawing.

See Also Fill, Pline, 3dface, Trace

N E W

SOLID MODELING

Prior to Release 13, solid modeling was available only in the AutoDESK Advanced Modeling Extension (AME). With Release 13, a full range of solid modeling commands have been implemented, providing an easy method to build 3D models. As well as creating basic solids (solid primitives), you can additionally create solids from 2D objects by extruding and revolving them (swept solids), and create more complex solids out of either of these by adding and subtracting volumes and calculating interferences. Solids are native AutoCAD objects, which means that they compute faster than AME objects and generally respond to standard AutoCAD commands—for example, **Chamfer**, **Fillet**, and **Scale**.

NOTES Solid objects resemble surface objects and are created in approximately the same way. The critical difference is that the solid objects have mass, which allows measurement based upon volume. It also allows edits that change the mass by addition, subtraction, and by combination with other solid objects.

The Solids commands that create composite objects (**Union**, **Subtract**, **Intersect**) can also be used to manipulate 2D regions.

Solid Primitives

The six solid primitives—box, cone, cylinder, sphere, torus, and wedge—are basic three-dimensional objects, which can be used to build more complex solids.

To Draw a Box

The Box command creates a three-dimensional solid box. The command line is **Box.**

1. In **Windows**, choose Solids toolbar ➤ Box flyout ➤ Center or Corner button. In **DOS**, choose Draw ➤ Solids ➤ Box ➤ Center or Corner.

2. Center/<Corner of box><0,0,0,>: Pick the first corner point (or the center point) for your box or enter a value.

3. Cube/Length/<other corner>: Pick a second corner point or enter a value.

4. <Height>: Provide the box height by dynamically picking two points or entering a value.

 **OPTIONS**

Center Allows you to create a 3D box using a specified center point.

Cube Allows you to create a 3D box with all sides equal.

Length Allows you to enter values for *Length, Width,* and *Height.*

To Draw a Cone

Cone offers several methods for drawing a three-dimensional solid cone. The default is to choose a center point, then pick or enter the diameter/radius and apex. The command line is **Cone**.

1. In **Windows**, choose Solids toolbar ➤ Cone flyout ➤ Elliptical or Center button. In **DOS**, choose Draw ➤ Solids ➤ Cone Elliptical or Center.

2. Elliptical/<center point> <0,0,0>: Pick a center point.

3. Diameter/<Radius>: Provide a Diameter or <Radius> (or Axis endpoint for an elliptical cone by dynamically picking or entering a value).

4. Apex/<Height>: Provide an apex or height by dynamically picking the point(s) or entering a value.

 OPTIONS

Center Allows you to create a cone with a circular base.

Elliptical Allows you to create a cone with an elliptical base.

Apex Allows you to specify the apex of the cone solid.

Height Allows you to specify the height of the cone solid.

To Draw a Cylinder

Cylinder offers several methods for drawing a three-dimensional solid cylinder. The default is to choose a center point, then pick or enter the diameter/radius and apex. The command line is **Cylinder**.

1. In **Windows**, choose Solids toolbar ➤ Cylinder flyout ➤ Elliptical or Center button. In **DOS**, choose Draw ➤ Solids ➤ Cylinder ➤ Elliptical or Center.

2. Elliptical/<center point> <0,0,0>: Pick a center point.

3. Diameter/<Radius>: Provide a Diameter or <Radius> (or an Axis endpoint for an elliptical cylinder) by dynamically picking or entering a value.

4. Center of other end/<Height>: Provide a cylinder top or height by dynamically picking the point(s) or entering a value.

 **OPTIONS**

Center   Allows you to create a cylinder with a circular base.

Elliptical   Allows you to create a cylinder with an elliptical base.

Center of other end   Allows you to specify the top end of the cylinder.

Height   Allows you to specify the height of the cylinder.

To Draw a Sphere

The Sphere command creates a three-dimensional solid sphere with its central axis parallel to the Z axis of the current UCS. The overall dimensions of the sphere can be specified using either the radius or the diameter. The command line is **Sphere**.

1. In **Windows**, choose Solids toolbar ➤ Sphere button. In **DOS**, choose Draw ➤ Solids ➤ Sphere.

2. Center of sphere <0,0,0>: Pick a center point.

3. Diameter/<Radius> of sphere: Provide a diameter or radius by dynamically picking or entering a value.

Solid Modeling

 **OPTIONS**

Radius Allows you to specify the overall dimension of the sphere using its radius.

Diameter Allows you to specify the overall dimension of the sphere using its diameter. Type **D** at step 3 to use this option.

To Draw a Torus

The Torus command creates a three-dimensional donut-shaped solid. The torus is defined by specifying two radius (or diameter) values, one from the center of the torus to the center of the tube, and one for the actual tube. You can create a torus with no center hole (a self-intersecting torus) by specifying the radius of the tube greater than the radius of the torus. The command line is **Torus**.

1. In **Windows**, choose Solids toolbar ➤ Torus button. In **DOS**, choose Draw ➤ Solids ➤ Torus.

2. Center of torus <0,0,0>: Pick a center point.

3. Diameter/<Radius> of torus: Provide a diameter or radius for the torus by dynamically picking or entering a value.

4. Diameter/<Radius> of tube: Provide a diameter or radius for the tube by dynamically picking or entering a value.

 **OPTIONS**

Radius Allows you to specify the overall dimension of the torus or the tube using its radius.

Diameter Allows you to specify the overall dimension of the torus or the tube using its diameter. Type **D** at step 3 or step 4 to use this option.

To Draw a Wedge

Wedge creates a three-dimensional wedge-shaped solid. The base is parallel to the Z axis and the sloped face is tapered along the X axis. You may create a wedge based on the first corner point, or on a specified center point. The command line is **Wedge**.

1. In **Windows**, choose Solids toolbar ➤ Wedge flyout ➤ Center or Corner button. In **DOS**, choose Draw ➤ Solids ➤ Wedge ➤ Center or Corner.

2. Center/ <corner of wedge> point> <0,0,0>: Specify a corner point, or type **C** and pick a center point.

3. Cube/ Length <other corner>: Pick a point for the other corner.

4. Height: Provide height by dynamically picking the point(s) or entering a value.

 OPTIONS

First Corner   Allows you to create a cylinder starting from the first corner point.

Center   Allows you to create a wedge centered on a specified point.

Cube   Allows you to create a cubic (equal-sided) wedge. Only one length value is required to create this type of wedge.

Length   Allows you to create a wedge by specifying separately the length, width, and height.

To Create Swept Solids

Solid objects can also be created from 2D objects. You can draw new solids by extruding (adding height) to a 2D object along a specified path or by revolving a 2D object about an axis. For example, extruding a circle produces a cylinder, and revolving a circle about an axis produces a torus. These commands create a solid object from a common profile and are particularly useful for profiling objects that have fillets or chamfers which would otherwise be very difficult to profile.

To Create a Solid by Extruding a 2D Object

You can extrude closed objects such as circles, ellipses, closed splines and polylines, polygons, rectangles, donuts, and regions, but not 3D objects, objects within a block, and polylines that self-cross or intersect or are not closed. At the command line, use **Extrude**.

1. In **Windows**, choose the Solids toolbar ➤ Extrude button. In **DOS**, choose Draw ➤ Solids ➤ Extrude.

2. Select Objects: Select the object(s) to extrude.

3. Path <Height of Extrusion:> Specify the height or enter **P** and pick an object that describes the path.

4. Extrusion taper angle <0>: Enter a value for tapering the extruded object, if required, or press ↵.

NOTES   If you wish to extrude an object that contains lines or arcs, you should first join them using the **Pedit** command to form a single polyline object, or make them into a region before you extrude them. If you are extruding a polyline, it must contain at least 3 but not more than 500 vertices. If an object you have selected to extrude has width or thickness (in the case of a polyline), AutoCAD will ignore it. A thick polyline is extruded from the center of its path.

To Create a Solid by Revolving a 2D Object

Revolve works with the same kinds of objects as **Extrude**. You can revolve closed objects such as circles, ellipses, splines and poly-lines, polygons, rectangles, donuts, and regions, but not 3D objects, objects within a block, and polylines that self-cross or intersect or are not closed. At the command line, use **Revolve**.

1. In **Windows**, choose the Solids toolbar ➤ Revolve button. In **DOS**, choose Draw ➤ Solids ➤ Revolve.

2. Select Objects: Select the object(s) to revolve.

3. Axis of revolution: Object/X/Y/<Start point of axis>: Specify the start point and endpoint of the axis; type **X** or **Y** to specify the X axis or Y axis; or type **O** and select an object as the axis of revolution.

4.   Angle of revolution <full circle>: Specify the required angle of rotation, or press ↵ to accept the default (360 degrees).

To Create Composite Solids

Complex solids can be created from both Solid Primitives and Swept solids. Boolean operations can be used to create composite solids from two or more solids. The Subtract, Union, and Intersect command options are available on the Modify toolbar ➤ Explode Flyout in **Windows**, and on the Construct menu in **DOS**. Interfere is available on the Solids toolbar in **Windows**, and on the Draw ➤ Solids pull-down menu in **DOS**.

 **OPTIONS**

Union   Allows you to combine the volume of two or more solids (or regions) into one. Select the objects to join, and AutoCAD creates a single composite object.

Subtract   Allows you to remove the common area shared by two sets of solids (or regions). You must first select the solid(s) from which to subtract and then the solid(s) which are to be subtracted.

Intersect   Allows you to create a composite solid that contains only the common volume of two or more overlapping solids (or regions). It effectively joins the solids, leaving only the area where the solids intersect.

Interference   This option performs essentially the same operation as the **Intersect** command. Interfere, however, allows you to keep the original objects after it has created a further object based on their overlapping volumes. The original objects are kept, minus the overlapping areas.

To Slice a Solid

The Slice command allows you to create a new solid or set of solids by slicing an existing solid with a plane and removing a selected side. You may choose to keep only one or both sides of the solids. At the command line, use **Slice**.

1. In **Windows**, choose Solids toolbar ➤ Slice. In **DOS**, choose Draw ➤ Solids ➤ Slice.

2. Select objects: Pick the required objects.

3. Slicing plane by Object/Zaxis/View//XY/YZ?ZX/ <3points>: Specify a point or enter an option.

NOTES By default, you specify 3 points to define the cutting plane: the first point defines the origin of the slicing plane; the second point defines the X axis; and the third point defines the Y axis. You may also define the cutting plane using another Object, or by the current View, the Z axis, or the XY, YZ, or ZX plane.

To Create a Cross-section of a Solid

The Section command allows you to create a cross-section through any solid.

1. In **Windows**, choose Solids toolbar ➤ Section. In **DOS**, choose Draw ➤ Solids ➤ Section.

2. Select objects: Pick the required objects.

3. Section plane by Object/Zaxis/View//XY/YZ?ZX/ <3points>: Specify a point or enter an option.

NOTES See the "Notes" section above in regard to this command.

To Convert an AME Solid Model

Ameconvert allows you to convert solid models created using the AutoDESK Advanced Modeling Extension into AutoCAD solid objects. The command line is **Ameconvert**.

1. In **Windows**, choose Solids toolbar ➤ AMEConvert button. In **DOS**, choose Draw ➤ Solids ➤ AME Convert.

2. Select objects: Pick the solid models you wish to convert.

NOTES The objects you select must be regions or solids created using AME Release 2 or 2.1. AutoCAD ignores all other objects. Improved accuracy in the Release 13 solid modeler may cause AME models to display differently, particularly filleted and chamfered objects.

To Calculate a Solid's Mass Properties

Massprop calculates and displays the mass properties of 2D and 3D objects. For Solids, it provides volumetric information such as center of gravity principal axes and moments of inertia. At the command line, use **Massprop**.

1. In **Windows**, choose the Object Properties toolbar ➤ Inquiry flyout ➤ Mass Properties button. In **DOS**, choose Assist ➤ Inquiry ➤ Mass Properties.

2. Select objects: Pick the solid model(s) you wish to analyze. Massprop will display all of the properties of the object(s) on the text screen.

3. Write to a file <N>: If you want the information written to a file, type **Y** and provide a file name, or press ↵ to return to the command prompt.

NOTES The Massprop command can be used to list the properties of 2D regions as well as solid objects.

See Also *Import/Export:* Stlout; Pedit, Pline, Solid; *System Variables:* Isoline

SPELL

The Spell command checks the spelling of text in your drawing, including dimension text. You may select between several different dictionaries, which are available in different languages. You can customize any of the main dictionaries to include words that you commonly use. At the command line, use **Spell**.

To Check Spelling

1. In **Windows**, choose the Standard toolbar ➤ Spelling, or Tools ➤ Spelling. In **DOS**, choose Tools ➤ Spelling.

2. Select the objects you want to check or type **all** to select all text objects.

3. If a misspelled word is found, the Check Spelling dialog box identifies the misspelled word and offers alternative suggestions.

4. Choose one of the options offered.

 **OPTIONS**

Change/Change All   Allows you to select a word from the Suggestions list box or type in the correct spelling.

Change All   Changes all instances of the flagged word without further prompting.

Ignore/Ignore All   Leaves a flagged word unchanged. Ignore All will not flag further instances of the word.

Add   Leaves the flagged word unchanged and adds it to a custom dictionary. This button is not selectable if you are using a standard dictionary.

Lookup   Checks the spelling of a word in the Suggestions list box.

Change Dictionaries   Allows you to change dictionaries during a spell check.

Cancel   Allows you to exit the Check Spelling dialog box.

NOTES   You may create custom dictionaries containing a list of spelling exceptions that you have identified. You may edit (add and delete words) from existing dictionaries, or combine dictionaries using any ASCII text editor. You may also edit and create dictionaries via the Check Spelling ➤ Change Directories subdialog box. To create a new dictionary, select the *Change Dictionaries* button and select a new Main Dictionary or Custom Dictionary.

 **See Also**   *System Variables:* Dctcust, Dctmain

N E W

SPLINE

The Spline command fits a smooth curve to a set of points within a defined tolerance. The particular kind of spline created by Auto-CAD is a NURBS (nonuniform rational B-spline) curve. Splines can be used to produce irregularly shaped curves for mapping. At the command line, use **Spline**.

To Draw a Spline

1. In **Windows**, choose the Draw toolbar ➤ Polyline flyout ➤ Spline button. In **DOS**, choose Draw ➤ Spline.

2. Object/<Enter first point>: Specify a point.

3. Continue to enter points until you have defined the spline curve. After the second point, you will be prompted: Close/Fit Tolerance/<Enter point>:. Enter **C** to close the spline; **F** to change the tolerance, or continue to enter points.

4. When you have added all of the required spline segments, press ↵.

5. Enter start tangent: If desired, specify the tangency of the spline, or press ↵ to terminate the spline.

 **OPTIONS**

Object   This option allows you to convert 2D or 3D spline-fit polylines to corresponding splines. In step 2 above, type **O**, then select the polyline objects you wish to convert. If the *Delobj* system variable is set to zero, the original polylines will be deleted.

Close   Closes the spline curve so that the last point coincides with the first point and is tangent to the joint.

Fit Tolerance   Allows you to change the tolerance for fitting the spline curve. Tolerance defines how closely the spline fits the set of points you specify. A lower tolerance produces a closer fit to the specified points. When you adjust the tolerance, the current spline curve is redrawn so that it still fits the specified points, but is adjusted per the new tolerance.

Tangent   Allows you to redefine the spline start- and endpoint tangents. You may do this dynamically by picking a point, or enter **Tan** or **Perp**. Using these object snaps, you may make the spline tangent or perpendicular to existing objects. The spline is redrawn through the defined points.

NOTES   Once you have created a spline object, you can manipulate it easily using **Grips**. The spline retains the smoothness of the curves no matter where you position the grips.

See Also   Grips; Polyline; Splinedit; *System Variables:* Delobj

SPLINEDIT

Splinedit allows you to edit spline objects. You can add or delete fit points and control points, remove fit points or control vertices, open or close a spline, change the fit tolerance, and edit the start and end fit point tangents. At the command line, use **Splinedit**.

To Edit a Spline

1. In **Windows**, choose the Modify toolbar ➤ Special Edit fly-out ➤ Edit Spline. In **DOS**, choose Modify ➤ Edit Spline.

2. Select Spline: Select a spline. Grips appear on the control points and also on fit data points, if they have not been purged.

3. Fit Data/Close/ Move Vertex/ Refine / rEverse/Undo/ eXit<X>: Enter an option, then press ↵.

 **OPTIONS**

Fit Data   Allows you to edit the spline fit data. Fit data includes all fit points' fit tolerance, and all tangents associated with the spline. If a spline has no fit data, the *Fit Data* option does not appear in the prompt. Type **F** to edit fit data. To add a fit point, type **A** at the next prompt, then select an existing fit point (grip). The grips for this point and the next point are highlighted with a rubber-banding line. Enter a new point. AutoCAD interpolates the new point between the two highlighted points and refits the spline curve. To delete a fit point, type **D**, then select the point(s) you wish to delete. The spline is redrawn to fit the remaining fit points. To move fit points to a new position, type **M**, then type **N** (Next) or **P** (Previous) to move sequentially along the fit points until you reach the desired point, or type **S** (Select Point) and pick a specific point; pick a new point or enter a coordinate to relocate the fit point. To Purge the fit data from the drawing, type **P**. To change the start or end tangent of the spline, type **T**, and then specify a new point or type **S** to accept the System Defaults. Type **X** to return to the main prompt.

Close   Closes an open spline and creates a smooth curve through the start/endpoint. Type **C** and select the spline to close it. A spline may have the same start- and endpoint and still be an open spline. It will, however, lack the smoothness (tangent continuity) of a closed spline.

Open Opens a closed spline.

Move Vertex Moves the control points on the spline. When you select this option, the start point of the spline is highlighted. Type **N** (Next) or **P** (Previous) to move sequentially along the control vertices until you reach the desired point, or type **S** (Select Point) and pick a specific vertex. Pick a new point or enter a coordinate to relocate the control point. Type **X** to return to the main prompt.

Refine Allows you to increase the accuracy of a spline's definition. You may increase the number of points on a given portion or across the whole spline, or manipulate the distance between the spline and the control points. The *Add control point* option allows you to increase the number of control points by picking them directly. The *Elevate Order* option allows you to increase the number of control points on the spline by a specified order of magnitude (up to 26). The *Weight* option allows you to assign a greater "weight" to any selected control point. Selecting a point will pull the spline more to that point.

Reverse Reverses the direction of the spline.

Undo Cancels the last edit performed using Splinedit.

Exit Exits the current Splinedit mode.

 NOTES A spline can lose its fit data, if it is purged or refined. It may also lose its fit data if you fit the spline to a tolerance and then move its control vertices, or open or close the spline.

See Also Pedit, Pline, Spline

STATUS

Displays the current settings of a drawing, including the drawing limits and the status of all drawing modes. It also displays the current memory usage. The command line is **Status**.

To Display Current Drawing Settings

Choose Data ➤ Status.

NOTES   AutoCAD uses many defaults and modes. They are all displayed using the Status command. All measurements are shown in the standard units specified for the drawing.

Modelspace limits and *Modelspace uses* change to *Paperspace limits* and *Paperspace uses* when you are in the Paperspace mode.

STRETCH

Stretch stretches objects while maintaining the continuity of connected lines. At the command line, enter **Stretch**.

To Stretch an Object

1. In **Windows**, choose the Modify toolbar ➤ Resize flyout ➤ Stretch button. In **DOS**, choose Modify ➤ Stretch.

2. Select objects to stretch by crossing-window or -polygon:

- Enter **W** (Window) to select objects that lie entirely within a specified window. This option will move the entire object.

- Enter **C** (Crossing-window) to select objects that lie wholly or partially within a specified window.

- Enter **CP** (Crossing-polygon) to select only objects that lie wholly or partly with a user-specified polygon.

3. Select objects: Enter **R** to remove objects from the set of selected objects or press ↵ to confirm your selection.

4. Base point: Pick the base reference point for the stretch.

5. Second point: Pick the second point in relation to the base point, indicating the distance and direction you wish to move.

 **NOTES**   You cannot stretch blocks or text. If the insertion point of a block or text is included in a crossing window, the entire block will be moved.

See Also   Copy, Move

STYLE

Allows you to create a text style by specifying the AutoCAD font on which it is based, its height, its width factor, and the obliquing angle. You can change a font to be backwards, upside down, or vertical. You can also use Style to modify an existing text style. At the command line, use **Style**. Figure 16 shows the standard AutoCAD fonts. See Appendix C of the *User's Guide* for symbol fonts, PostScript fonts, and TrueType fonts.

To Create or Modify a Text Style:

1. Choose Data ➤ Text Style.

2. Text style name (or ?) <current style>: Enter a style name or a question mark to display a list of styles that have been defined in the drawing. Wildcards are accepted.

3. Font file <default font file>: Enter a font file name, select one from the Select Font File dialog box, or press ↵ to accept the default.

4. Height <default height>: Enter the desired height or press ↵ to accept the default.

This is CIBT______.pfb
This is COBT______.pfb
This is EUR______.pfb
This is EURO_____.pfb
This is PAR.pfb
This is ROM______.pfb
This is ROMB____.pfb
This is ROMI____.pfb
This is SAS______.pfb
This Is SASB____.pfb
This Is SASBO___.pfb
This is SASO____.pfb
This is SUE.pfb
THIS IS TE______.PFB
THIS IS TEB______.PFB
THIS IS TEL______.PFB
Τηισ ισ ΘΜΑΤΗ·ττφ
This is SWISSLI.ttf
This is VINET.ttf
This is SWISSL.ttf
This Is SWISSEK.ttf
This Is SWISSKO.ttf
This Is SWISSEB.ttf
This Is SWISSE.ttf
This Is SWISSKI.ttf
This Is SWISSK.ttf
This is SWISSI.ttf
This is SWISSCLI.ttf
This is SWISSEL.ttf
This is SWISSCL.ttf
THIS IS BGOTHL.TTF
THIS IS BGOTHM.TTF
.%%® %® '_'_÷★™ (compl.ttf)
This is COMSC.ttf
This is DUTCH.ttf
This is DUTCHB.ttf
This is DUTCHBI.ttf
This is DUTCHEB.ttf
This is DUTCHI.ttf
This is MONOS.ttf
This is MONOSB.ttf
This is MONOSBI.ttf
This is MONOSI.ttf
This is STYLU.ttf
This is SWISS.ttf
This Is SWISSB.ttf
This Is SWISSBI.ttf
This Is SWISSBO.ttf
This is SWISSC.ttf
This Is SWISSCB.ttf
This Is SWISSCBI.ttf
This Is SWISSCBO.ttf
This is SWISSCI.ttf
This Is SWISSCK.ttf
This Is SWISSCKI.ttf

Figure 16: Standard AutoCAD fonts

5. Width factor <default width factor>: Enter the desired width factor or press ↵.
6. Obliquing angle <default angle>: Enter the desired width obliquing angle or press ↵.
7. Backwards? <N>: Enter **Y** if you want the text to read backward, or press ↵ to accept N, the default.
8. Upside-down? <N>: Enter **Y** if you want the text to read upside-down or press ↵ to accept N, the default.
9. Vertical? <N>: Enter **Y** if you want the text to read vertically, or press ↵ to accept N, the default.

 OPTIONS

Text style name   Allows you to enter either a new name to define a new style or the name of an existing style to redefine the style.

Font file   Allows you to choose from several fonts. In Windows, you can select from a set of predefined fonts by picking Find File from the Select Font File dialog box. This opens the Browse/Search dialog boxes. Valid font types are shape files (.SHX), PostScript Type 1 fonts, (.PFB) and TrueType fonts (.TTF). If you are using TrueType or Type 1 fonts, you can improve drawing speed by resetting the system variables *Txtfill* and *Txtqlty*. These affect both display and plotting.

Height   Allows you to determine a fixed height for the style being defined. A value of 0 allows you to determine text height as it is entered.

Width factor   Allows you to make the style appear expanded or compressed.

Obliquing angle   Allows you to "italicize" the style.

Backwards   Allows you to make the style appear backwards.

Upside down   Allows you to make the style appear upside- down.

Vertical   Allows you to make the style appear vertical.

NOTES   If you modify a style's font, text previously entered in that style is updated to reflect the modification. If any other style option is modified, previously entered text is not affected. Once you use the Style command, the style created or modified becomes the new current style.

A 0 value at the **Height:** prompt causes AutoCAD to prompt you for a text height whenever you use this style with the **Dtext** or **Text** commands. At the **Width factor:** prompt, a value of 1 generates normal text. A greater value expands the style; a smaller value compresses it. At the **Obliquing angle:** prompt, a value of 0 generates normal text. A greater value slants the style to the right, creating italics. A negative value slants the style to the left.

👁 **See Also**   Change; Ddedit; Dtext; Qtext; *System Variables:* Txt fill, Txtqlty; Wildcard characters

SUBTRACT

Subtract allows you to remove the common area shared by two sets of solids (or regions) and create a new composite region or solid. You must first select the object(s) from which to subtract and then the object(s) that are to be subtracted. At the command line, use **Subtract**.

To Subtract Solids or Regions

1. In **Windows**, choose the Modify toolbar ➤ Explode flyout ➤ Subtract button. In **DOS**, choose Construct ➤ Subtract.

2. Select solids and regions to subtract from: Click on the overlapping solid(s) or region(s) that will form the basis of the new object.

3. Select solids and regions to subtract: Click on the objects you wish to subtract.

AutoCAD removes all of the objects selected in step 3 above.

 NOTES   Subtract can be used only for regions or solids. In steps 2 and 3 above, you may select both regions and solids at the same time, and you may select objects from any number of planes. AutoCAD will group the selection set into subsets by region/solid and by plane before subtracting the common areas and creating the new object.

👁 **See Also**   Intersect, Region, Solid Modeling, Union

SYSTEM VARIABLES

The system variables control AutoCAD's many settings. Many of the settings controlled by the system variables can be adjusted by the user. At the command prompt, type the name of the system variable you wish to manipulate.

To Adjust System Variables

1. Choose Options ➤ System Variables ➤ Set.

2. You will be prompted for a new value. Enter the appropriate integer value or decimal value. (Values are usually numeric, but in some cases you may also use Off and On in place of 0 and 1 values.)

Alternatively, you may use the **Setvar** command to list and/or set system variables:

1. Enter **Setvar** (or **'Setvar** to use transparently).

2. Variable name or ?: Enter the desired system variable name or a question mark for a list of variables.

 OPTIONS

Table 10 lists all of the system variables. They fall into two categories: adjustable variables and read-only variables. Read-only system variables such as DWGNAME cannot be directly modified by the user, but are modified by AutoCAD program. Each adjustable variable has a unique set of values.

Table 10: System Variables

Variable	Description
Acadprefix	Read-only. Displays the name(s) of the directory path or paths saved in the DOS environment variable *Acad*, using the DOS command **SET**.
Acadver	Read-only. Displays the AutoCAD version number.
Aflags	Controls the attribute mode settings: 0 = no mode, 1 = invisible, 2 = constant, 4 = verify, 8 = preset. For more than one setting, use the sum of the desired settings. See **Attdef**.
Angbase	Controls the direction of the 0 angle. Can also be set with the **Units** command.
Angdir	Controls the positive direction of angles: 0 = counterclockwise, 1 = clockwise. Can also be set with the **Units** command.
Aperture	Controls the Osnap cursor target height in pixels. Can also be set with the **Aperture** command.
Area	Read-only. Displays the last area computed. See **Area, List** commands.
Attdia	Controls the attribute dialog box for the **Insert** command: 0 = no dialog box, 1 = dialog box.
Attmode	Controls the attribute display mode: 0 = off, 1 = normal, 2 = on. Can also be set with the **Attdisp** command.
Attreq	Controls the prompt for attributes. 0 = no prompt or dialog box for attributes. Attributes use default values. 1 = normal prompt or dialog box upon attribute insertion. Can also be set with the **Units** command.
Auditctl	Controls the creation of Audit log (.ADT) files. 0 = create, 1 = do not create. See **Audit**.

Table 10: System Variables (continued)

Aunits	Controls angular units: 0 = decimal degrees, 1 = degrees- minutes-seconds, 2 = grads, 3 = radians, 4 = surveyors' units.
Auprec	Controls the precision of angular units determined by decimal place. Can also be set with the **Units** command.
Backz	Read-only. Displays the distance from the Dview target to the back clipping plane. See **Dview**.
Blipmode	Controls the appearance of blips: 0 = off, 1 = on. See **Blipmode**.
Cdate	Read-only. Displays calendar date/time read from DOS. See **Time**.
Cecolor	Displays/sets current object color. See **Color**.
Celtscale	Displays/sets current global line type scale for objects. See **Linetype, Ltscale**.
Celtype	Displays/sets current object line type. See **Linetype**.
Chamfera	Displays/sets first chamfer distance. See **Chamfer**.
Chamferb	Displays/sets second chamfer distance. See **Chamfer**.
Chamferc	Displays/sets thirdchamfer distance. See **Chamfer**.
Chamferd	Displays/sets fourth chamfer distance. See **Chamfer**.
Chammode	Chamfer method. 0 = two distances, 1 = one distance plus angle. See **Chamfer**.
Circlerad	Sets a default value for circle radius. Enter 0 for no default.
Clayer	Displays/sets current layer. See **Layer** and **Ddlmodes**.

Table 10: System Variables (continued)

Cmdactive	Read-only. Shows status of commands, scripts, and dialog boxes: 1 = ordinary command is active, 2 = ordinary and transparent commands are active, 4 = script is active, 8 = dialog box is active. If more than one setting is active, the variable shows the active sum.
Cmddia	Controls dialog box for **Plot** command: 1 = use dialog box, 0 = use command-line prompts.
Cmdecho	Used with AutoLISP to control what is displayed on the prompt line. 0 = not echoed to screen, 1 = echoed. See the AutoLISP manual for details.
Cmdnames	Read-only. Displays in English current active command name, including transparent command.
Cmljust	Multiline object justification. 0 = Top, 1 = Middle, 2 = Bottom.
Cmlscale	Scales the width of a multiline object. 0 = single line. < 0 reverses line sequence.
Cmlstyle	Displays/sets the multiline object style name.
Coords	Controls coordinate readout: 0 = coordinates are displayed only when points are picked. 1 = absolute coordinates are dynamically displayed as cursor moves. 2 = distance and angle are displayed during commands that accept relative distance input. Also controlled by the F6 function key.
Cvport	Shows/sets ID number for current viewport
Date	Read-only. Displays Julian date/time. See **Time**.
Dbmod	Read-only. Identifies drawing database modification status: 0 = drawing database not modified, 1 = entity database modified, 2 = symbol table modified, 4 = database variable modified, 8 = window modified, 16 = view modified.

Table 10: System Variables (continued)

Dctcust	Display/sets custom spelling dictionary (.DCT).
Dctmain	Display/set main spelling dictionary (.DCT).
Delobj	Controls retention of polyline when coverting splinefit polylines to the new spline objects. 0 = delete, 1 = retain.
Diastat	Read-only. Dialog box exit method: 0 = via Cancel, 1 = via OK.
Dispilh	Controls display of silhouette curves in 3D objects. 0 = on, 1 = off.
Distance	Read-only. Displays last distance read using **Dist**. See **Dist**.
Donutid	Sets inside diameter default value for **Donut** command.
Donutod	Sets outside diameter default value for **Donut** command.
Dragmode	Controls dragging: 0 = no dragging, 1 = on if requested, 2 = automatic drag. See **Dragmode**.
Dragp1	Controls regen-drag input sampling rate.
Dragp2	Controls fast-drag input sampling rate. Higher values force the display of more of the dragged image during cursor movement, and lower values display less.
Dwgcode-page	Current drawing code page.
Dwgname	Read-only. Displays drawing name. See **Status**.
Dwgprefix	Read-only. Displays drive and directory prefix or path for the current drawing file.
Dwgtitled	Read-only. Drawing name status: 0 = drawing is unnamed, 1 = drawing is named.
Dwgwrite	Controls drawing's read-only status: 0 = drawing open as read-only, 1 = drawing open for reading and editing.
Edgemode	Controls definition of boundary edge for **Trim** and **Extend**. 0 = as selected, 1 = extend selected edge to apparent intersection.

Table 10: System Variables (continued)

Elevation	Controls current three-dimensional elevation. See **Elev**.
Errno	Displays/sets code for errors from AutoLISP and ADS applications.
Expert	Controls prompts, depending on level of user's expertise. 0 issues normal prompts. 1 = suppresses the About to Regen: and Really want to turn the current layer off? prompts and the Verify Regenauto OFF setting. 2 = suppresses previous prompts plus Block already defined... Redefine it? and A drawing with this name already exists. 3 = suppresses previous prompts plus line type warnings. 4 = suppresses previous prompts plus **UCS** and **Vports** *Save* warnings. 5 = suppresses previous prompts plus DIM Save and DIM Override warnings.
Explmode	Controls exploding of non-uniformly scaled blocks. 0 = explode, 1 = do not explode
Extmax	Read-only. Displays upper-right corner coordinate of drawing extent.
Extmin	Read-only. Displays lower-left corner coordinate of drawing extent.
Facetres	Control resolution of 3D objects. Values are 0.01 to 10.0.
Fflimit	Defines limit of PostScript and TrueType fonts. Values are 1 to 100, 0 = unlimited.
Filedia	Controls use of dialog boxes. 0 = off unless requested by ~ (tilde), 1 = on.
Fillmode	Controls fill status: 0 = off, 1 = on. See **Fill**.
Fontalt	Defines alternate font to be used when font specified in drawing is not found.
Fontmap	Defines location of substitute fonts to be used in place of fonts defined in drawing.
Frontz	Read-only. Displays the distance from the Dview target to the front clipping plane. See **Dview**.

Table 10: System Variables (continued)

Gridmode	Controls grid: 0 = off, 1 = on. See **Grid**.
Gridunit	Controls grid spacing. See **Grid**.
Gripblock	Sets the appearance of grips in blocks: 0 = grip appears at block insertion only (default value), 1 = grips assigned to all entities within blocks.
Gripcolor	Sets color for nonselected grips.
Griphot	Sets color for selected grip.
Grips	Displays grips for **Stretch**, **Move**, **Rotate**,
Gripsize	Sets grip box size. Default value is 3.
Handles	Read-only. Handles status. On is the only valid option with R13.
Highlight	Controls object-selection ghosting: 0 = no ghosting, 1 = ghosting.
Hpang	Sets default hatch pattern angle.
Hpbound	Sets object type created by **Hatch** and **Boundary**. 0 = region, 1 = polyline
Hpdouble	Sets default double hatch for user-defined pattern: 0 = single hatch, 1 = double hatch.
Hpname	Sets default hatch pattern name and style.
Hpscale	Sets default hatch pattern scale.
Hpspace	Sets default line spacing for user-defined hatch pattern.
Insbase	Controls insertion base point of current drawing. See **Base**.
Insname	Default block name for **Ddinsert** or **Insert** command.
Isolines	Sets number of lines displayed per surface on solids: default = 4, values = 0 to 2047.
Lastangle	Read-only. Displays the end angle of last arc or poly arc.
Lastpoint	Displays coordinates of last point entered. Same point referenced by at sign (@).
Lenslength	Read-only. Displays the current lens focal length used during the **Dview** command *Zoom* option.

Table 10: System Variables (continued)

Limcheck	Controls limit checking: 0 = no checking, 1 = checking. See **Limits**.
Limmax	Stores the coordinate of drawing's upper-right limit. See **Limits**.
Limmin	Stores the coordinate of drawing's lower-left limit. See **Limits**.
Locale	Read-only. Displays ISO language code of the version of AutoCAD.
Loginname	Read-only. Displays user's login name set during configuration.
Ltscale	Global line type scale factor. See **Psltscale, Celtscale**.
Lunits	Controls unit styles: 1 = scientific, 2 = decimal, 3 = engineering, 4 = architectural, 5 = fractional. See **Units, DDunits**.
Luprec	Stores unit accuracy by decimal place or size of denominator. See **Units**.
Maxactvp	Maximum number of viewports to regenerate at one time.
Maxsort	Sets the maximum number of symbol or file names to be sorted by any listing command.
Menuctl	Controls swapping of the screen menus whenever a command is entered: 0 = doesn't switch, 1 = switches.
Menuecho	Controls the display of commands and prompts issued from the menu. A value of 1 suppresses display of commands entered from menu (can be toggled on or off with Ctrl-P); 2 suppresses display of commands and command prompts when command is issued from AutoLISP macro; 3 is a combination of options 1 and 2; 4 disables Ctrl-P menu echo toggle; 8 enables the printing of all input and output strings to the screen for debugging DIESEL macros.
Menuname	Read-only. Stores the current menu file name. See **Menu**.

Table 10: System Variables (continued)

Mirrtext	Controls text mirroring: 0 = no text mirroring, 1 = text mirroring.
Modemacro	Allows display of text or special strings like current drawing name, time, date, or specials modes at the status line. See DIESEL macro language in AutoCAD Customization manual.
Mtexted	Name of program for text editing.
Offsetdist	Offset default distance. Negative value = offset through point.
Orthomode	Controls the Ortho mode: 0 = off, 1 = on. See **Ortho**.
Osmode	Sets the current default Osnap mode: 0 = none, 1 = endpoint, 2 = midpoint, 4 = center, 8 = node, 16 = quadrant, 32 = intersection, 64 = insert, 128 = perpendicular, 256 = tangent, 512 = nearest, 1024 = quick, 1028 = appint. If more than one mode is required, enter the sum of those modes. See **Osnap**.
Pdmode	Sets the display style for point object. See **Point, Ddptype**.
Pdsize	Controls the display size of the point object. See **Point**, **Pdmode**.
Pellipse	Controls the type of ellipse created with the ellipse command. 0 = true ellipse, 1 = polyline ellipse.
Perimeter	Read-only. Displays the perimeter value currently being read by Area, List, or Dblist. See **Area**, **List**, and **Dblist**.
Pfacevmax	Read-only. Defines maximum number of vertices for mesh entity faces.
Pickadd	Controls ability to add or remove entities from a selection set using the Shift key. 0 = disabled, 1 = enabled.
Pickauto	Controls automatic windowing for **Select objects:** prompt: 0 = disabled, 1 = enabled.

Table 10: System Variables (continued)

Pickbox	Sets object selection target height in screen pixels.
Pickdrag	Controls how a selection window is drawn: 0 = click mouse at each corner, 1 = Click mouse at one corner, hold mouse down while dragging, then release at other corner.
Pickfirst	Lets you select first, then use an edit/inquiry command: 0 = disabled, 1 = enabled.
Pickstyle	Sets group and associative hatch selection. 0 = None, 1 = Group, 2 = Associative hatch, 3 = Group and Associative hatch.
Platform	Read-only. Message indicating AutoCAD version, such as Microsoft Windows, 386 DOS Extended, Apple Macintosh.
Plinegen	Controls line type pattern to adjust its appearance between vertices. 0 = line type displays dash at vertices, 1 = line type continuous around vertices.
Plinewid	Default polyline width.
Plotid	Changes default plotter based on text description.
Plotter	Changes default plotter based on its assigned configuration number.
Plotrot-mode	Sets plot orientation, 0 = landscape, 1 = portrait.
Plotter	Changes default plotter using its assigned configuration number.
Polysides	**Polygon** command's default for number of sides, can be 3 to 1024.
Popups	Read-only. Displays the availability of the Advanced User Interface based on the display driver. 0 = not available, 1 = available.
Projmode	Sets projection mode for **Trim/Extend**. 0 = True 3D (no projection), 1 = XY plane of the current UCS, 2 = Current view plane.

Table 10: System Variables (continued)

Psltscale	Sets line type scale for Paperspace. 0 = regular line type scaling, 1 = adjust all line types to use the current ltscale, including XREF's, viewed from Paperspace.
Psprolog	Assigns a name for the prologue section in file *acad.PSF* for **Psout** command.
Psquality	Sets rendering quality PostScript image when imported into a drawing. 0 = disabled.
Qtextmode	Controls the Quicktext mode: 0 = off, 1 = on. See **Qtext** command.
Regenmode	Controls the Regenauto mode: 0 = off, 1 = on. See **Regenauto**.
Re-init	Resets I/O ports, digitizer, display, plotter, and *Acad.PGP* file.
Riaspect	Sets the image aspect ratio for the screen display.
Ribackg	Sets background color for the screen display.
Riedge	Sets edge detection when **Rasterin** command is used to import an image file. 0 = no edge tracing, 1 to 255 = threshold for edge detection.
Rigamut	Sets the number of colors **Rasterin** uses when importing a color image file.
Rigrey	Controls gray-scale imported image file. 0 = off.
Rithresh	Controls luminance on imported image file. 0 = off, only pixels brighter than threshold value will be imported
Savefile	Read-only. Displays current auto-save file name.
Savename	Read-only. File name assigned to the currently saved file.
Savetime	Automatic-save time interval: 0 = disabled.
Screen-boxes	Read-only. Number of boxes displayed on screen menu of graphics area.

Table 10: System Variables (continued)

Screen-mode	Read-only. Controls grpahics/text screens: 0 = text screen, 1 = graphics mode, 2 = dual screen. Values are additive.
Screensize	Read-only. Reads the size of the graphics screen in pixels.
Shadedge	Sets shading parameters: 0 = faces shaded, edges not highlighted, 1 = faces shaded with edges drawn using background color, 2 = faces unfilled with edges in entity color, 3 = faces in entity color, edges with background color.
Shadedif	Sets the ratio (in percent) of diffuse reflective light to ambient light.
Shpname	Stores default shape name.
Sketchinc	Sets the sketch record increment. See **Sketch**.
Skpoly	Controls whether the **Sketch** command uses regular lines or a connected lines in a polyline. 0 = lines, 1 = polyline.
Snapang	Controls snap and grid angle. See **Snap**.
Snapbase	Controls snap, grid, and hatch pattern origin. See **Snap**.
Snapisopair	Controls isometric plane: 0 = left, 1 = top, 2 = right. See **Snap** command.
Snapmode	Controls snap toggle: 0 = off, 1 = on. See **Snap** command.
Snapstyl	Controls snap style: 0 = standard, 1 = isometric. See **Snap**.
Snapunit	Sets snap spacing given in X and Y values. See **Snap**.
Sortents	Controls entity sorting order: 0 = disabled, 1 = object selection, 2 = object snap, 4 = redraws, 8 = Mslide slide creation, 16 = regens, 32 = plotting, 64 = PostScript output. Values are additive.

Table 10: System Variables (continued)

Splframe	Controls the display of spline vertices, surface-fit three-dimensional meshes, and invisible edges of 3dfaces. 0 = no display of Spline vertices of invisible 3dface edges. Displays only defining mesh or surface-fit mesh. 1 = display of Spline vertices or invisible 3dface edges. Displays only surface-fit mesh.
Splinesegs	Controls the number of line segments used for each spline patch.
Splinetype	Controls the type of curved line generated by the **Pedit Spline** command. 5 = quadratic B-spline, 6 = cubic B-spline.
Surftab1	Controls the number of mesh control points for the **Rulesurf** and **Tabsurf** commands and the number of mesh points in the M direction for the **Revsurf** and **Edgesurf** commands.
Surftab2	Controls the number of mesh control points in the N direction for the **Revsurf** and **Edgesurf** commands.
Surftype	Controls the type of surface fitting generated by the **Pedit Smooth** command. 5 = quadratic B-spline, 6 = cubic B-spline, and 8 = Bezier surface.
Surfu	Controls the accuracy of the smoothed surface models in the M direction.
Surfv	Controls the accuracy of the smoothed surface models in the N direction.
Syscode-page	Read-only. Indicates system code page of *Acad.XMF*.
Tabmode	Sets tablet mode: 0 = disabled, 1 = enabled.
Target	Read-only. Displays the coordinate of the target point used in the **Dview** command.

Table 10: System Variables (continued)

Tdcreate	Read-only. Displays time and date of drawing creation. See **Time**.
Tdindwg	Read-only. Displays total editing time.See **Time**.
Tdupdate	Read-only. Displays time and date of last save. See **Time**.
Tdusrtimer	Read-only. Displays user-elapsed time. See Time.
Tempprefix	Read-only. Displays the name of the directory where temporary AutoCAD files are saved.
Texteval	Controls whether prompts for text and attribute input to commands are taken literally or as AutoLISP expressions. 0 = literal, 1 = text you input with left parens and exclamation points will be interpreted as AutoLISP expression. **Dtext** takes all input literally, regardless of this setting.
Textfill	Controls the display of PostScript and TrueType fonts. 0 = outline, 1 = filled.
Textqlty	Controls the resolution of PostScript and TrueType fonts. values are 0 to 100.0.
Textsize	Controls default text height except for styles with an assigned fixed height. See **Dtext**, **Text**, and **Style**.
Textstyle	Sets the current text style. See **Style**.
Thickness	Controls three-dimensional thickness of objects being drawn. See **Elev**.
Tilemode	Toggle between Paperspace and Modelspace: 0 = enable paper space, 1 = exit paper space.
Tooltips	Controls the display of tooltips (windows only). 0 = off, 1 = on.
Tracewid	Sets default trace width. See **Trace**.

Table 10: System Variables (continued)

Treedepth	Lets you set a four-digit integer coding that ultimately affects AutoCAD's quickness for searching a database to execute commands. Changing the value of this variable forces a drawing regeneration regardless of **Regenauto** setting.
Treemax	Limits memory (RAM) usage during regen operations.
Trimmode	Controls whether corner lines are trimmed during **Chamfer** and **Fillet** commands. 0 = no trim, 1 = trim.
Ucsfollow	Controls whether changing the current UCS automatically displays the plan view of the new current UCS. 0 = displayed view does not change, 1 = automatic display of new current UCS in plan.
Ucsicon	Controls UCS icon display: 0 = off, 1 = on, 2 = at origin and off, 3 = at origin and displayed when origin is visible.
Ucsname	Read-only. Displays the name of the current UCS. See **UCS**.
Ucsorg	Read-only. Displays the current UCS origin point. See **UCS**.
Ucsxdir	Read-only. Displays the X direction of the current UCS. See **UCS**.
Ucsydir	Read-only. Displays the Y direction of the current UCS. See **UCS**.
Undoctl	Read-only. Displays state of **Undo**: 1 = set if Undo enabled, 2 = set for one undo, 4 = set if Auto-group mode enabled, 8 = set if group currently active.
Undomarks	Read-only. Desplays the number of Undo's by *Mark* and *Back* options placed in the current drawing.

Table 10: System Variables (continued)

Unitmode	Sets how fractional, feet-and-inches, and surveyors' angles are displayed on the status line. 0 = normal (for example, 1'– 6 1/2"). 1 = same as input format (for example, 1'6– 1/2").
Useri1-5	Five variables for storing integers for custom applications.
Userr1-5	Five variables for storing real numbers for custom applications.
Users1-5	Five variables for storing text strings for custom applications.
Viewctr	Read-only. Displays the current UCS coordinates of the center of the current viewport.
Viewdir	Read-only. Displays the view direction of the current view port. This also describes the camera point as a 3D offset from the TARGET point.
Viewmode	Read-only. Controls view mode for current viewport: 1 = perspective on, 2 = front clipping plane on, 4 = back clipping plane on, 8 = UCS follow mode on, 16 = front clipping plane not at eye level.
Viewsize	Read-only. Displays the height of the current view in drawing units.
Viewtwist	Read-only. Displays the view twist angle for the current viewport. See **Dview**.
Visretain	Stores Xref freeze/thaw, on/off, color and linetype layer settings. 0 = Xref layer settings are as defined in the Xref drawing itself. 1 = Xref layer settings are controlled and stored by the current drawing. One xref may be called into multiple drawings with different layer settings, if Visretain is set in the calling drawing, the Xref's will conform to each of the called layer definitions.

Table 10: System Variables (continued)

Vsmax	Read-only. Displays the three-dimensional coordinate of the upper-right corner of the current viewport's virtual screen relative to the current UCS.
Vsmin	Read-only. Displays the three-dimensional coordinate of the lower-left corner of the current viewport's virtual screen relative to the current UCS.
Worlducs	Read-only. Displays the status of the world coordinate system. 0 = WCS is not current, 1 = WCS is current. See **UCS**.
Worldview	Controls whether point input to the **Dview** and **Vpoint** commands is relative to the WCS or the current UCS. 0 = commands use the current UCS to interpret point value input, 1 = commands use WCS to interpret point value input.
Xrefctl	Controls creation of external .*XLG* files: 0 = not written, 1 = written.

N E W

SYSWINDOWS

Windows Only

Syswindows allows you to arrange (tile or cascade) the AutoCAD windows or arrange the window icons. It works in AutoCAD in the same way as the Window menu in the Windows Program Manager works.

To Arrange AutoCAD Windows

1. At the command line, type **Syswindows**.

2. Cascade tileHorz/tileVert/Arrangeicons: Select an option.

 **OPTIONS**

Cascade Overlaps the windows with visible title bars.

tileHorz Arranges the windows horizontally, in non-overlapping tiles.

tileVert Arranges the windows vertically, in non-overlapping tiles.

Arrangeicons *Arranges the window icons.*

TABLET

Tablet is useful only if you have a digitizing tablet. Use it to set up your tablet for accurate tracing. At the command line, type **Tablet**.

To Set Up a Tablet

1. Choose Options ➤ Tablet.

2. Option (ON/OFF/CAL/CFG): Enter an option. If you do not have a digitizing tablet, you will get the message "Your pointing device cannot be used as a tablet."

 **OPTIONS**

ON/OFF Toggles the Calibrated mode on or off. When on, you cannot access the screen menus. In Windows, use the F4 key to toggle On/Off. In DOS, use the F10 key. Alternatively, you may set the *Tabmode* system variable: 0=Off, 1=On.

CAL Allows you to calibrate a tablet so distances on the tablet correspond to actual distances in your drawing. The calibration is effective only for the space (Paper/Modelspace) in which it is performed. After calibrating the tablet, set the transformation to Orthogonal, Affine, or Projective, depending on the drawing dimensions and the digitizing requirements.

CFG Allows you to configure your digitizing tablet for a tablet menu like the one provided by AutoCAD.

NOTES The *CAL*, or Calibrate, option allows you to set specific distances on the tablet to correspond to actual distances in your AutoCAD drawing. You are prompted to pick a first known point on the tablet and enter its corresponding coordinate in your AutoCAD drawing. This point should be at the lowest-left corner of a known origin—for example, one corner of a property line. Then you are prompted to pick a second known point on your tablet and enter its corresponding coordinate in your drawing. This second point should be the upper-right end of the line of known length. For best results, this line should be as long as possible and should be horizontal or vertical, not diagonal. You may want to include a graphic scale in your drawing to be digitized just for the purpose of calibrating your tablet.

You may not be able to calibrate your tablet if you have configured it to have menus and a small screen pointing area. If this is the case, you may have to reconfigure it so that its entire surface is designated for the screen pointing area.

The *CFG*, or Configure, option allows you to control the location and format of tablet menus as well as the pointing area on your tablet. You are first prompted for the number of tablet menus you want. The AutoCAD tablet menu contains four menus. Then you are prompted to pick the upper-left, lower-left, and lower-right corners of the tablet menus. The AutoCAD template shows a black dot at these corners. Next, you are prompted for the number of columns and rows that each menu contains. Finally, you are asked if you want to specify the screen pointing area. This is the area on the tablet used for actual drawing. If you answer Yes to this prompt, you are prompted to pick the lower-left and upper-right corners of the pointing area.

To Use the Tablet Menu

The Tablet menu allows you to use a pointing device to activate commands from a digitizing tablet. To use it, load the Tablet menu. You can activate a command from the tablet by moving your pointing device to a box that represents the desired command and pressing the pick button. Commands you pick from the tablet menu often display a corresponding screen menu to allow you to pick the command options. The blank area at the top of the tablet menu is reserved for additional custom menu options.

 See Also   Sketch; *System Variables:* Tabmode

TABSURF

Tabsurf draws a surface by extruding a curve in a straight line, as shown in Figure 17. Before using Tabsurf, you must draw a curve defining the extruded shape and a line defining the direction of the extrusion (the direction vector). At the command line, type **Tabsurf**.

To Straighten a Curved Surface

1. In **Windows**, choose Surfaces toolbar ➤ Extruded Surfaces button. In **DOS**, choose Draw ➤ 3D Surfaces ➤ Extruded Surface.

2. Select path curve: Pick a curve defining the surface shape.

3. Select direction vector: Pick a line defining the direction of the extrusion.

NOTES   The point at which you pick the direction vector at the Select direction vector: prompt determines the direction of the extrusion. The endpoint nearest the pick point is the base of the direction vector, and the other end indicates the direction of the extrusion.

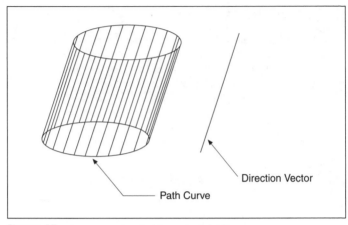

Figure 17: A curve extruded in a straight line

You can draw the curve with a line, arc, circle, two-dimensional polyline, or three-dimensional polyline. The direction vector can be a three-dimensional line. Tabsurf has an effect similar to changing the thickness of an object, but extrusions using Tabsurf are not limited to the Z axis. The *Surftab1* system variable will affect the number of facets used to form the surface.

 **See Also** Pedit, *System Variables:* Surftab1

AutoCAD for Windows comes with a set of standard toolbars that provide access to groups of commonly used commands. See **Toolbar** for further information. The Toolbars dialog box allows you to create new toolbars, delete toolbars, customize the supplied tool-bars by adding or removing commands to meet your current needs, and modify properties on toolbars. At the command line, use **Tbconfig**.

To Create or Modify a Toolbar

1. Choose Tools ➤ Customize Toolbars.

2. When the Toolbars dialog box appears, select a toolbar, then choose the desired option button.

 **OPTIONS**

Toolbars The toolbars list box displays all available toolbars, both hidden and shown. Highlight the toolbar whose properties you wish to customize, delete, or modify.

Close Exits the Toolbar dialog box and implements any changes that you have made.

New Opens the New Toolbar subdialog box. Enter a *Toolbar Name* for the new toolbar. This is the name that will appear above the tools on the toolbar. In the *Menu Group* drop-box, select the menu group associated with the new toolbar. This list box contains all menus currently loaded, including the ACAD standard menu and any others you may have created and loaded (see **Menuload**). The internal AutoCAD name (or alias) of a toolbar consists of the tool-bar name prefixed by the menu group name—for example, ACAD.*CUSTOM*. When you choose OK, an empty toolbar will appear on your drawing area. You should now use the *Customize* option to add tools to the toolbar.

Delete Use this option to delete any toolbar. You may create tempo-rary toolbars and then delete them when you no longer need them.

Customize This option opens the Customize Toolbars subdialog box. The new or existing toolbar(s) that you wish to modify must be visible on your screen. To delete a tool from the displayed tool-bar, simply drag it off the toolbar. To add a new tool to a displayed toolbar, select the relevant tool category from the *Categories* drop-box. When you select a category (for example, Solids or Attributes), all of the tool icons for that category appear in the Categories box. Click on any tools that you want and drag them to the onscreen toolbar that you are customizing. You may also move and copy tools from one displayed toolbar to another. To *move* a tool from another toolbar, drag the tool to the new toolbar. To *copy* a tool from another toolbar, press the Ctrl key as you drag the tool to the new toolbar. During all of the above operations, the displayed toolbar resizes itself as tools are added or deleted. Choose the *Close* button to save the toolbar changes.

Properties Opens the Toolbar Properties subdialog box and allows you to change the toolbar *Name*, and *Hide* or display that particular toolbar.

Large buttons This check box allows you to change the icons on the toolbars from the standard 16×16 pixels to 32×32 pixels.

Show Tooltips This check box allows you to turn on or off the display of the tool name each time a pointing device passes over any tool icon. It is controlled by the system variable *Tooltips*.

 **NOTES** You can open the Toolbars dialog box directly from a displayed toolbar by clicking on a tool icon with the Return button (right button) of your pointing device. Double-clicking on a tool icon with the Return button will open the Button Properties dialog box for that tool. You may change the name, command, and tool icon associated with that tool. If you double-click on a flyout toolbar icon (➤), the Flyout Properties dialog box will open. You may change the flyout name, toolbar, and icon.

Any changes made to toolbars are saved to the associated compiled menu (.MNC) file.

◉ See Also Toolbar; *System Variables:* Tooltips

TEXT

See **Dtext**.

The 3D command creates basic 3D surface objects. You may select from a predefined set of 3D shapes: box, cone, dish, dome, mesh, pyramid, sphere, torus, or wedge. The objects initially display as wire-frame objects, although they are actually faceted surfaces. You may use **Hide**, **Shade**, or **Render** on them to simulate solid objects. At the command line, type **3D**.

To Create a Simple 3D Surface Object

1. In **Windows**, choose the Surfaces toolbar ➤ Predefined Surface Object buttons. In **DOS**, choose Surfaces ➤ 3D Objects….

2. Box/Cone/Dish/DOme/Mesh/Pyramid/Sphere/Torus/ Wedge: Select a 3D shape. When you select 3D objects in DOS, an icon menu displays the predefined surface objects for selection.

   • In Windows, the simple mesh option is not available on the Surfaces Toolbar. Choose Miscellaneous toolbar ➤ Mesh.

3. Depending on the 3D shape chosen, you will be prompted for Diameter, Radius, Height, etc.

4. Number of Segments <current value>: Enter the number of facets desired on the surface. This prompt appears

only for curved surface objects, not for flat-sided objects such as a box or pyramid. For dish, dome, and sphere, you will be prompted for both latitudinal and longitudinal segments; for torus you will be prompted for segments around tube circumference and segments around torus circumference.

 NOTES Surface objects fall somewhere between wire-frame models and solid objects. They initially display as wire-frames, but can be shaded or rendered to appear as solid objects. Unlike solids, they provide no information about physical properties (such as mass, weight, or center of gravity), cannot be combined into more complex shapes, or used to calculate interferences.

See Also Hide, Render, Shade, Solid Modeling, 3D mesh

3DFACE

Allows you to draw a 3D face in three-dimensional space. 3D faces are surfaces defined by four points in space picked in circular fashion. Although they appear transparent, 3D faces are treated as opaque when you remove hidden lines from a drawing. After the first face is defined, you are prompted for additional third and fourth points, which allow the addition of adjoining 3D faces. At the command line, use **3Dface**.

To Draw a 3D Face

1. In **Windows**, choose the Surfaces toolbar ➤ 3Dface button. In **DOS**, choose Draw ➤ Surfaces ➤ 3D Face.

2. First point: Select the first corner.

3. Second point: Select the second corner.

4. Third point: Select the third corner.

5. **Fourth point:** Select the fourth corner.

6. **Third point:** Continue to pick pairs of points defining more faces or press ↵ to end the command.

Entering **Invisible** or **I** at the first point of an edge makes that edge of the 3D face invisible.

NOTES Use the *Invisible* option if you want to hide the joint line between joined 3D faces. Do this by entering **I** just before you pick the first defining point of the side to be made invisible. Make invisible edges visible by setting the *Splframe* system variable to a nonzero value. See **Setvar** for more on *Splframe*.

The Edge command can also be used to change the visibility of 3D faces. All meshes are composed of 3D faces. If you explode a 3D mesh, each facet of the mesh will be a 3D face.

See Also Edge, Solid Modeling, *System Variables:* Pfacevmax, Splframe

3DMESH

Draws a three-dimensional surface mesh using coordinate values you specify. 3Dmesh can be used when drawing three-dimensional models of a topography or performing finite element analysis. 3Dmesh is designed for programmers who want control over each node of a mesh. You may also use 3Dmesh along with scripts and LISP routines to automate the process. At the command line, type **3Dmesh**.

To Draw a Rectangular Mesh

1. In **Windows**, choose the Surfaces toolbar ➤ 3D Mesh button. In **DOS**, choose Draw ➤ Surfaces ➤ 3D Mesh.

2. **Mesh M size:** Enter the number of vertices in the M direction (2 to 256).

3. **Mesh N size:** Enter the number of vertices in the N direction (2 to 256).

4. **Vertex (0,0):** Enter the XYZ coordinate value for the first vertex in the mesh.

5. **Vertex (0,1):** Enter the XYZ coordinate value for the next vertex in the N direction of the mesh.

6. **Vertex (0,2):** Continue to enter XYZ coordinate values for the vertices.

NOTES To use 3Dmesh to generate a topographical model, arrange your XYZ coordinate values in a rectangular array, roughly as they would appear in the plan. Fill any blanks in the array with dummy or neutral coordinate values. Start the 3Dmesh command and use the number of columns for the mesh M size and the number of rows for the N size. At the prompts, enter the coordinate values row by row, starting at the lower-left corner of your array and reading from left to right. Include any dummy values. 3Dmesh creates a polygon mesh which is open in both directions (M and N). Use the Grip editor or Pedit to edit the mesh.

See Also Grips; Pedit; Pface; Solid Modeling; *System Variables:* Surftype, Surfu

3DPOLY

Allows you to draw a polyline in three-dimensional space using XYZ coordinates or object snap points. Three-dimensional polylines are like standard polylines, except that you can't give them a width or use arc segments. Also, you cannot use the **Pedit** command's *Fit curve* option with 3dpoly. To create a smooth curve using three-dimensional polylines, use the **Pedit** *Spline* option. This creates a Spline fit curve. To convert this into a true spline, use the **Spline** command *Object* option. At the command line, use **3Dpoly**.

To Draw a 3Dpolyline

1. In **Windows,** choose the Draw toolbar ➤ Polyline flyout ➤ 3Dpolyline button. In **DOS,** choose Draw ➤ 3D Polyline.

2. From point: Enter the beginning point.

3. Close/Undo/<Endpoint of line>: Enter the next point of the line.

4. Close/Undo/<Endpoint of line>: Continue to pick points for additional line segments or press ↵ to end the command.

 **OPTIONS**

Close   Connects the first point with the last point in a series of line segments.

Undo   Moves back one line segment in a series of line segments.

 See Also   Pedit, Pline, Spline

TILEMODE

The Tilemode system variable allows you to toggle between Modelspace and Paperspace in AutoCAD. Modelspace is where you do basic design and drafting. In Paperspace you can create and manipulate different views of your model for plotting. When Tilemode is On (=1), you are working in Modelspace and the Modelspace UCS icon is visible in the lower-left corner. When Tilemode is Off (=0), you are in Paperspace and the triangular Paperspace icon is visible in the lower-left corner. At the command line, enter **Tilemode**.

While you are in Paperspace (Tilemode = 0), you may create *floating viewports* of your Modelspace drawing using **Mview**, and then switch to *floating Modelspace* (Tilemode still = 0) to edit the views. Moving between Paperspace and Modelspace can be accomplished using Tilemode to toggle Modelspace On and Off. Switching between Paperspace and the floating viewports can be accomplished using the **Mspace** and **Pspace** commands. These operations are now menu and/or status bar options.

To Turn On Paperspace

• Choose View ➤ Paper Space.

The above menu option performs two functions. It moves you from regular Modelspace to Paperspace, and it can also be used to switch from floating Modelspace back into Paperspace. So it activates both the Tilemode toggle and starts the **Pspace** command.

In Windows you can use the status bar to turn on Paperspace. Double-click on the MODEL button. The button changes to PAPER.

To Switch to Floating Modelspace

• Choose View ➤ Floating Modelspace.

This menu option activates the **Mspace** command, and allows you to work in Modelspace via a floating viewport. You may edit the Modelspace objects while keeping the Paperspace layout visible.

In Windows, you can use the Status bar PAPER/MODEL button to toggle back and forth between Paperspace view and the floating Modelspace. Note that as long as you are in Paperspace, MODEL on the status bar indicates floating Modelspace, not regular Modelspace.

NOTES When you wish to return to regular Modelspace, you may either reset Tilemode to 1 (On), or choose View ➤ Tiled Modelspace to perform the same function.

Floating viewports and tiled viewports should not be regarded as the same. In floating viewports you have more control over the contents of each view. You can turn off layers within different floating viewports, and scale and align views with more flexibility.

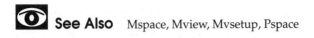 **See Also** Mspace, Mview, Mvsetup, Pspace

TIME

Keeps track of the time you spend on a drawing. The time is displayed in "military" format, using the 24-hour count. At the command line, enter **Time** (or **'Time** to use transparently).

To Display Drawing-Time Data

1. Choose Data ➤ Time.

2. Current time: Enter date and time.

3. Times for this drawing:

- **Created:** Displays date and time.
- **Last updated:** Displays date and time.
- **Total editing time:** Displays days and time.
- **Elapsed time (on):** Displays days and time.
- **Display/On/Off/Reset:** Enter an option.

 **OPTIONS**

Display Redisplays time information.

On Turns elapsed timer on.

Off Turns elapsed timer off.

Reset Resets elapsed timer to 0.

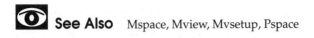 **See Also** *System Variables:* Tdcreate, Tdindwg, Tdupdate, Tdusrtimer

Tolerance allows you to specify maximum allowable variations of form, profile, orientation, location, or runout from those that are defined by the geometry shown in the drawing. These geometric tolerances define the maximum variations on the specified dimensions that will still allow the drawn object to function and to fit as required. AutoCAD positions the specified tolerances on the drawing in a *feature control frame*. At the command line, use **Tolerance**.

To Add Geometric Tolerances to Object Dimensions

1. In **Windows**, choose the Dimensioning toolbar ➤ Tolerance button. In **DOS**, choose Draw ➤ Dimensioning ➤ Tolerance.

2. When the Symbols dialog box appears, select the desired feature control symbol, then choose OK.

3. When the Geometric Tolerance subdialog box appears, enter the relevant tolerance information for the feature selected. In addition to the tolerance value, you may add a diameter symbol and supplementary datums and symbols pertaining to material conditions and projected tolerances. Choose OK when you have entered all of the required information.

4. Enter tolerance location: Pick the point at which the tolerance information is to be located. The symbol(s) selected, surrounded by a standard frame, will appear at the selected location.

 **OPTIONS**

Feature Control Symbols The Symbols dialog box provides an icon menu of the geometric feature symbols: the first three symbols pertain to *Location* (position, concentricity, and symmetry); the next three symbols to *Orientation* (parallelism, perpendicularity, and angularity); the next three symbols to *Form* (flatness, roundness, and straightness); then come two symbols for *Profile* (surface profile and line profile); and the final two symbols pertain to *Runout* (circular runout and total runout). When you select a feature symbol, AutoCAD closes the Symbols dialog box and inserts the symbol into the *Sym* text box in the Geometric Tolerance subdialog box.

Tolerance 1/Tolerance 2 You may enter up to two tolerance values for the object dimension. The tolerance *Value* specifies the amount by which the dimensions of the built object may deviate from the dimensions indicated on the drawing. Two additional modifiers may be added to value. You may optionally insert a diameter symbol (if appropriate) before the value by clicking on the *Dia* box. You may also add material condition information; clicking on the *MC* box opens the Material Condition subdialog box and allows you to specify *maximum material condition* (symbol M), *least material condition* (symbol L) or *regardless of feature size* (symbol S). Material conditions apply to features that can vary in size.

Datum 1/2/3 You may add up to three optional *datum reference letters* (A, B, C) after the tolerance values. Each datum represents a point, axis, or plane from which you can measure and verify dimensions. Usually these are three mutually perpendicular planes called the *datum reference frame*. Each datum may be followed by a material condition modifier symbol (M, L, or S) as described immediately above.

Height/Projected Tolerance Zone You may define projected tolerances in additional to positional tolerances to increase accuracy. Specify a *Height* value. This value specifies the minimum projected tolerance zone. Selecting the *Projected Tolerance Zone* box will add the projected tolerance symbol (P) after the height value.

Datum Identifier Allows you to specify a datum-identifying symbol. This identifier consists of a reference letter preceded and followed by a dash (-A-).

NOTES AutoCAD inserts all of the tolerance information and symbols into a feature control frame. A feature control frame will at minimum contain two elements: the symbol of the geometric characteristic being defined and the tolerance value. The tolerance value field will additionally contain all modifiers and datum references selected. The projected tolerance height and P symbol (if any) are inserted in a frame below the feature control frame, and the datum identifier is placed in a frame below these frames. Feature control frames are a single AutoCAD object, and you may copy, move, stretch, scale, and rotate them. You may use **Osnap** and **Grips**, and you may edit them using **Ddedit**.

Feature control frame characteristics are controlled by the dimension variables as follows: color (*Dimclre*); text color (*Dimclrt*); text gap (*Dimgap*); size of text (*Dimtxt*); and text style (*Dimtxtsty*).

See Also Ddedit; Dimensioning Commands; *Dimension Variables:* Dimclre, Dimclrt, Dimgap, Dimtxt, Dimtxtsty

N E W

TOOLBAR

Windows Only

AutoCAD Release 13 for Windows has a set of standard toolbars with frequently used commands grouped for easy access. You may display multiple toolbars on the screen at once, and you may hide them when you are not using them. The Toolbar command allows you to display, hide, and position the toolbars. At the command line, use **Toolbar**.

The most commonly used commands are grouped on the *top level* toolbars. The Standard toolbar provides access to all of these toolbars, either directly or via the Tool Windows toolbar. Toolbars are also available under Toolbars on the Tools menu.

Toolbars may be either *docked* or *floating*. If a toolbar is docked, it locks into position along the top, bottom, or sides of the screen. A floating toolbar can be moved around with your pointing device, and may overlap other toolbars.

To Display Top Level Toolbars

• Choose Tools ➤ Toolbars ➤ Predefined Options from Menu.

The toolbar immediately appears on your screen. You may reposition it by dragging it across the screen, and resize or reorient it using the "handles." To close it, click on the upper-left corner.

If you wish to "dock" a floating toolbar, drag it to a dock location at the top, bottom, or sides of the screen, and release the pick button.

Almost all of the toolbars have *flyouts*, or mini-toolbars that contain more tool icons. For example, the Special Edit flyout on the Modify toolbar contains tools to Edit Polyline, Edit Multiline, Edit Spline, Edit Text, and Edit Hatch. For specific tasks you may wish to display this "toolbar" on your screen rather than access it repeatedly via the Modify toolbar.

To load the lower level toolbars, use the Toolbar command. You will need to know the internal system name or *alias* for the toolbar. The aliases are shown below each toolbar graphic in Figure 18.

To Use the Toolbar Command

1. At the command prompt, type **Toolbar**.

2. Toolbar name (or ALL): Enter the full alias for the toolbar, and press ↵.

3. Show/Hide/Left/Right/Top/Bottom/Float <current>: Enter an option or press ↵.

 OPTIONS

All Type **All** to activate this option. Choose Hide or Show all toolbars. If you choose Show, every toolbar both top level and lower

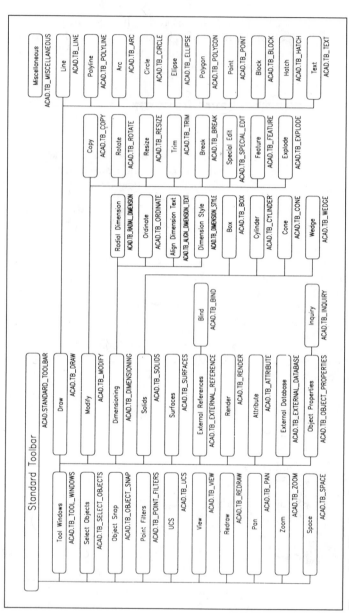

Figure 18: The AutoCAD toolbars

level will display on your screen. If you choose Hide, every toolbar including your default toolbars will close.

Show   Displays the named toolbar.

Hide   Closes the named toolbar.

Left/Right/Top/Bottom   Docks the named toolbar at the left, right, top, or bottom of the screen. The Position prompt sets the position of the toolbar relative to an existing docked toolbar.

Float   Changes the named toolbar from docked to floating. The Position prompt sets the position of the floating toolbar in XY coordinates. The Rows prompt allows you to define the number of rows in the toolbar.

NOTES   Each tool icon on a tool bar has a *ToolTip* that serves as a label, When you pass your pointing device slowly across the icon, the Tooltip appears and a line of help text is displayed on the status bar.

The position of tools on a flyout customizes itself based upon your usage. The flyout tool most recently used moves to the first position for easier access.

All of the toolbars are flexible and can be customized extensively to meet your specific needs. See **Tbconfig** for more information on customizing toolbars.

See Also   Tbconfig

TRACE

You can use Trace where a thick line is desired. Alternatively, you can accomplish the same thing using the **Pline** command. If you draw a series of Trace line segments, the corners are automatically joined to form a sharp corner. At the command line, type **Trace**.

To Draw a Thick Line

1.   In **Windows**, choose the Miscellaneous toolbar ➤ Trace. In **DOS**, type **Trace** at the command prompt.

2.   Trace width <default width>: Enter the desired width.

3.   From point: Pick the start point for the trace.

4.   To point: Pick the next point.

As with the **Line** command, you can continue to pick points to draw a series of connected line segments. Trace lines appear only after the next point is selected.

 NOTES   If you draw a series of Trace line segments, the corners are automatically joined to form a sharp corner. For this reason, traces do not have an Undo option, and the starting and ending segments will not join and bevel properly. To make traces bevel properly for the start and end segments, begin the trace not on the desired corner/endpoint but at any point midway on the desired first segment, and then make the end segment complete the actual first segment.

👁 **See Also**   Fill, *System Variables:* Tracewid

TRANSPARENT COMMANDS

The transparent commands can be used while AutoCAD is still executing another command. Control is transferred temporarily to the transparent command until it is completed, or until you terminate it by pressing Ctrl-C in DOS and ESC in Windows. Not all commands can be used transparently. See Table 11 for a list of Transparent commands.

To Use a Command while Another Is Executing

Type an apostrophe preceding the command name. (This only works for commands that are identified as transparent commands in Table 11 and throughout this book.)

Table 11: AutoCAD Transparent Commands

Transparent Commands		
About	Dist	Redrawall
Aperture	Dragmode	Regenauto
Appload	Files	Resume
Attdisp	Fill	Script
Base	Grid	Setvar
Blipmode	Help / ?	Snap
Cal	Id	Status
Color	Isoplane	Style
Ddemodes	Layer	Time
Ddgrips	Limits	Units
Ddlmodes	Linetype	View
Ddosnap	Ltscale	Zoom
Ddrmodes	Ortho	
Ddselect	Osmode	
Ddunits	Pan	
Delay	Redraw	

TREESTAT

Displays data regarding the drawing's current spatial index, allowing you to improve drawing efficiency via the *Treedepth* system variable. Information is provided separately for model space and paper space.At the command line type **Treestat**.

NOTES The number of nodes being reported is shown in the Modelspace branch and Paperspace branch. Each node requires approximately 80 bytes of memory. Setting the *Treedepth* system variable to a large number increases disk swapping, negating the performance benefits of the spatial index. The objective is to have fewer objects per node to take advantage of spatial indexing, the optimum number being dependent on the amount of memory your computer has. The more memory you have, the more you can take advantage of spatial indexing. The use of *Treedepth* and *Treestat* is best suited to large drawings in order to optimize performance.

See Also *System Variables:* Maxtreenodes, Treedepth, Treestat

TRIM

Trim shortens an object to meet another object or objects. In AutoCAD Release 13, objects may also be trimmed to a point of *implied* intersection—that is, to the point at which they *would* intersect with the cutting edge if the cutting edge were extended out. Additionally, objects may be trimmed to the current UCS plane or along the current view direction—that is, to an apparent intersection in the current view. These options are controlled by the system variables *Projmode* and *Edgemode*. At the command line, type **Trim**.

To Trim an Object

1. In **Windows**, choose the Modify toolbar ➤ Trim flyout ➤ Trim button. In **DOS**, choose Modify ➤ Trim.

2. Select cutting edge(s)(Projmode - UCS, Edgemode - No extend: Choose object(s) that define the cutting edge(s) at which you want to trim other objects.

3. <Select objects to trim>: Pick the objects you want to trim, one at a time or using the Fence selection set option, or select an option:

- If you type **P**, you will be prompted None/Ucs/View/<current value>:.

- If you type E, you will be prompted Extend/ No extend <current value>:.

 OPTIONS

Project Specifies the projection mode for AutoCAD to use when trimming objects: *None* specifies that only objects that actually intersect the cutting edge will be trimmed; *UCS* specifies projection onto the XY plane of the current UCS; *View* trims all selected objects which intersect with the cutting edge in the current view. The system variable *Projmode* settings control the projection mode.

Edge Allows cutting edges to be extended to the point where they *would* intersect with an option. You may select either *Extend* or *No Extend* (system variable *Edgemode* settings 1 and 0). If you choose No extend, only objects that *actually* intersect the cutting edge will be trimmed.

NOTES Objects that may be trimmed include arcs, circles, elliptical arcs, lines open 2D and 3D polylines, rays and splines. These same objects may be selected as cutting edges. Regions, floating viewports, text, and xlines may also be used to define cutting edges.

At the **Select cutting edge:** prompt, you can pick several objects that intersect the objects you want to trim. Once you've selected the cutting edges, press ↵ and the **Select object to trim:** prompt appears, allowing you to pick the sides of the objects to trim. You cannot trim objects within blocks or use blocks as cutting edges.

See Also Break, Change, Extend, *System Variables:* Edgemode, Projmode

U

The U command reverses the most recent command. You can undo as many commands as you have issued during any given editing session. At the command line, type **U**.

To Reverse a Command

In **Windows**, choose the Standard toolbar ➤ Undo button. In **DOS**, choose Assist ➤ Undo.

 NOTES   The Auto, End, and Control options under the **Undo** command affect the results of the U command. U is essentially the Undo command with 1 as the parameter.

See Also   Redo, Undo

UCS

The user coordinate system, or UCS, is a tool for creating and editing three-dimensional drawings. A UCS can be described as a plane in three-dimensional space on which you can draw. Using the UCS command, you can create and shift between as many UCS's as you like. It determines the orientation in which two-dimensional objects are drawn and the direction in which objects are extruded. At the command line, use **UCS**.

To Modify a UCS

1. In **Windows,** choose the Standard toolbar ➤ UCS fly-out. In **DOS,** choose View ➤ Set UCS ➤ Predefined UCS Settings.

2. Origin/ZAxis/3point/Object/View/X/Y/Z/Prev/Restore/ Save/Del/?/<World>: Enter or select an option.

 **OPTIONS**

Origin Determines the origin of a UCS.

ZAxis Defines the direction of the Z-coordinate axis. You are prompted for an origin for the UCS and for a point along the Z axis of the UCS.

3point Allows you to define a UCS by selecting three points: the origin, a point along the positive direction of the X axis, and a point along the positive direction of the Y axis.

Object Defines a UCS based on the orientation of an object.

View Defines a UCS parallel to your current view. The origin of the current UCS will be used as the origin of the new UCS.

X/Y/Z Allows you to define a UCS by rotating the current UCS about its X, Y, or Z axis.

Prev Places you in the previously defined UCS. The *UCS Previous* option under the Settings pull-down menu has the same effect.

Restore Restores a saved UCS.

Save Saves a UCS for later recall.

Del Deletes a previously saved UCS.

?/List Displays a list of currently saved UCS's. You can use wild-card filter lists to search for specific UCS names.

World Returns you to the world coordinate system.

NOTES The world coordinate system, or WCS, is the base from which all other UCS's are defined. The WCS is the default coordinate system when you open a new file. You may additionally set the *UCSfollow* system variable by choosing Options ➤ UCS ➤ Follow. This automatically shifts your drawing into the appropriate plan view whenever the UCS is moved.

If you use the *Objects* option, the way the selected object was created affects the orientation of the UCS. Table 12 correlates selected objects with UCS orientation.

Table 12: UCS Orientation Based on Objects

Object Type	UCS Orientation
Arc	The center of the arc establishes the UCS origin. The X axis of the UCS passes through one of the endpoints nearest to the picked point on the arc.
Circle	The center of the circle establishes the UCS origin. The X axis of the UCS passes through the pick point on the circle.
Dimension	The midpoint of the dimension text establishes the UCS origin. The X axis of the UCS is parallel to the X axis that was active when the dimension was drawn.
Line	The endpoint nearest the pick point establishes the origin of the UCS, and the XZ plane of the UCS contains the line.
Point	The point location establishes the UCS origin. The UCS orientation is arbitrary.
2D Polyline	The starting point of the polyline establishes the UCS origin. The X axis is determined by the direction from the first point to the next vertex.

Table 12: UCS Orientation Based on Objects (continued)

Solid	The first point of the solid establishes the origin of the UCS. The second point of the solid establishes the X axis.
Trace	The direction of the trace establishes the X axis of the UCS, with the beginning point setting the origin.
3Dface	The first point of the 3Dface establishes the origin. The first and second points establish the X axis. The plane defined by the face determines the orientation of the UCS.
Shapes, Text, Blocks, Attributes, *and* Attribute Definitions	The insertion point establishes the origin of the UCS. The object's rotation angle establishes the X axis.

👁 **See Also**   Dducs; Dducsp; Dview; Elev; Plan; Rename; *System Variables:* Ucsfollow, Ucsicon, Ucsname, Ucsorg, Ucsxdir, Ucsydir, Vsmax, Vsmin, Worlducs; Thickness; Ucsicon; Vpoint; Wildcard characters

UCSICON

Ucsicon controls the display and location of the UCS icon. The UCS icon tells you the orientation of the current UCS. It displays an L-shaped graphic symbol showing the positive X and Y directions. The icon displays a *W* when WCS is the current default coordinate system. If the current UCS plane is perpendicular to your current view, the UCS icon displays a broken pencil to indicate that you will have difficulty drawing in the current view. The UCS icon changes to a cube when you are displaying a perspective view. When you are in Paperspace, it turns into a triangle.

To Modify the UCS Icon

1. Choose Options ➤ UCS ➤ Icon.

2. ON/OFF/All/Noorigin/ORigin <ON>: Enter an option.

 **OPTIONS**

ON Turns the UCS icon on.

OFF Turns the UCS icon off.

All Forces the Ucsicon settings to take effect in all viewports if you have more than one viewport. Otherwise, the settings will affect only the active viewport.

Noorigin Places the UCS icon in the lower-left corner of the drawing area, regardless of the current UCS's origin location.

ORigin Places the UCS icon at the origin of the current UCS. If the origin is off the screen, the UCS icon will appear in the lower-left corner of the drawing area.

 NOTES Instead of selecting the *ORigin* option as shown above, achieve the same effect by selecting Options ➤ UCS ➤ Icon Origin. The UCS icon will always move automatically with the origin, unless the origin is not within the drawing view window.

See Also UCS, Viewports. *System Variables:* Ucsicon

UNDEFINE

See **Redefine**.

UNDO

Allows you to undo parts of your editing session. This can be useful if you accidentally execute a command that destroys part or all of your drawing. Undo also allows you to control how much of a drawing is undone.

To Reverse Commands

1. At the command prompt, type **Undo**.

2. Auto/Control//BEgin/End/Mark/Back/<default number>:
   Enter an option to use or the number of commands to undo.

 OPTIONS

Auto Makes AutoCAD view menu macros as a single command. If Auto is set to On, the effect of macros issued from a menu will be undone regardless of the number of commands the macro contains.

Control Allows you to turn off the Undo feature to save disk space or to limit the Undo feature to single commands. You are prompted for **All**, **None**, or **One**. All fully enables the Undo feature, None disables Undo, and One restricts the Undo feature to a single command at a time.

Begin, End *Begin* marks the beginning of a sequence of operations. All edits after that point become part of the same group. *End* terminates the group. This allows you to mark a group of commands to be undone together.

Mark, Back Allows you to experiment safely with a drawing by first marking a point in your editing session to which you can return. Once a mark has been issued, you can proceed with your experimental drawing addition. Then, you can use *Back* to undo all the commands back to the place that Mark was issued.

NOTES Many commands offer an Undo option. The Undo option under a main command will act more like the **U** command and will not offer the options described here.

See Also Redo; *System Variables:* Undoctl, Undomarks; U

Union creates a composite object by combining the total area or volume of two or more regions or solids. At the command line, use **Union**.

To Combine Regions or Solids

1. In **Windows**, choose the Modify toolbar ➤ Explode flyout ➤ Union button. In **DOS**, choose Construct ➤ Union.

2. "Courier"Select objects:$ Click on the overlapping solids or regions that you want to combine.

 NOTES Union can be used only for regions or solids. In step 2 above, you may select both regions and solids at the same time, and you may select objects from any number of planes. Auto-CAD will group the selection set into subsets by region/solid and by plane (in the case of regions) before combining them.

See Also Intersect, Region, Solid Modeling, Subtract

UNITS

Sets AutoCAD to the unit format appropriate to the drawing. For
example, if you are drawing an architectural floor plan, you can set
up AutoCAD to accept and display distances using feet, inches,
and fractional inches. You can also set up AutoCAD to accept and
display angles as degrees, minutes, and seconds of an arc rather
than the default decimal degrees. The dialog box equivalent of this
command is **Ddunits**.

To Change Drawing Units

1. At the command line, type **Units** (or **'Units** to use transparently).

2. Report formats: Enter choice, 1 to 5 <2>: Enter the number corresponding to the desired unit system, as described
below. With the exception of the Engineering and Architectural modes, you can use these modes with any basic unit
of measurement.

3. Number of digits to right of decimal point (0 to 8): <4>:
Enter a number to specify the degree of precision.

4. Systems of angle measure: Enter choice, 1 to 5 <1>: Enter the number corresponding to the desired angle measure
system, as described below.

5. Number of fractional places for display of angle (0 to
8) <0>: Enter a number to specify the degree of precision.

6. Direction for angle 0: Enter direction for angle 0 <0>:
Enter the desired angle for the 0 degree direction, as described below.

7. Do you want angle measured clockwise? <N>: Enter **Y**
if you want angles measured clockwise; otherwise, press ↵.

OPTIONS

System of units Sets format of units that AutoCAD will accept as input:

Report Format	Example
1. Scientific	1.55E+01
2. Decimal	15.50
3. Engineering	1′–3.50″
4. Architectural	1′–3 1/2″
5. Fractional	15 1/2

System of angle measure Sets format of angle measurement Auto-CAD will accept as input:

Measurement Format	Example
1. Decimal degrees	45.0000
2. Degrees/minutes/seconds	45d0′0″
3. Grads	50.0000g
4. Radians	0.7854r
5. Surveyor's units	N 45d0′0″ E

Direction for angle 0 Sets direction for the 0 angle:

East   3 o'clock = 0
North   12 o'clock = 90
West   9 o'clock = 180
South   6 o'clock = 270

NOTES   You can set decimal or fractional input regardless of the unit format being used. This means you can enter 5.5′, as well as 5′6″ when using the Architectural format. Decimal mode is perfect for metric units as well as decimal English units.

See Also   Ddunits, Mvsetup, *System Variables:* Aflags, Angbase, Angdir, Aumits, Luprec, Unitmode

VIEW

View allows you to save views of your drawing. Instead of using the **Zoom** command to zoom in and out of your drawing, you can save views of the areas you need to edit, and then recall them using the *Restore* option of the View command. The corresponding dialog box command is **Ddview**. (To use **Ddview**, choose View ➤ Named Views.)

To Save Views of Your Drawing

1.   At the command prompt, type **View**.

2.   ?/Delete/Restore/Save/Window: Enter an option.

OPTIONS

?   Lists all currently saved views. Wildcard filter lists are accepted.

Delete   Prompts you for a view name to delete from the drawing database.

Restore   Prompts you for a view name to restore to the screen.

Save   Saves the current view. You are prompted for a view name.

Window   Saves a view defined by a window. You are prompted first to enter a view name and then to window the area to be saved as a view.

NOTES   AutoCAD provides a Select Initial View check box to restore a previously saved view in the Open Drawing dialog box when you open an existing drawing. View will save three-dimensional orthographic projection views, perspective views, and Paperspace or Modelspace views. View does not save hidden-line views or shaded views.

 See Also   Open

VIEWPORTS

See **Vports**.

VIEWRES

Controls whether AutoCAD's virtual screen feature is used and how accurately AutoCAD displays lines, arcs, and circles.

To Invoke Fast Zoom Mode

1.   At the command prompt, type **Viewres**.

2.   Do you want fast zooms? <Y>: Enter **Y** or **N**. If you respond with **Y**, the following prompt appears: Enter circle zoom percent (1-20000) <current setting>:. Enter a value from 1 to 20,000, or press ↵ to accept the default.

 OPTIONS

Yes Sets up a large virtual screen within which zooms, pans, and view/restores occur at redraw speeds. You are prompted for a circle zoom percent (based on the current zoom magnification). This value determines how accurately circles and noncontinuous lines are shown.

No   Turns off the virtual screen. All zooms, pans, and view/restores will cause a regeneration.

NOTES   The circle zoom percent value also affects the speed of redraws and regenerations. A high value slows down redraws and regenerations; a low value speeds them up. Differences in redraw speeds are barely noticeable unless you have a very large drawing.

Use a high percent value for circle zoom to display smooth circles and arcs and to accurately show noncontinuous lines. A low value causes arcs and circles to appear as a series of line segments when viewed up close. Noncontinuous lines, however, may appear continuous. This does not mean that prints or plots of your drawing will be less accurate; only the display is affected.

The default value for the circle zoom percent is 100, but at this value dashed or hidden lines might appear continuous, depending on the Ltscale setting and how far you are zoomed into the drawing. A value of 2000 (i.e., 20×) or higher reduces or eliminates this problem with little sacrifice of speed.

A low circle zoom value causes object endpoints, intersections, and tangents to appear inaccurately placed when you edit a close-up view of circles and arcs. Often, this results from the segmented appearance of arcs and circles and does not necessarily mean the object placement is inaccurate. It may also be hard to distinguish between polygons and circles. Setting the circle zoom percent to a high value also reduces or eliminates these problems.

The drawing limits affect redraw speed when the virtual screen feature is turned on. If the limits are set to an area much greater than the actual drawing, redraws are slowed down.

To force the virtual screen to contain a specific area, set your limits to the area you want, set the limit's checking feature to On, and issue a **Zoom**/*All* command. The virtual screen will conform to these limits until another **Regen** is issued or until you pan or zoom outside of the area set by the limits.

 See Also   Limits, Redraw, Regen, Regenauto

VPLAYER

Controls the visibility of layers for each individual viewport and allows display of different types of information in each viewport, even though the views are of the same drawing. You can use Vplayer in conjunction with overlapped viewports to create clipped views.

To Modify Viewport Layer Visibility

1. In Paperspace (Tilemode = 0), choose Data ➤ Viewport Layer Controls.

2. ?/Freeze/Thaw/Reset/Newfrz/Vpvisdflt: Enter the desired option.

 OPTIONS

? Displays the names of layers that are frozen in a given viewport. You are prompted to select a viewport. If you are in Modelspace, AutoCAD temporarily switches to Paperspace during your selection.

Freeze Lets you specify the name of layers you want to freeze in selected viewports. You are first prompted for the names of **Layer(s) to freeze:**, then **All/Select/<current>:** appears for the viewport(s) in which to freeze them.

Thaw Thaws layers in specific viewports. You are prompted for the layer names to thaw, then the viewports in which the layers are to be thawed.

Reset Restores the default visibility setting for layers in a given viewport. See the *Vpvisdflt* option for information on default visibility.

Newfrz Creates a new layer that is automatically frozen. You can then turn this new layer on for each viewport individually. The option *Vp Frz* in the Ddlmodes dialog box performs the same function.

Vpvisdflt   Presets the visibility of layers for new viewports to be created using *Mview* by prompting:

- **Layer name(s) to change default viewport visibility:** Enter layer name.

- **Change default viewport visibility to Frozen/<Thawed>:** Enter an option.

NOTES   All options that prompt you for layer names allow use of wildcard characters to select multiple layer names. You can also use comma delimiters for lists of layers with dissimilar names.

See Also   Ddlmodes; Layer Mview; Mvsetup; Pspace; *System Variables:* Tilemode, Visretain

VPOINT

Vpoint selects an orthographic, three-dimensional view of your drawing. At the command line, type **Vpoint**.

To Set a Viewing Point

1.   Choose View ➤ 3D Viewpoint.

2.   Select the Rotate, Tripod, or Vector option.

If you are operating from the command line **Rotate/<View point> <current setting>:**, enter a coordinate value, enter **R** for the Rotate option, or press ↵ to set the view with the compass and axes tripod.

 **OPTIONS**

Rotate   Allows you to specify a view in terms of angles from the XY plane and from the X axis. You are first prompted to enter an

angle in the XY plane from the X axis. Next, you are prompted to enter an angle from the XY plane.

View point/Vector Allows you to specify your viewpoint location by entering an X,Y,Z coordinate value.

⏎/Tripod Allows you to visually select a view by using the compass and axes tripod.

NOTES There are three methods for selecting a view: Enter a value in X, Y, and Z coordinates that represents your view point. For example, entering 1,1,–1 will give you the same view as entering 4,4,–4.

Use the *Rotate* option to specify a viewpoint as horizontal and vertical angles in relation to the last point selected. Use the **ID** command to establish the view target point (the last point selected) before you start Vpoint, as shown in Figure 19.

Press ⏎ at the Vpoint prompt, and visually select a view point using the compass and axes tripod. To select a view, move your pointing device until the tripod indicates the desired X-, Y-, and Z-axis orientation. A

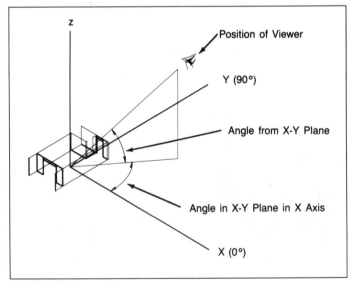

Figure 19: The viewpoint angles and what they represent

cross on the compass indicates your location in plan. For example, placing the cross in the lower-left quadrant of the compass places your viewpoint below and to the left of your drawing. Your view elevation is indicated by the distance of the cross from the compass center. The closer the cross is to the center, the higher the elevation. The circle inside the compass indicates a 0 elevation. If the cross falls outside of this circle, your view elevation becomes a minus value and your view will be from below your drawing (see Figure 20).

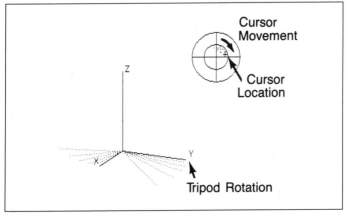

Figure 20: How the tripod rotates as you move the cursor
around the target's center

 **See Also**   Dview

VPORTS/VIEWPORTS

Displays multiple views, or tiled viewports, of your drawing at one time. This command is disabled when the *Tilemode* system variable is set to 0.

To Display Multiple Viewports

1. Choose View ➤ Tiled Viewports ➤ Preset options.

2. Save/Restore/Delete/Join/Single/?/2/<3>/4: Enter the desired option.

 **OPTIONS**

Save Saves the current viewport arrangement.

Restore Restores a previously saved viewport arrangement.

Delete Deletes a previously saved viewport arrangement.

Join Joins two adjacent viewports of the same size to make one larger viewport.

Single Changes the display to a single viewport.

? Displays a list of saved viewport arrangements along with each viewport's coordinate location.

2 Splits the display to show two viewports. You are prompted for a horizontal or vertical split.

3 Changes the display to show three viewports.

4 Changes the display to show four equal viewports.

Layout If you are working from the pull-down View menu, you may select Layout to open the Select Layout dialog box. This displays an icon menu of predefined viewport arrangements from which you may select the desired layout.

NOTES   Each viewport can contain any type of view you like. For example, you can display a perspective view in one viewport and a plan view of the same drawing in another viewport.

You can only work in one viewport at a time. To change active viewports, pick any point inside the desired viewport. The border around the selected viewport will thicken to show that it is active. The standard cursor appears only in the active viewport. (When you move the cursor into an inactive viewport, it changes into an arrow.) Any edits made in one viewport are immediately reflected in the other viewports.

Each viewport has its own virtual display within which you can pan and zoom at redraw speeds. For this reason, the **Regen** and **Redraw** commands affect only the active viewport. To regenerate or redraw all the viewports at once, use the **Regenall** and **Redrawall** commands.

👁 **See Also**   Mview; Redraw; Regen; *System Variables:* Cvports, Maxactvp, Viewctr, Viewdir, Viewtwist, Vsmax, Vsmin; Viewres

VSLIDE

Vslide displays raster image slide files in the current viewport. Slides are individual files with the extension .SLD. You may combine individual slide files into a slide library file by using the extension .SLB.

To Display Slide Files

1. Choose Tools ➤ Slide ➤ View.
2. File name <current file name>: Enter the name of the slide file to be displayed. If *Filedia* is set to 1, the Select Slide file dialog box will appear.

To View a Slide from a Slide Library

1.   Choose Tools ➤ Slide ➤ View.

2.   File name <current file name>: Enter the slide library
name followed by the slide's name in parentheses, as in

```
library-name(slide-file-name)
```

👁 **See Also**   Mslide, Script, Slidelib.EXE

WBLOCK

Wblock lets you create a new file from a portion of the current file
or from a block of the current file. At the command line, type
Wblock.

To Write a Block to Disk

1.   In **Windows**, type **Wblock**. In **DOS**, choose File ➤ Export
➤ Block.

2.   At the command line or in the Create Drawing File dialog
box, enter the file name for the new drawing file.

3.   Block name: Enter the block name or press ↵ to select objects.

The block or set of objects will be written to your disk as a drawing file.

NOTES If you are exporting a block from your drawing and you want the file name to be the same as the block name, enter an equals sign at the **Block name:** prompt, or enter the same block name again. If you enter the name of an existing file at the **File name:** prompt, you receive the prompt:

```
A drawing with this name already exists.
Do you want to replace it? <N>:
```

You can replace the file name or return to the command prompt to restart Wblock.

To write a portion of the current drawing view to a file, press ↵ without entering anything at the **Block name:** prompt. You receive the following two prompts:

- **Insertion base point:** Enter a coordinate or pick a point.

- **Select objects:** Select objects using the standard AutoCAD selection options.

The objects you select are written to your disk as a drawing file. The point you select at the **Insertion base point:** prompt becomes the origin of the written file. The current UCS (user coordinate system) becomes the WCS (world coordinate system) in the written file. When you save a block to disk, the UCS active at the time you create the block becomes the WCS of the written file.

Entering an asterisk (*) at the **Block name:** prompt writes the entire current file to disk, stripping it of all unused blocks, layers, line types, and text styles. This can reduce a file's size and access time. (See **Purge**.)

Objects are placed in the Modelspace of the output file unless the asterisk is used. In that case, objects are placed in the space they are in.

See Also Base; *System Variables:* Handles, Insbase

WILDCARD CHARACTERS

Wildcard characters allow you to list file names by using a filter to include or exclude files according to similarities in their names. AutoCAD wildcard characters are extensions of the standard DOS wildcard characters. Here are the wildcard characters you can use:

Character	Description
#	Matches any number. For example, **C#D** selects all names that begin with *C*, end with *D*, and have a single-digit number between.
@	Matches any alphabetical character. For example, **C@D** selects any name that begins with *C*, ends with *D*, and has a single alphabetical character between.
. (period)	Matches any character not numeric or alphabetical. For example, **C.D** might select the name C-D.
* (asterisk)	Matches any string of characters. For example, ***CD** selects all names of any length that end with *CD*.
? (question mark)	Matches any single character. For example **C?D** selects all names of three characters that begin with *C* and end with *D*.
~ (tilde)	Matches anything but the set of characters that follow. For example, **~CD** selects all names that do *not* include *CD*.

Character	Description
[ ] (brackets)	Typing any set of characters between two brackets matches any one of the characters enclosed in brackets. For example, **[CD]X** selects the names CX and DX, but not CDX. Brackets can be used in conjunction with other wildcard characters. For example, you could use **[~CD]X** to find all names except CX and DX.
– (hyphen)	Lets you specify a range of characters when used within brackets. For example, **[C-F]X** selects the names CX, DX, EX, and FX.
' (single quote)	Forces the character that follows to be read literally. (The reverse quote is the character that is located to the left of the 1 key on most keyboards.) For example, ' selects the name *CD, instead of all names that end in *CD*.

XBIND

Imports a block, dimension style, layer, line type, or text style from an external reference (xref). At the command line, type **Xbind**.

To Bind Symbols into Your Drawing

1. In **Windows**, choose the External References toolbar ➤ Bind flyout ➤ Bind button. In **DOS**, choose File ➤ Bind.

2. Block/Dimstyle/LAyer/LType/Style: Enter the desired option.

3. You are then prompted for the name of the item to import. Enter a single name, a list of names separated by commas, or use wildcard characters to specify a range of names.

342 Xline

NOTES Named variables from an xref file must be prefixed with their source file name. Be sure to include the full xref file name, including the vertical bar symbol, or pipe character (|), for example, xref-*filename | blockname*. When you use Xbind to import the named block, its name will change to xref-*filename*0*blockname* to reflect its source file. If a block of the same name already exists, the 0 is replaced with a 1, as in xref-*filename*1*blockname*.

See Also Xref

Allows you to create construction lines anywhere in three-dimensional space. By default, Xline creates an infinite line based on two input points. The first point specified, the root, becomes the "midpoint" of the infinite line. You may specify the Xline's orientation in a variety of ways. At the command line, type **Xline**.

To Draw a Construction Line

1. In **Windows**, choose the Draw toolbar ➤ Line flyout ➤ Xline button. In **DOS**, choose Draw ➤ Construction Line.

2. Hor/Ver/Ang/Bisect/Offset/<from Point>: Pick a first point (the Xline "root" or midpoint) or select an option.

3. Through point: Pick a second point to orient the Xline. Continue to pick additional through points as required to create additional construction lines radiating from the midpoint.

 **OPTIONS**

Hor/Ver Allows you to draw a construction line parallel to the X axis (Hor) or Y axis (Ver). You need only pick a single point to define Xlines of this type. Continue picking through points to create as many parallel construction lines as are required.

Ang Allows you to draw an Xline at a specified angle to the X axis by either entering an angle value or by dynamically picking two points. Continue picking through points to create as many parallel construction lines as are required.

Bisect Creates a construction line that bisects a specified angle. First pick the angle vertex point, then points to mark the lines of the angle.

Offset Allows you to draw a construction line parallel to a selected line object (including plines) at a specified offset. First specify the offset by picking two points or entering a numeric value. Then select a line object and pick a point to indicate the side on which to offset the construction line.

Xlines are ignored by commands that display the drawing extents.

 **See Also** Line, Ray

Lets you explode multiple compound objects and blocks, including non-uniformly scaled objects. You may also control and change the color, layer, and line type, either of individual objects or of all of the objects globally.

To Explode Compound Objects

1. At the command line, enter **Xplode**.

2. Select objects to Xplode: Select objects: Use a selection method to pick all of the objects you wish to explode. (AutoCAD will show how many were selected and how many are valid compound objects.)

3. Xplode Individually: Press ↵, or enter **I** if you wish to control color, layer, or line type individually.

4. All/ Color/ LAyer/LType/Inherit from parent block/ <Explode>: Press ↵ to explode all of the selected objects without changing any of their characteristics. Type in an option—A/C/LA/LT/I—if you wish to change all or any of the selected object's characteristics.

 **OPTIONS**

Global/Individual If you choose the default global option in step 3, Xplode will apply your choices to all objects in a single pass. If you chose the **I** option in step 3, Xplode will cycle through each of the selected objects one at a time.

All If you select this option, Xplode will prompt you though all of the other options in turn, allowing you to select or enter new values.

Color Allows you to specify any of the standard colors, or to choose color *BYLayer* or *BYBlock*.

Linetype Allows you to specify a new line type or to choose line type BYLAYER. The prompt BYBlock/BYLayer/CONTinuous/other loaded linetypes/<BYLayer>: lists the line types that are loaded.

Layer Xplode onto what layer? <current setting>: Enter a new layer name, or press CR to explode the block into the current layer.

 See Also Block, Explode, Wblock, Xbind, Xref

XREF

Xref lets you attach and detach, list, and reload or bind external drawing files to your current drawing file. You may also overlay external files over your current drawing to check the consistency or relationship between the drawings. Xrefs should be regarded as read-only files for reference purposes only.

To Import an External File

1. In **Windows**, choose the External References toolbar ➤ Preset Options button. In **DOS**, choose Files ➤ External Reference ➤ Preset menu options.

2. ?/Bind/Detach/Path/Reload/Overlay<Attach>: Enter the desired option.

 **OPTIONS**

?/List Displays a list of a cross-referenced files in your current drawing. The name of the file as well as its location on your storage device is shown. You can filter the Xref'd file names by using wild-card characters.

Bind Causes a cross-referenced file to become a part of the current file. Once Bind is used, the Xref file becomes an ordinary block in the current file and AutoCAD replaces the pipe character (|) with a number (usually 0) between two dollar signs($$) . If you are working from the pull-down File menu and not the command line. You are prompted for the name of the Xref'd file to be bound **Xref(s) to bind:**. Enter name or names separated with commas or a wildcard.

Detach Detaches a cross-referenced file, so it is no longer referenced to the current file:

- **Xref(s) to detach:** Enter name or names separated with commas or wildcard.

Path   Lets you specify a new DOS path for a cross-referenced file. This is useful if you have moved a cross-referenced file to another drive or directory. You are prompted for the file's name:

- **Old Path:** Enter old path.

- **New Path:** Enter new path.

Reload   Lets you reload a cross-referenced file without exiting and reentering the current file. This option is useful if you are in a network environment and you know that someone has just finished updating a file you are using as a cross-reference. AutoCAD creates a temporary lock file if the drawing you are editing is externally referenced during an Xref Reload operation and, if it encounters an error while reloading, ends the Xref command undoing the entire reload sequence:

- **Xref(s) to reload:** Enter name or names separated with commas or wildcard.

Attach   Lets you attach another drawing file as a cross-reference. You are prompted for a file name, notified if the file exists, then requested for an insertion point, scale factor(s), and rotation angle for the cross-reference.

- **Xref to Attach <default>:** Enter name or a ~ (tilde) to open the Select Drawing File dialog box.

- **Xref (filename) has already been loaded. Insertion point:** Enter a location.

- **X scale factor <1> / Corner XYZ:** Enter a new value or press ↵.

- **Y Scale factor (default =X):** Enter a new value or press ↵.

- **Rotation angle <0>:** Pick a rotation angle dynamically or enter a value.

Overlay   Lets you overlay another drawing file as a cross-reference for comparison purposes. It operates in a very similar way to the *Attach* option. You are prompted, in the same way, for a file name, notified if the file exists, then requested for an insertion point, scale factor(s), and rotation angle for the cross-reference. However, overlaid cross-references cannot be nested—that is, if you reference a drawing with an overlaid cross-reference, the overlaid cross-reference will not be referenced into your drawing. The overlay option allows multiple users to access the same drawings without circularity of Xrefs.

 NOTES   Xref'd files act like blocks; they cannot be edited from the file they are attached to. The difference between blocks and Xref'd files is that Xref'd files do not become part of the current file's database. Instead, the current file "points" to the Xref'd file. The next time the current file is opened, the Xref'd file is also opened and automatically attached. This has two advantages. First, since the Xref'd file does not become part of the current file, the current file size remains small. Second, since the Xref'd file stays independent, any changes made to it are automatically reflected in the current file whenever it is reopened.

In most of the options, you can enter a single name, a list of names separated by commas, or a name containing wildcard characters. Named variables from the Xref'd files will have the file name as a prefix. For example, a layer called "wall" in an Xref'd file called "house" will have the name House | wall in the current file.

At a file name prompt, you can assign a name to an Xref'd file that is different from its actual file name by appending to the file name an equals sign followed by the new name. For example, at the prompt, enter a statement in the form of

> *newplan=oldplan*

where *newplan* is the new name and *oldplan* is the file name of the Xref'd file.

AutoCAD keeps a log of Xref activity in an ASCII file. This file has the same root name as your current drawing file and has the extension .XLG. You can delete this file with no effect on your drawing.

See Also   Block; Insert; *System Variables:* Xrefctl; Xbind

ZOOM

Zoom controls the display of your drawing. At the command line, enter **Zoom** (or **'Zoom** to use transparently).

To Use Zoom

1. In **Windows**, choose the Standard toolbar ➤ Zoom In/Out buttons, or choose View ➤ Zoom. In **DOS**, choose View ➤ Zoom ➤ Zoom menu options.

2. All/Center/Dynamic/Extents/Left/PreviousVmax/Window/<Scale(X/XP)>: Enter the desired option.

 OPTIONS

In/Out   These buttons on the Windows standard toolbar allow you to zoom in and out by a predefined scale factor. Zoom *In* doubles the size of the drawing display; Zoom *Out* shrinks the display to half of the current size so that you can view double the drawing area.

All   Displays the area of the drawing defined by the drawing's limits or extents, whichever are greater (see **Limits**).

Center   Displays a view based on a selected point. You are first prompted for a center point for your view and then for a magnification or height. A value followed by an **X** is read as a magnification factor; a lone value is read as the desired height in the display's drawing units.

Dynamic   Displays the virtual screen and allows you to use a view box to select a view. The drawing extents, current view, and the current virtual screen area are indicated as a solid white box, a dotted green box, and red corner marks, respectively. You can pan, enlarge, or shrink the view by moving the view box to a new location, adjusting its size, or both. Whenever the view box moves into an area that will cause a regeneration, an hourglass appears in the lower-left corner of the display. When the view box appears, press the pick button to adjust the view box size, then pick again to re-store the X in the view box. Press enter to set the new view.

Extents Displays a view of the entire drawing. The drawing is forced to fit within the display and is forced to the left. The drawing limits are ignored (see **Limits**).

Left Similar to the *Center* option, but the point you pick at the prompt becomes the lower-left corner of the display.

Previous Displays the last view created by a **Zoom**, **Pan**, or **View** command. AutoCAD will store up to four previous views.

Vmax Displays an overall view of the current virtual display. Un-like the *Extents* and *All* options, no regeneration occurs.

Window Enlarges a rectangular area of a drawing, based on a de-fined window.

Scale(X) Expands or shrinks the drawing display. If an X follows the scale factor, it will be in relation to the current view. If no X is used, the scale factor will be in relation to the area defined by the limits of the drawing. A value of .5x displays a view half the size of the current view

Scale(XP) Sets a viewports scale in relation to the Paperspace scale. For example, if you have set up a title block in Paperspace at a scale of 1″ = 1″ and your full-scale Modelspace drawing is to be at a final plot scale of ¼″ = 1′, you can enter **1/48xp** at the Zoom prompt to set the viewport at the appropriate scale for Paperspace. You must be in Modelspace to use this option.

NOTES Zoom can be used transparently as long as the Viewres Fast Zoom option is on. Zoom cannot be used transpar-ently while viewing a drawing in perspective. Use the **Dview** com-mand's *Zoom* option instead. Zoom cannot be used transparently in Paperspace.

See Also Limits; Mspace; Mview; Mvsetup; Pspace; Redraw; Regen; Regenauto; *System Variables:* Viewsize; Viewres

Index

Note to the reader: Throughout this index, **boldfaced** page numbers indicate primary discussions of a topic. *Italicized* page numbers indicate illustrations.

Symbols & Numbers

\# wildcard character, 340
.$A file extension, 127
.$AC file extension, 127
* (asterisk) wildcard character,
    340
~ (tilde)
  to override Filedia OFF, xiii
  as wildcard character, 340
➤, on icons, xiv
<> (angle brackets), for
    dimension value, 88
. (period) wildcard character,
    340
[] (brackets) wildcard
    characters, 340
- (hyphen) wildcard character,
    341
? (Help) command, **142–143**
? (question mark) wildcard
    character, 340
@ (at sign)
  to reference last-entered
    point, 286
  for relative coordinates, 219
  as wildcard character, 340
2D objects
  creating enclosed areas, 237
  properties of regions, 269
  solids from, 265
2D polyline, UCS orientation
    based on, 322
3D axis, rotating object about,
    245
3D command, **303–304**
3D meshes, Pedit for, 201,
    205–207

3D objects. *See also* solid models
  creating surface, 303–304
  resolution of, 285
  shading, 253
3D StudioFiles
  exporting to, 148
  importing, 145
3D view
  hiding portions of, 111
  setting, 76
3DArray command, **9–11**
3Dface
  UCS orientation based on, 323
  visibility of edges, 65, 113
3Dface command, **304–305**
3DMesh command, **305–306**
3Dpoly command, **306–307**
.3DS file extension
  exporting to, 148
  importing files with, 144, 145
3DSIN command, 145
3DSOUT command, 148
3point option, to define UCS,
    321

A

About command, **1**
absolute coordinate, for points,
    219
.AC$ file extension, 127
Acad.DWG file, 192
Acad environment variable,
    23, 120
Acad.INI file, **1**
Acad.LIN file, 163, 164
Acad.log file, 167
Acad.LSP file, 23

Acad.MLN file, 179
Acad.MNS file, 1
Acad.MNU file, 200, 220
  customizing, 170
Acad.MSG message file,
  displaying, 1
ACAD.PAT file, 25, 139
Acad.PGP file, **2**
  re-initializing, 238
Acad.PSF PostScript file, 226
ACADALTMNU environment
  setting, 120
ACADCFG environment
  setting, 120
ACADDRV environment
  setting, 120
ACADHELP environment
  setting, 120
ACADLOGFILE environment
  setting, 120
ACADMAXMEM
  environment setting, 120
ACADMAXPAGE
  environment setting, 120
ACADPAGEDIR environment
  setting, 120
ACADPLCMD environment
  setting, 120, 225
Acadprefix system variable,
  281
Acadver system variable, 281
ACISIN command, 146
ACISOUT command, 148
Add (Select command), 252
Add mode, for Area
  command, 8
Administration (External
  Database menu), 11–12
ADS applications, loading and
  unloading, 4
.ADT file name extension, 22
Aerial view window, opening,
  105
Aflags system variable, 281
alias, for toolbar, 313, *314*
Align command, **3**

aligning
  dimensions, 87–89, *88*
  text, 107
All (Select command), 252
Alt key, and dialog boxes, xiii
alternate font, 285
alternate measurement
  systems, 79
alternate tolerance zero
  suppression, 80
AME solid models, converting,
  268–269
Ameconvert command, 149,
  268–269
Angbase system variable, 281
Angdir system variable, 281
angle brackets (<>), for
  dimension value, 88
Angle (Chamfer command), 32
Angle to fill, for object array, 10
angle unit format, 81
angles
  of arc, 6, 64
  of dimension text, 89, 98
  editing for attribute, 16
  measurement units for, 56,
    74, 328
  system variable for, 281
  viewpoint, 334
angular dimension, *78*
Annotation Gap option, 56
Annotation sub-dialog box,
  56–58
annotations
  inserting, 158
  line to connect to object, 157
Aperture command, **4**, 66
aperture size, 66
Aperture system variable, 281
apex of cone, 262
appending text to alternate
  dimension, 80
applications, system variables
  for custom, 295
Appload command, **4–5**
Appload dialog box, 23

Arc Cascading menu, 6
Arc command, **5–7**
Arc mode, for Pline command, 210
architectural measurement units, 328
arcs
  adding radius dimension to, 96
  calculating areas including, 8
  center point of, 90–91
  changing angle, 64
  changing properties, 32
  dimension label for angle of, 89
  dimensions for diameter, 92
  elliptical, 117
  erasing with Break command, 29
  from Fillet command, 131
  UCS orientation based on, 322
Area command, 7–9, 238
Area system variable, 281
Array command, **9–11**, 71
arrows
  appearance of, 54–55
  custom, 81, 83
  for leader line, 158
  placement for dimensions, 55
  size for dimension, 80
ASCII files
  Acad.INI, 1
  for audit report, 22
  converting attributes to, 18, 46–47
  for log of Xref activity, 347
  shape/font description file as, 38
  writing text window contents to, 167
ASCII.PCP file, 212
ASE application, **11–12**
Aseadmin command, 12
Aseexport command, 12
Aseselect command, 12
Asesqled command, 12

aspect ratio, of drawing editor screen, 39
Assist menu (DOS)
  ➤ Distance, 101
  ➤ Group Objects, 137
  ➤ Inquiry
    Area, 8
    List, 165
    Locate Point, 143
    Mass Properties, 269
  ➤ Object Snap, 199
  ➤ Ortho, 198
  ➤ Redo, 234
  ➤ Select Objects, 251
  ➤ Selection Filters, 133
  ➤ Undo, 320
Associative (Bhatch command), 26
associative dimensions, 80
associative hatch block, modifying, 141–142
at sign (@)
  to reference last-entered point, 286
  for relative coordinates, 219
  as wildcard character, 340
Attach setting, and overflow text, 184
Attdef command, **13–14**
Attdia system variable, 281
Attdisp command, 14–15
Attedit command, 46
Attext command, 13, **18–20**
Attmode system variable, 281
Attredef command, **21**, 152
Attreq system variable, 152, 281
Attribute Definition dialog box, 13, 45
attribute definitions
  changing, 49–50
  creating, 13–14, 45
Attribute Edit dialog box, 59
Attribute Extraction dialog box, 46
Attribute toolbar (Windows)
  ➤ Ddattdef, 45

➤ Ddatte, 46
➤ Edit Attribute Globally, 15
➤ Redefine Attribute, 21
attributes
  controlling display and
    plotting, 14–15
  displaying invisible, 15
  editing values, 15–17
  prompt for, 281
Audit command, **22**
Audit log files, system variable
    for, 281
Auditctl system variable, 281
Aunits system variable, 282
Auprec system variable, 282
Auto
  for Drag mode, 104
  for Undo command, 325
AUto (Select command), 252
Auto.sv$ file name, 248
AutoCAD
  arranging windows, 296
  configuring input and output
    devices, 38
  DOS commands without
    exiting, 255
  Release 13 new features,
    xiv–xvi
  temporary files for, 127
  version number of, 281
AutoCAD fonts, 277
  creating style from, 276
AutoCAD menu system,
    AutoLISP code embedded
    in, 24
AutoDESK Advanced
    Modeling Extension, 268
AutoLISP, **23–24**
  error codes for, 285
  file routines in .MNL files, 170
  loading files, 4
  and prompt line display, 283
  using undefined command
    with command function,
    233
AutoLISP command, 253

automatic save, 40
  file name for, 290
  preferences, 223
  time interval, 248, 290
automatic updates, of linked
    objects, 195
autoregeneration, 15
AutoShade, 253
AVECFG environment setting,
    120
AVEDFILE environment
    setting, 120
AVEFACEDIR environment
    setting, 120
AVEPAGEDIR environment
    setting, 120
axis endpoint, for ellipse, 117
axis of revolution for extruded
    surface, 242
axis of rotation, 3D, 245

B

background color, 290
Backspace, for script, 251
Backz system variable, 282
.BAK file extension, 118, 248
Base command, **24**
base point, 24
  for mirror-line axis, 175
beep sound, after errors, 40
Bezier surface, 207
Bhatch command, **25–26**, 138,
    141
  and regions, 238
Bind, for cross-referenced file,
    345
Bisect (Xline command), 343
bitmap images, exporting to,
    148
bitmap window repair, 223
Blipmode command, **26–27**, 69
Blipmode system variable, 282
blips, 26, 69

Block command, **27–28**, 71
blocks
  alphabetic list of, 58
  attribute values of, 46
  converting to drawing files, 28
  displaying properties of, 165
  exploded version of, 59
  extracting information about, 20
  grips for, 52
  importing from external reference, 341–342
  inserting, 58, 150, 172–173
  as marking device for Divide command, 101
  redefining, 21
  reducing to component objects, 124
  replacing with external drawing, 152
  vs. shapes, 255
  stripping unused from file, 339
  Trim command and, 319
  writing to disk, 338–339
  vs. Xref'd files, 347
.BMP file extension, exporting to, 148
BMPOUT command, 148
Boolean operations, 267
boundaries
  of drawing, 161
  extending objects to, 126
  for hatches, 25
Boundary command, **28–29**
Box command, 261–262
BOX (Select command), 252
Bpoly command, 9
Break command, xv, **29–30**
broken pencil, UCS icon as, 323
browse, before opening file, 197
Button Properties dialog box, 302
Byblock, for color setting, 36, 49
Bylayer, as color, 36, 49

C

C programming language, 23
Cal command, **30–31**
calculation of area, 7
calculator, 30–31
calendar date/time, displaying, 282
calibration option, for tablet, 298
CAmera option (Dview command), *109*, 109
Camfera system variable, 282
Cdate system variable, 282
CDF (comma-delimited file), for exported attributes information, 18
Cecolor system variable, 282
Celtscale system variable, 282
Celtype system variable, 282
center marks
  appearance of, 55
  size of, 81
center point
  for 3D box, 262
  of arc or circle, 5, 6, 90–91
  of ellipse, 117
  of object array, 10
  for zoom, 348
centering
  dimension text, 56
  text, 107
chained dimension measurements, 91
Chamfer command, xv, **31–32**
Chamferb system variable, 282
Chamferc system variable, 282
Chamferd system variable, 282
chamfers, for swept solids, 265
Chammode system variable, 282
Change command, **32–34**, 71
Change Properties dialog box, 48
check boxes, xiii
Chprop command, **34–35**, 71

Circle command, **35–36**
circle zoom percent value, 331
Circlerad system variable, 282
circles
  adding radius dimension to,
    96
  center point of, 90–91
  changing properties, 32
  for cylinder base, 263
  dimension for diameter, 92
  erasing with Break
    command, 29, 30
  UCS orientation based on, 322
circular array, 10
circumscribed polygon, 221
Clayer system variable, 282
clearing dimension variable
  overrides, 96
clip art, inserting, 153
CLip (Dview command), 111, *112*
Clipboard, xvi
  cut and paste with, **42–44**
Cmdactive system variable, 283
Cmddia system variable, xiii,
  40, 212, 213, 283
Cmdecho system variable, 283
Cmdnames system variable, 283
Cmljust system variable, 283
Cmlscale system variable, 283
Cmlstyle system variable, 283
color
  of attributes, 17
  background, 290
  of dimension lines, 54, 81
  of extension lines, 54, 81
  of face, 208
  of grips, 52
  of layers, 61, 156
  in Modify dialog boxes, 63
  of nonselected grips, 286
  of objects, 33, 34, **36–37**, 48, 51
  setting preferences, 224
  system variable for, 282
Color command, **36–37**
color image file, importing, 290
columns, in object array, 9

comma-delimited file (CDF),
  for exported attributes
  information, 18
command alias definitions,
  location, 2
command line
  dimensioning from, 87
  plotting drawing at, 213–216
  working from, xiii
command prompts, supplying
  values with calculator, 31
command window, setting
  number of lines to display,
  225
commands
  and cursor as pick box, 71
  help for, 142
  repeating, 186
  reversing, 320, 325
  script to play back, 250–251
  status of, 283
  suppressing, 233
  system variable to display,
    287
  transparent, **316–317**
  using while another is
    executing, 317
Compile command, **38**
composite objects, from Union
  command, 326
composite regions, creating,
  237
composite solids, 267
compound objects, exploding,
  343–344
compressed text, 278
CompuServe, Autodesk
  forum, 23
Cone command, 262
Config command, 38–41
Constant (Attdef command), 14
Construct menu (DOS), 267
  ➤ 3D Rotate, 245
  ➤ 3DArray, 9
  ➤ Array, 9
  ➤ Attribute, 45

➤ Block, 27
➤ Boundary, 29
➤ Chamfer, 31
➤ Copy, 41
➤ Fillet, 131
➤ Intersection, 154
➤ Mirror, 173
➤ Offset, 192
➤ Region, 237
➤ Subtract, 279
➤ Union, 326
construction lines, creating, 342
context-sensitive help, 142
control points, moving on
 spline, 274
Control (Undo command), 325
Coons surface patch, 114, *115*
coordinates
 displaying for point, 143–144
 edit boxes for relocating, 64
 system variable for readouts,
 283
Coords system variable, 283
Copy command, **41–42**, 71
Copy file (File Utilities dialog
 box), 127
Copyclip command, 43
copying, tool between
 toolbars, 302
Copylink command, 43
corners
 multiline options for, 176
 for Trace line segments, 316
 trimming lines, 294
corrupted data
 checking drawing file for, 22
 recovering files, 231
CPolygon (Select command),
 253
CRC (Cyclic Redundancy
 Check) validation, 40
Create … File dialog box, 147
Create Drawing File dialog
 box, 118, 338
Create Extract File dialog box, 18
Create Plot File dialog box, 215

Create Slide File dialog box, 181
crosses. *See also* blips
 multiline options for, 176
cross-hatching, 139. *See also*
 hatching
cube, UCS icon as, 323
cube option, for Box
 command, 262
current drawing
 saving, 118–119
 as template, 191–192
current global line type scale, 282
current layer, 156, 282
 identifying, 60
current object line type, 282
cursor
 commands permitting as pick
 box, 71
 operation for user-positioned
 text, 86
 rotating, 11, 198
 switching orientation of, 155
Cursor menu, 200, 219
curved surface
 extruded, *242*, 242
 straightening, 299
curves
 creating smooth from
 polyline, 202
 generating polygon mesh
 surface between, 246–247
 smooth for polyline, 211
 types of lines, 292
custom applications, system
 variables for, 295
custom menu, 171
 loading file, 170
custom shapes, 254–255
Customize Toolbars dialog
 box, 301–302
Cut and Paste command, **42–44**
cutting edge, for Trim, 319
Cvport system variable, 283
Cyclic Redundancy Check
 (CRC) validation, 40
cycling, xvi

Cylinder command, 262–263

D

dashed lines, 163
Data menu
➤ Drawing Limits, 161
➤ Layer, 59
➤ Linetype, 62
➤ Multiline Style, 178
➤ Purge, 228
➤ Rename, 68
➤ Shape File, 166
➤ Status, 275
➤ Text Style, 276
➤ Time, 309
➤ Units, 74
➤ Viewport Layer Controls, 332
Data menu (DOS)
➤ Color, 49
➤ Dimension Style, 53
➤ Object Creation, 51
databases, linking AutoCAD to external, 11
data-exchange format (DXF)
for exported attributes information, 19
importing from, 144
Date system variable, 283
datum, ordinate dimension string based on, 95
datum reference frame, 311
dBASE, 11
Dblist command, **44–45**
Dbmod system variable, 283
Dctcust system variable, 284
Dctmain system variable, 284
Ddattdef command, 13, **45–46**
Ddatte command, 13, **46**
Ddattext command, 13, **46–47**
Ddchprop command, 34, **48**, 71
Ddcolor command, 36, **49**
Ddedit command, **49–50**

for feature control frame, 312
Ddemodes command, **51–52**
Ddgrips command, **52–53**, 136
Ddim command, **53–58**
Ddim dialog box, 89, 97
Ddinsert command, **58–59**, 149
Ddlmodes command, **59–61**, 156
Ddltype command, **62**, 163
Ddmodify command, **63–65**
Ddosnap command, 4, 65–67, 199
Ddptype command, **67**, 169
Ddrename command, **68**, 239
Ddrmodes command, **69–70**, 131
Ddrmodes dialog box, 198
Ddselect command, **70–72**
Dducs command, **72–73**
Dducsp command, **73**
Ddunits command, **74**
Ddview command, **75**
Ddvpoint command, **76**
decimal measurement units, 328
decimal places, for alternate dimension, 79
default settings
changing attribute assignment, 64
for layer, 157
for plot file name, 40
restoring dimension style as, 97
for Z-axis elevation, 115
Define New View dialog box, 75
Defpoints layer, 157
delay, in script file, 250
Delay command, **76–77**
Delete file (File Utilities dialog box), 127
deleting
objects, 122–123
toolbars, 301

UCS (user coordinate
   system), 72, 321
views, 75, 329
Delobj system variable, 272, 284
detaching cross-referenced file,
   345
dialog boxes
   controlling, xiii
   exit method, 284
   status of, 283
   system variable for, 285
   working with, xiii–xiv
Dialog Colors dialog box, 102
diameter
   defining for circle, 36
   dimensions for, *78*, 91–92
Diastat system variable, 284
dictionaries for spelling,
   270–271
   custom, 284
digitizer
   configuring, 39
   input preferences, 223
   re-initializing, 238
   for Sketch, 257
digitizing tablet, setting up,
   297–299
Dim1 command, 87
Dim: Hometext command, 77
Dim: Horizontal command, 77,
   93
Dim: Newtext command, 77
Dim: Rotate command, 77, 93
Dim: Trotate command, 77
Dim: Vertical command, 77, 93
Dim command, 87
Dimaligned command, 87–89
Dimalt variable, 79
Dimaltd variable, 79
Dimaltf variable, 80
Dimalttd variable, 80
Dimalttz variable, 80
Dimaltu variable, 80
Dimaltz variable, 80
Dimangular command, 89–90
Dimapost variable, 80

Dimaso variable, 80
Dimasz variable, 54, 80, 159
Dimaunit variable, 81
Dimbaseline command, 90
Dimblk1 variable, 81
Dimblk2 variable, 81
Dimblk variable, 54, 81, 159
Dimcen variable, 81
Dimcenter command, 90–91
   custom marks and lines for,
      55
Dimclrd variable, 54, 81, 159
Dimclre variable, 54, 81, 312
Dimclrt variable, 58, 81, 159,
   312
Dimcontinue command, 91
Dimdec variable, 57, 81
Dimdiameter command, 91–92
   custom marks and lines for,
      55
Dimdle variable, 54, 81
Dimdli variable, 54, 82
Dimedit command, 77, 92–93
dimension arrow. *See* arrows
dimension line, 54, *79. See also*
   extension lines
   suppressing, 83–84
dimension range, 82
dimension strings, 90
dimension styles, 97
   activating, 53
   Annotation options, 56–58
   current, 84
   Format options, 55–56
   Geometry options, 54–55
   importing from external
      reference, 341–342
Dimension Styles dialog box,
   53
dimension text, *79*
   color of, 81
   editing and customizing,
      88–89
   minus tolerance value of, 85
   placement, 55, 56
   setting for, 82

style of, 86
UCS orientation based on, 322
Dimensioning toolbar
    (Windows), 87
➤ Align Dimension Text, 98
➤ Aligned Dimension, 87
➤ Angular Dimension, 89
➤ Baseline Dimension, 90
➤ Center Mark, 91
➤ Continue Dimension, 91
➤ Dimstyle, Dimstyle, 53
➤ Leader, 158
➤ Linear Dimension, 94
➤ Ordinate, Automatic, 95
➤ Radial Dimension
  Diameter Dimension, 92
  Radius, 96
➤ Tolerance, 310
dimensions, **77–100**
  adding geometric tolerances
    to, 310
  aligned or rotated, 87–89, *88*
  changing individual
    properties, 95–96
  components of labels, *79*
  continuing, 91
  mode subcommands, 99–100
  new features, xv
  saving variable settings, 97
  starting processing, 87
  types of, *78*
  variables to control, **78–86**
Dimexe variable, 54, 82
Dimexo variable, 54, 82
Dimfit variable, 55, 82
Dimgap variable, 57, 82, 159,
    312
Dimjust variable, 56, 82
Dimlfac variable, 57, 82
Dimlim variable, 82
Dimlinear command, 77, 93–94
Dimordinate command, 95
Dimoverride command, 95–96
Dimpost variable, 56, 83
Dimradius command, 96–97

custom marks and lines for,
  55
Dimrnd variable, 58, 83
Dimsah variable, 55, 83
Dimscale variable, 55, 83, 86
Dimsd1 variable, 83
Dimsd2 variable, 83
Dimse1 variable, 83
Dimse2 variable, 84
Dimsho variable, 84
Dimsoxd variable, 84
Dimstyle command, 97–98
Dimstyle variable, 84
Dimtad variable, 56, 84
Dimtedit command, 98
Dimtfac variable, 84
Dimtih variable, 56, 84
Dimtix variable, 84
Dimtm variable, 85
Dimtofl variable, 55, 85
Dimtoh variable, 56, 85
Dimtol variable, 85
Dimtolj variable, 85
Dimtp variable, 85
Dimtsz variable, 85
Dimtvp variable, 85
Dimtxsty variable, 57, 312
Dimtxt variable, 57, 312
Dimunit variable, 56
Dimupt variable, 55
Dimzin variable, 57
direction, for arc, 6
directories
  for plot spool, 40
  preferences, 224
directory path, displaying, 281
Dispilh system variable, 284
Dist command, **100–101**
Distance (Chamfer command),
  32
Distance (Dview command),
  110
Distance system variable, 284
Divide command, 67, **101–102**
Dlgcolor command, **102**
docked toolbars, xiv, 313, 315

Docked Visible Lines, setting preferences, 225
Donut command, **103–104**
  default diameter values, 284
Donutid system variable, 284
Donutod system variable, 284
donut-shaped solid, 3D, 264
DOS commands, without exiting AutoCAD, 255
DOS editor, for multiline text, 183
DOS environment, 119
DOS programs, launching within AutoCAD, 2
DOS Set command, 119, 222
DOS shell, opening, 255
dotted lines, 163
Doughnut command, **103–104**
dragging, to lengthen object, 160
Dragmode command, **104–105**
  speed of, 112
Dragmode system variable, 284
Dragp1 system variable, 284
Dragp2 system variable, 284
Draw menu (DOS)
➤ 3D Polyline, 307
➤ 3D Surfaces, Extruded Surface, 299
➤ Arc, 5
➤ Circle, 35
  Donut, 103
➤ Construction Line, 342
➤ Dimensioning, 87
  Align Text, 98
  Aligned, 87
  Angular, 89
  Baseline, 90
  Center Mark, 91
  Continue, 91
  Leader, 158
  Linear, 94
  Ordinate, Automatic, 95
  Radial, Diameter, 92
  Tolerance, 310

➤ Dimensions, Radial, Radius, 96
➤ Ellipse, 116
➤ Hatch, 25
  PostScript Fill, 227
➤ Insert
  Block, 58
  Multiple Blocks, 172
  Shape, 254
➤ Line, 162
➤ Multiline, 177
➤ Point, 217
  Divide, 101
➤ Polygon
  2D Solid, 260
  Polygon, 221
  Rectangle, 232
➤ Polyline, 210
➤ Ray, 231
➤ Sketch, 256
➤ Solids, 237, 267
  AME Convert, 268
  Box, 261
  Cone, 262
  Cylinder, 263
  Extrude, 266
  Revolve, 266
  Section, 268
  Slice, 268
  Sphere, 263
  Torus, 264
  Wedge, 265
➤ Spline, 271
➤ Surfaces
  3D Face, 304
  3D Mesh, 305
  Edge, 113
  Edge Surface, 114
  Revolved Surface, 242
  Ruled Surface, 247
➤ Text
  Dynamic Text, 106
  Text, 183
Draw toolbar (Windows)
➤ Arc, 5

➤ Block
  Block, 27
  Insert Block, 58
➤ Circle, 35
  Donut, 103
➤ Ellipse, 116
➤ Hatch
  Hatch, 25
  PostScript, 227
➤ Line
  Line, 162
  Ray, 231
  Xline, 342
➤ Point, 217
  Divide, 101
  Measure, 169
➤ Polygon
  Boundary, 29
  Polygon, 221
  Rectangle, 232
  Region, 237
  Solid, 260
➤ Polyline
  3Dpolyline, 307
  Multiline, 177
  Polyline, 210
  Spline, 271
➤ Text
  Dtext, 106
  Text, 183
Drawing Aids dialog box, 69, 134
drawing code page, 284
drawing editor, updating
    screen, 235
Drawing Exchange Format
  exporting, 147
  importing, 145
drawing files
  checking for errors, 22
  converting blocks to, 28
  displaying information, 45
  linking objects from other
    applications in, 194
  purging elements from, 228

drawing log, for information
    lost in Release 12 format,
    248
drawing process
  boxes, 261–262
  circles, 35–36
  cones, 262
  cylinders, 262–263
  freehand, 255–257
  new features, xv–xvi
  spheres, 263–264
  torus, 264
  wedges, 264–265
drawing scales, dimensioning
    and, 86
drawing units, changing,
    327–328
drawing window, maximizing,
    225
drawings
  boundaries of, 161
  current as template, 191–192
  displaying current settings, 274
  displaying multiple views,
    335–337
  exiting without saving, 230
  name status for, 284
  opening, 196
  orthographic 3D view of,
    333–335
  plotting, 211
  restoring deleted objects to,
    195–196
  saving, 118–119, 229
  saving views of, 329–330
  scale factor of, 55
  setting up Paperspace
    specifications, 188
  shifting display of, 200
  spatial index for, 317–318
  thumbnail images of, 197
  time and date of creation, 293
  tracking time spent on, 309
  Zoom to control display,
    348–349
Dsviewer command, **105**

Dtext command, **106–108**
Dview command, 71, **108–112**, 143
  zoom, 349
Dviewblock block, 112
Dwgcodepage system variable, 284
Dwgname system variable, 284
Dwgprefix system variable, 284
Dwgtitled system variable, 284
Dwgwrite system variable, 284
.DXB file extension
  exporting files to, 147
  importing files with, 144
DXBIN command, 145
  automatic audit after, 41
DXF (data-exchange format)
  for exported attributes information, 19
  importing files with, 144
DXFIN command, 145
  automatic audit after, 41
DXFOUT command, 147
dynamic dragging mode, to lengthen object, 160
dynamic zoom, 348

E

edge, of polygon, 221
Edge command, **113**
Edgemode system variable, 284, 318
Edgesurf command, **114**
Edit Attribute Definition dialog box, 50
Edit Attributes dialog box, 46
edit boxes, xiii
Edit menu (DOS)
  ➤ Paste, 43–44
  ➤ Paste Special, 43–44
Edit menu (Windows)
  ➤ Links, 195
  ➤ Redo, 234

➤ Select Objects, Insert Object, 153
Edit Mtext dialog box, 89, 158, 159, 183, 184
Edit Rows subdialog box, for external dialog box, 12
Edit Text dialog box, 50
editing
  grouping objects for, 137
  new features, xv–xvi
  polylines, 201–203
  spline objects, 272–274
  undoing, 325
Elev command, **115–116**
elevation for objects, 33, 52
  default, **115–116**
Elevation system variable, 285
ellipse
  for cylinder base, 263
  system variable for type, 288
Ellipse command, **116–118**
  for isometric ellipses, 259
elliptical cone, 262
embedding objects, 194
End command, **118–119**
endpoints
  of arc, 6
  circle zoom value and, 331
  joining in polyline, 202
engineering measurement units, 328
environment settings, **119–122**, 224
  DOS preferences, 222
  file for, 1
.EPS file extension, importing files with, 144, 146
Erase command, 71, **122–123**
erased objects, restoring, 196
Errno system variable, 285
errors, checking drawing file for, 22
Exit command, **123–124**
expanded text, 278
Expert system variable, 285
Explmode system variable, 285

Explode command, 71, **124**, 152
  and polylines, 211
exploded version of block, 59
exploding, compound objects,
    343–344
Export Links (External
    Database menu), 12
exporting, **147–148**
Extend command, xv, **125–126**
extension lines, *79*
  appearance of, 54
  color of, 54, 81
  dimensinon text placement
    and, 56, 84
  extension for, 82
extension offset, *79*
extension origin, *79*
Extents (Zoom command), 349
external commands, parts of, 2
External Database toolbar
    (Windows), ➤
    Administration, 11
external databases, linking
    AutoCAD to, 11
external files, 345–347
  inserting, 152
external references
  importing from, 341–342
  new features, xvi
External References toolbar
    (Windows)
  ➤ Bind, Bind, 341
  ➤ Preset Options, 345
Extmax system variable, 285
Extmin system variable, 285
Extrude command, 266
extruded curved surface, *242, 242*
extruding 2D object, 265, 266

F

Facetres system variable, 149,
    285
families of dimension styles, 53

fast zoom mode, 330
Fastdraw, 223
feature control frame, 310
  for tolerance information, 312
Fence (Select command), 253
Fflimit system variable, 285
file extensions, 128–130
file locking, 41
File menu
  ➤ Exit, 230
  ➤ Exit AutoCAD, 123
  ➤ Export, 147
  ➤ Import, 144
  ➤ Management
    Audit, 22
    Recover, 232
  ➤ Print, 211, 213
  ➤ Save, 229
File menu (DOS)
  ➤ Bind, 341
  ➤ Export
    Attributes, 47
    Block, 338
    Release 12 DWG, 248
  ➤ External Reference, Preset,
    345
  ➤ Import, PostScript,
    Display, 226
  ➤ Management, Utilities, 126
  ➤ New, 191
  ➤ Open, 196
File menu (Windows)
  ➤ Import, 144
  ➤ Management, Unlock
    Files, 126
  ➤ Options, PostScript
    Display, 226
file names
  changing, 127
  wildcard characters to filter
    list, 340–341
File Utilities dialog box, 127
Filedia system variable, xiii,
    119, 126, 127, 215, 232, 247,
    250, 285

files
creating from portion of
current file, 338
location for temporary, 40
preferences, 224
recovering corrupted, 231
saving, 247
writing plot to, 215
Files command, **126–130**
Fill command, **130–131**
fill status, system variable for,
285
Fillet command, xv, **131–132**
fillets, for swept solids, 265
Fillmode system variable, 259,
285
Filter command, 132–134
filters
for layers, 61
for points, 219–220
Find File dialog box, 197
finite element analysis, 3D
models for, 305
Fit (Ddim command), 55
Fit Data option, for editing
spline, 273
fitting text between points, 107
floating modelspace, switching
to, 308
floating toolbars, xiv, 313, 315
floating viewport, 308
switching to Paperspace,
227–228
Flyout Properties dialog box,
302
flyouts, xiv, 313
Fontalt system variable, 285
Fontmap system variable, 285
fonts
AutoCAD, 277
mapping, 225
setting preferences, 224
system variable for alternate,
285
Force Line Inside (Ddim
command), 55

form, geometric feature
symbols for, 311
Format sub-dialog box, for
dimension styles, 55–56
Fox Pro, 11
fractional measurement units,
328
freehand drawing, 255–257
freezing layers, 60, 61, 156, 332
Frontz system variable, 285
frozen layers, displaying list,
332

G

geometric points, picking, 198
Geometric Tolerance dialog
box, 158
geometric tolerances, 310
geometry, new features, xvi
Geometry subdialog box, for
dimension styles, 54–55
ghosting, 286
.GIF file extension, importing
files with, 144, 146
GIFIN command, 146
global line type scale, 282, 287
global scale factor, 57, 82
graphic objects, inserting, 153
Graphics Interchange format,
importing, 144, 146
Grid command, **134–135**
Grid mode, 70
Gridmode system variable, 286
Gridunit system variable, 286
Gripblock system variable, 286
Gripcolor system variable, 286
Griphot system variable, 286
grips
color for nonselected, 286
for mirroring, 174
for moving, 180
and Scale command, 249–250
Grips command, **136**

for feature control frame, 312
Grips dialog box, 52
Grips system variable, 286
Gripsize system variable, 286
group, selecting, 251
Group command, **137–138**
group of commands, marking
    for undo, 325

H

halfwidth, for polyline, 210
handles, in Modify dialog
    boxes, 63
Handles system variable, 286
Hatch command, 71, **138–140**
Hatchedit command, xv,
    141–142
hatching
  default settings for patterns,
      286
  editing block, 141
  new features, xv
  options, 25
  standard patterns, 140
height
  default for text, 293
  of dimension text, 86
  editing for attribute, 16
  of Mtext, 183
  of object, 64
  projected tolerance zone for,
      311
  of text, 106, 278
help, from Tooltip, 315
Help command, **142–143**
Help menu, ➤ About
    AutoCAD, 1
Hide (Dview command), 111
Hide command, **143**
Hideplot option, 187
Highlight system variable, 69,
    286

History lines, setting
    preferences, 225
Home (Dimedit command), 93
Home (Dimtedit command), 98
hook line, 157
Horizontal (Dimlinear
    command), 94
horizontal dimension text, 85
horizontal justification, for
    dimension text, 55, 56
horizontal text, 183
hot grip, 136
Hpang system variable, 286
Hpbound system variable, 286
Hpdouble system variable, 286
Hpname system variable, 286
Hpscale system variable, 286
Hpspace system variable, 286

I

icons, xiv
  size on toolbars, 302
ID command, **143–144**, 334
ID number, for viewports, 283
image tiles, xiv
implied intersection, trimming
    to, 318
Implied Windowing, for object
    selection, 71
Import command, **144–146**
Import File dialog box, 144
importing
  color image file, 290
  external files, 345
  from external reference,
      341–342
index, for Help, 142
Informix, 11
Inherit properties (Bhatch
    command), 26
input devices, configuring, 38
Input/Output ports,
    re-initializing, 238

Insbase system variable, 286
inscribed polygon, 221
Insert command, **149–152**
  dialog box for, 281
Insert dialog box, 58
Insert New Object dialog box,
  153
inserting
  blocks, 58, 150
  custom shapes, 254
Insertion point: prompt,
  options for, 151
Insertobj command, **153–154**
Insname system variable, 286
interference, with solids, 267
international preferences, 225
interrupting script file
  processing, 251
Intersect command, **154–155**, 237
intersection
  circle zoom value and, 331
  for solids, 267
  trimming to, 318
Invisible (Attdef command), 14
invisible attributes, displaying,
  15
invisible option, for joint line
  between joined 3D faces,
  305
Island Detection, 25, 26
ISO pen width, 62
Isolation level, for external
  database, 11
Isolines system variable, 286
isometric snap, 70, 116
Isometric Style option, 259
Isoplane command, **155**, 259
italicized text style, 278

J

Japanese Industrial Standards,
  56
joining unparallel lines, 31–32

justification, 64
  for dimension text, 56
  for multiline objects, 283
  for text, 106

K

keystrokes, setting preferences,
  223

L

landscape plotter orientation,
  289
Last (Select command), 252
Lastangle system variable, 286
Lastpoint system variable, 286
Layer command, **156–157**
Layer Control dialog box, 51,
  59
layers
  assigning line types to, 165
  changing for object, 33, 48
  controlling, 59–61
  creating new frozen, 332
  current, 282
  editing for attribute, 16
  importing from external
    reference, 341–342
  listing names, 60
  in Modify dialog boxes, 63
  stripping unused from file,
    339
  visibility of, 332
Leader command, xv, **157–159**
leader lines, placement for
  dimensions, 55
left justification, for dimension
  text, 56, 98
Left (Zoom command), 349
length of chord, for arc, 6
Lengthen command, xv–xvi, 7,
  159–160
Lenslength system variable,
  286

library file, loading multiline style from, 179
light sources, 239
Lights (Render command), 240
Limcheck system variable, 287
Limits command, **161**
Limmax system variable, 287
Limmin system variable, 287
Line command, **162**
line segments, changing smoothed polyline into, 2020
line type scale, current global, 282
linear dimension, *78*
  creating, 93–94
lines. *See also* dimension lines; extension lines
  construction, 342
  erasing with Break command, 29
  noncontinuous, 331
  Pline command to create, 210
  from Ray command, 231
  removing hidden, 143
  types of, 163
  UCS orientation based on, 322
Linetype command, **163–165**
linetypes
  changing, 65
  importing from external reference, 341–342
  for layer, 156
  in Modify dialog boxes, 63
  new features, xv
  for objects, 48, 51
  scale of, 167
  stripping unused from file, 339
  viewing, selecting and loading, 62
linked view, 43
linking objects, 194–195
Links (External Database menu), 12

list
  of blocks, 58
  of cross-referenced files, 345
  of layers, 60, 156
  of linked objects, 195
  of object properties, 44–45
  of patterns, 139
  saved UCS's, 321
  of saved views, 329
List command, 71, **165–166**
Load command, **166**, 254
Locale system variable, 287
location, geometric feature symbols for, 311
locked files
  configuring, 41
  unlocking, 127
locking layers, 60, 156
log, for information lost in Release 12 format, 248
Logfileoff command, **167**
Logfileon command, **167**
login name, 41, 287
Loginname system variable, 287
loops, 237
.LSF file name extension, 23
LtScale, 34, 48, 51
Ltscale command, **167–168**
Ltscale system variable, 287
LType (Change command), 33
luminance, for imported image file, 290
Lunits system variable, 287
Luprec system variable, 287

M

macros
  file for, 1
  treating as single command for Undo, 325
Makepreview command, **168**

manual update, of linked
    objects, 195
mass of solid objects, 261, 269
Massprop command, 269
Material Condition dialog box,
    311
Materials library (Render
    command), 240
Materials (Render command),
    240
Matlib command, 240
Maxactvp system variable, 287
maximize application on start
    up, 225
Maxsort system variable, 287
Measure command, 67, **169**
measurement units, 56
    alternate, 79
    for angles, 282
    format for dimension styles,
        86
    options for, 74
    setting preferences, 222, 225
measurements, rounding, 58
media clips, inserting, 153
memory
    setting preferences, 224
    Treestat command and, 318
memory usage, 274
Menu command, **170**
Menu Customization dialog
    box, 171
Menuctl system variable, 287
Menuecho system variable, 287
Menuload command, **171–172**
Menuname system variable,
    287
menus
    group associated with
        toolbar, 301
    swapping, 287
    for tablet, 298, 299
Menuunload command,
    171–172
mesh
    3D surface polygon, 114

control points, 292
drawing polygon, 207
editing 3D, 65, 201, 205–207
Method (Chamfer command),
    32
Metric measurement system,
    222
Microsoft ODBC, 11
Minsert command, 124,
    172–173
minus tolerance value, of
    dimension text, 85
Mirror3D command, **173–175**
Mirror command, 71, **173–175**
mirror image, inserting, 152
mirrored blocks, exploding, 124
mirroring of text, 288
Mirrtext system variable, 288
miscellaneous preferences, 225
Miscellaneous toolbar
    (Windows)
    ➤, Mesh, 303
    ➤ Insert Multiple Blocks, 172
    ➤ Oops, 196
    ➤ Shape, 254
    ➤ Sketch, 256
    ➤ Trace, 316
Mledit command, **175–176**
Mline command, **177–178**
Mlstyle command, **178–179**
.MNC file extension, 302
.MNL file extension, 170
mode
    changing settings, 69
    for Ddattdef, 45
model space units, 57
Modelspace, 228
    toggle with Paperspace, 182,
        293, 307–308
Modemacro system variable,
    288
Modify menu (DOS)
    ➤ Align, 3
    ➤ Attribute
    Edit, 46
    Edit Globally, 15

Redefine, 21
➤ Break, 29
➤ Edit Hatch, 141
➤ Edit Multiline, 175
➤ Edit Polyline, 201
➤ Edit Spline, 273
➤ Edit Text, 50
➤ Erase, 122
➤ Explode, 124
➤ Extend, 125
➤ Lengthen, 160
➤ Move, 180
➤ Oops!, 196
➤ Point, 33
➤ Properties, 63
➤ Rotate, 244
➤ Scale, 249
➤ Stretch, 275
➤ Trim, 318
Modify toolbar (Windows)
➤ Break, 29
➤ Copy
Array Options, 9
Copy, 41
Mirror, 173
fset, 192
e, 122
de, 124, 237, 267
ion, 154
79

gle
152
7
t other
s of
th, 169
ual divisions,

Edit Spline, 273
Hatch Edit, 141
Text Edit, 50
➤ Trim
Extend, 125
Trim, 318
Move command, 71, **180–181**
moving
control points on spline, 274
tool between toolbars, 302
toolbars, 313
vertices, 204
Mslide command, 149, **181**, 254
Mspace command, **182**, 308
Mtext command, xiv, **182–184**
for annotations, 158
text editor for, 225
vs. Dtext command, 107
Mtext object
changing properties, 185
pasted text as, 44
Mtext properties dialog box, 185
Mtexted system variable, 288
Mtprop command, **185**
Multiline Edit Tools dialog box, 176
multiline objects, xiv, 182, 183
drawing, 177
editing characteristics of, 175–176
justification, 283
Multiline Styles dialog box, 178–179
multimedia objects, inserting, 153
Multiple (Select command), 252
Multiple command, **186**
multiplication factor, for alternate measurement unit, 80
Mview command, **186–187**, 212, 308
etup command, 161, 88–190
setup.DFS file, 190

N

named variables, from xref file,
  342, 347
names
  changing, 68, 239
  changing for user coordinate
    system, 72
  for line type, 164
  for text styles, 278
nested blocks, purging, 228
network node name, 40
New (Dimedit command), 93
New command, **191–192**
Next Point: prompt, for Area
  command, 8
Node Osnap override, 217
noncontinuous lines, 331
nonuniform rational B-spline
  (NURBS) curve, 271
Noun/Verb Selection:, 70–71
null value, editing attributes
  with, 17
NURBS (nonuniform rational
  B-spline) curve, 271

O

object arrays, creating, 9
Object Creation Modes dialog
  box, 51
object grips, 136
Object Grouping, for object
  selection, 71
Object Grouping dialog box,
  137
object line type, current, 282
Object Linking and
  Embedding (OLE), xvi,
  153, **194**
object modes, setting, 70
Object Properties toolbar
  (Windows)
  ➤ Color Control, 49

➤ Inquiry
  Area, 8
  Distance, 101
  List, 165
  Locate Point, 144
  Mass Properties, 269
➤ Layers, 59
➤ Linetype, 62
➤ Multiline Style, 178
➤ Object Creation, 51
➤ Properties, 63
Object Selection Filters dialog
  box, 132–134
Object Selection Settings dialog
  box, 70
object snap modes
  multiple active, 65
  setting, 198
object sort method, 71–72
objects. See also properties of
    objects
  aligning, 3
  for Area command, 8
  changing length, 159–160
  changing name, 239
  changing size of, 249–250
  color for new, 49
  color of, 33, 34, **36–37**, 48, 51
  copying, **41–42**
  creating parallel to original
    192
  deleting, 122–123
  dragging, 104–105
  elevation for, 52
  grouping multiple as sin
    object, 27
  inserting from block,
  leader line to connec
    annotation to, 15
  lengthening to mee
    object, 125–126
  marking division
    specified leng
  marking into e
    101–102
  moving, 180

opening dialog box to modify, **63–65**
reducing to component objects, 124
restoring to drawing, 195–196
rotating, 244
selecting, 251
shortening to meet another, 318
stretching, 275–276
UCS orientation based on, 322–323
Oblique (Dimedit command), 93
obliquing, 64
obliquing angle for text, 278
Offset command, **192–193**
Offsetdist system variable, 288
OLE (Object Linking and Embedding), xvi, 153, **194**
Olelinks command, **194–195**
Oops command, **195–196**
Open command, **196–197**
Open Drawing dialog box, 196, 329
operating parameters, configuring, 40
Optimizing Pen Motion dialog box, 212
Options menu
➤ Configure, 39
➤ Dialog Box colors, 102
➤ Display
  Attribute Display, 14
  Point Style, 67
➤ Drawing Aids, 134
  QuickText, 230
➤ Grips, 52
➤ Linetypes, Global Linetype Scale, 168
➤ Preferences, 1
➤ Running Object Snap, 66
➤ System Variables, Set, 280
➤ Tablet, 297
➤ UCS
  Follow, 322
  Icon, 324

Options menu (DOS)
➤ AutoSave Time, 248
➤ Log Files, 167
➤ Selection, 70
Options menu (Windows)
➤ Preferences
  Environment, 167
  Misc, 184
  System, 248
Oracle, 11
ordinate dimension, *78*, 95
orientation, for plot, 212
origin
  for block written to file, 339
  for plot, 212–213
  of UCS, 321
origin point, ordinate dimension string based on, 95
Ortho command, **198**
Ortho mode, 32, 69
  and sketch, 257
Orthomode system variable, 288
Osmode system variable, 288
Osnap command, 66
  for feature control frame, 312
Osnap cursor target height, 281
Osnap target box, size of, 4
Osnap toolbar (Windows), ➤ Running Object Snap, 4
Osnap variable, **198–200**
output devices, configuring, 38
overall scale (Ddim command), 55
overlapping objects, polyline boundary from, 28
overlay mode, xvi
overlaying, drawing file as cross-reference, 346

P

Paint program format, importing, 146

pan, virtual screen for, 330
PAn (Dview command), 111
Pan command, 108, **200–201**
paper size, for plot, 212
Paperspace, 57, 228
  creating viewports, 186–187
  line type scale for, 290
  setting up specifications, 188
  switching floating viewport
    to, 227–228
  toggle with Modelspace, 182,
    293, 307–308
  turning on, 308
Paradox, 11
paragraph text, 182
parallel lines, drawing
    multiple, 177
parallel projection, scale factor
    for, 111
Pasteclip command, 44
pasting from Clipboard, 43–44
path curve, 242
path of extrusion, 242
paths, for cross-referenced file,
    346
patterns
  listing, 139
  properties for hatch, 25
pause, in script file, 250
.PCX file extension, importing
    files with, 144, 146
PCXIN command, 146
Pdmode system variable, 101,
    102, 169, 217, 288
Pdsize system variable, 101,
    169, 288
Pedit command, 7, **201–207**
  for smooth curve, 306
Pellipse system variable,
    117–118, 288
pen parameters, for plot, 212
Pen width prompt, for plot, 216
pencil, UCS icon as broken, 323
pen-down mode, 256
pen-up mode, 256

performance, optimizing,
    317–318
Perimeter system variable, 288
perpendicular lines, drawing, 198
Perspective mode, turning on,
    110
Pface command, **207–208**
Pfacevmax system variable, 288
.PFB file extension, 38
pick box, cursor as, 71
pick location, and osnap
    modes, 66
pick point, 64
Pickadd system variable, 288
Pickauto system variable, 288
Pickbox system variable, 289
Pickdrag system variable, 289
Pickfirst system variable, 289
Pickstyle system variable, 289
Plan command, **209**
  and Fillet command, 132
planar view, from wire-frame
    view, 111
Platform system variable, 289
Pline command, **210–211**
  for thick line, 315
Plinegen system variable, 211,
    289
Plinewid system variable, 289
Plot command, **211–217**
Plot Configuration dialog box,
    211
plot file name, default for, 40
plot spooling, setting
    preferences, 225
Plotid system variable, 289
Plotrotmode system variable, 289
plotter
  automating setup, 251
  configuring, 40
  optimization, 39
  selecting, 214
Plotter system variable, 289
plus tolerance value, 85
Point command, **217–218**

point objects
  creating, 217
  display style for, 288
point size, 67
Point Style dialog box, 67
pointing device, configuring, 39
points
  appearance of, 67
  defining circle based on, 35
  displaying X, Y, and Z
      coordinates for, 143–144
  distance between, 100
  fitting smooth curve to set of, 271
  fitting text between, 107
  selecting, **218–220**
  UCS orientation based on, 322
POints (Dview command),
      110–111
Polar array, 9, 10
polar coordinates, relative, 219
Polygon command, **221–222**
polygon mesh, drawing, 207
polygon mesh surface,
      generating between
      curves, 246–247
polygons
  creating solid-filled, 259
  drawing, 221
polyline boundary, from
      overlapping objects, 28
polyline outlines, filling with
      PostScript pattern, 226
polylines, 210–211
  chamfering line segments
      within, 32
  changing properties, 32
  converting lines to, 162
  creating smooth curve from,
      202
  default width, 289
  donuts as, 104
  drawing in 3D space, 306–307
  editing, 65, 201–203
  editing vertices, 203–205
  erasing with Break
      command, 29

rectangular, 232
reducing to component
      objects, 124
from Sketch, 257
solid fills for, 130–131
UCS orientation based on, 322
Polysides system variable, 289
pop-up list, xiv
Popups system variable, 289
portrait plotter orientation, 289
position, editing for attribute, 16
PostScript fonts, xiv, 276, 278
  displaying, 293
PostScript images
  appearance of, 226
  importing, 146
precision, of measurement units,
      57, 74
pre-defined hatch patterns, 25
Preferences (Render
      command), 241
Preferences command, 119,
      222–225
  for environment, 224
  international, 225
  Misc, 225
  for rendering, 224
  for system, 223–224
presentation, automating with
      script, 251
Preset (Attdef command), 14
Press and Drag, for object
      selection, 71
preview
  creating, 168
  of plot, 213
Preview Hatch (Bhatch
      command), 26
Previous (Select command), 252
Previous (Zoom command), 349
primary units for
      measurement, 56
printer, automating setup, 251
problem solving
  Audit report for, 22
  plot rotation, 217

profile, geometric feature symbols for, 311
ProGram Parameters ASCII file, 2
projected tolerance zone, for height, 311
projection mode, 125
  when trimming objects, 319
Projmode system variable, 125, 289, 318, 319
prompts
  changing label, 64
  user expertise and, 285
properties of objects
  changing, 32, 34, **48**
  listing, 44–45, 165
  for Mtext, 185
prototype drawing file, 40, 222, 225
  retaining drawing as, 192
Psdrag command, **226**
Psfill command, **226–227**
PSIN command, 146
Psout command, 226
Pspace command, **227–228**, 308
Psquality system variable, 149, 226
puck configuration, 39
Purge command, **228–229**

Q

Qsave command, **229**
Qtext command, 69, **229–230**
Quadrant Osnap, 92
quadratic B-spline surface, 207
Quick Text, 69
Quit command, 123, **230**

R

radial dimension, *78*
radio buttons, xiii

radius
  adding dimension to arcs and circles, 96
  of arc, 6
  default value for circle, 282
  editing, 65
  of polygon, 222
RAM disk, for temporary files, 40
raster images
  file formats for importing, 145, 146
  saving view as, 181
  setting preview preferences, 224
  as slide files, 337–338
ray casting, 26
Ray command, **231**
Rconfig command, 241
RDPADI environment setting, 120
Read Only mode, for opening drawing, 197
Read-only system variables, 280
Record increment: prompt, for sketch, 257
Recover command, **231–232**
Rectang command, **232–233**
rectangular array, 9, 10, 65
  creating for block, 172
rectangular mesh, drawing, 305–306
rectilinear areas, Solid command to fill, 259
Redefine command, **233**
Redo command, **234**
Redraw command, **234–235**, 337
Redrawall command, 234–235, 337
Regen command, **235**, 337
  Qtext and, 230
Regenall command, **235**, 337
Regenauto command, 235, **236**
Region command, **237–238**

regions
  combining, 326
  subtracting, 279
Reinit command, 2, **238**
Re-initialization dialog box, 238
relative coordinates, for points,
  219
reloading cross-referenced file,
  346
Remove (Select command), 252
Rename command, **239**
Rename dialog box, 68
Render command, **239–241**
Render toolbar (Windows)
  ➤ Hid, 143
  ➤ Render, 240
  ➤ Shade, 253
rendering, preferences for, 224
repair of window, 223
repeating
  commands, 186
  script, 250
Replay command, 241
resolution of 3D objects, 285
restoring, dimension style as
  default, 97
resume, for script, 250
Retain Boundaries (Bhatch
  command), 26
reversing commands, 320, 325
Revolve command, 266–267
revolving 2D object, to create
  solid, 266–267
Revsurf command, **242–243**
RHPADI environment setting,
  120
Riaspect system variable, 149
Ribackg system variable, 149
Riedge system variable, 149
Rigamut system variable, 149
right-hand rule, 243
right justification
  for dimension text, 56, 98
  for text, 107
Rithresh system variable, 149
Rmat command, 240

Rotate3D command, **245**
Rotate (Dimedit command), 93
Rotate (Snap command), 259
Rotate command, 71, **244**
rotated dimensions, *88*
Rotated (Dimlinear
  command), 94
rotation
  for block insertion, 150
  for ellipse, 117
  for Mtext, 183
  for object, 64
  for object arrays, 10
  for plot, 212–213, 215
  positive direction of, 243
  for text, 106
rounding dimensions, 58, 83
rows, in object array, 9
Rpref command, 241
Rulesurf command, **246–247**
Running Object Snap dialog
  box, 4, 65
runout, geometric feature
  symbols for, 311
Rx applications, loading and
  unloading, 4

S

.SAT file extension
  exporting to, 148
  importing files with, 144, 146
Save command, **247–248**
Save Drawing As dialog box,
  118, 191
Saveas command, **247–248**
Saveasr12 command, 248
Saveimg command, 241
saving
  automatic, 40
  current drawing, 118–119
  dimension variable settings,
  97
  drawing, 229

filter list, 133
rendered image, 241
setting automatic
    preferences, 223
UCS, 321
view with hidden lines
    removed, 143
views of drawing, 329–330
Scale command, 71, **249–250**
scale factor
    for dimension variables, 83
    for drawing, 55
    for linetypes, 62
    for plot, 212–213
    for text height, 84
    for viewports, 187, 189
    for zoom, 348
Scale(X) (Zoom command), 349
Scenes (Render command), 240
scientific measurement units,
    328
screen display
    aspect ratio for, 290
    automatic regeneration, 236
    configuring, 39
    refreshing, 234–235
    re-initializing, 238
    system variable for, 291
    Zoom command and, 348–349
Screenmode system variable,
    291
Screensize system variable, 291
Script command, **250–251**
script files, 108
    designating time periods for
        slides in, 76–77
    status of, 283
SDF (space-delimited file), for
    exported attributes
    information, 18–19
Select Color dialog box, 49, 51,
    58
Select command, **251–253**
Select Drawing File dialog box,
    59, 150

Select Initial View check box,
    329
Select Intial View dialog box,
    197
Select Layer dialog box, 63
Select Linetype dialog box, 51,
    61, 62
Select Objects (External
    Database menu), 12
Select Objects toolbar, 251
Select Shape File dialog box,
    166, 254
Select Slide dialog box, 337
Select Template File dialog list
    box, 18
Select Text Style dialog box, 51
selecting, points, **218–220**
selection modes, 70–71
selection window, system
    variable for, 289
serial number, identifying, 1
series of related dimensions, 91
Set command (DOS), 119, 222
Set Layer Filters dialog box, 61
Setvar command, 257, 280
Sh command, **255**
Shade command, 143, **253–254**
    and regions, 238
Shadedge system variable, 253,
    291
Shadedif system variable, 253,
    291
Shape command, **254–255**
shape files, 278
    compiling, 38
    loading, 166
.SHB file extension, 38
Shell command, **255**
Shift to Add, for object
    selection, 71
.SHP file extension, xv
    loading file with, 166
Shpname system variable, 291
.SHX font files, xiv, 278
silhouette curves, display of,
    284

SIngle (Select command), 252
Sketch command, **255–257**
Sketchinc system variable, 291
Skpoly system variable, 291
.SLD file extension, 337
  saving, 181
Slice command, 267–268
slide bar, xiii
Slide files, saving view as
    raster image in, 181
slide library file, 257–258
  viewing slide from, 338
Slidelib.EXE program, **257–258**
slides, time period for viewing,
    76–77
smooth curves
  from 3D polylines, 306
  fitting to set of points, 271
  for polyline, 211
Snap Angle edit box, 69–70
Snap command, **258–259**
  Rotate option, 10
  system variable for, 291
Snap mode, 69
  Isometric style for, 155
  settings for, 258–259
  and sketch, 257
snap origin, and Hatch
    command, 140
Snap spacing, grid spacing
    and, 135
Snapang system variable,
    10–11, 198, 259, 291
Snapbase system variable, 291
Snapisopair system variable,
    291
Snapmode system variable, 291
Snapstyl system variable, 291
Snapunit system variable, 291
Solid command, **259–260**
solid fill, 69
solid models, xvi, **260–269**
  calculating mass properties,
    269
  combining, 326
  composite solids, 267

creating from conversion of
    overlapping objects,
    154–155
cross-section, 268
exporting, 138
importing, 146
primitives, 261–265
rendering, 239
revolving 2D object to create,
    266–267
from Shade command,
    253–254
Slice command, 267–268
solid fills for, 130–131
subtracting, 279
swept solids, 265–267
UCS orientation based on, 323
vs. surface objects, 304
Solids toolbar (Windows)
  ➤ AMEConvert, 269
  ➤ Box, 261
  ➤ Cone, 262
  ➤ Cylinder, 263
  ➤ Extrude, 266
  ➤ Revolve, 266
  ➤ Section, 268
  ➤ Slice, 268
  ➤ Sphere, 263
  ➤ Torus, 264
  ➤ Wedge, 265
sort methods, for objects, 71–72
Sortents system variable, 291
sound clips, inserting, 153
space-delimited file (SDF), for
    exported attributes
    information, 18–19
spacing for grid, 135
spatial index, for drawing,
    317–318
speed
  of Dragmode command, 112
  Fill command and, 260
  of redraw, 223, 331
  Regen and, 236
Spell command, xiv, **269–271**
Sphere command, 263–264

Splframe system variable, 203,
207, 292, 305
spline, 307
for leader line, 158
Spline command, **271–272**
spline objects, editing, 272–274
Splinedit command, xvi,
272–274
spline-fit curve, 202, 203
Splinesegs system variable, 292
Splinetype system variable,
203, 292
spool directory, for plot, 40
spreadsheets, inserting, 153
SQL Editor (External Database
menu), 12
Standard measurement
system, 222
Standard toolbar (Windows),
312
➤ ?, 142
➤ Aerial View, 105
➤ Copy, 43
➤ New, 191
➤ Object Group, 137
➤ Object Snap, Calculator, 31
➤ Open, 196
➤ Osnap, 199
➤ Pan, 200
➤ Point Filters, 219
➤ Print, 211, 213
➤ Redo, 234
➤ Redraw, Redraw View, 235
➤ Save, 229
➤ Select Objects, Selection
Filters, 133
➤ Spelling, 270
➤ UCS, 321
Preset UCS, 73
➤ Undo, 320
➤ USC, 72
➤ Zoom In/Out, 348
start point, for arc, 6
Statistics (Render command),
241
Stats command, 241

status bar
icon function on, xiv
MODEL/PAPER, 227
ORTHO, 198
PAPER/MODEL, 308
Status Bar menu (Windows)
➤ Grid, 134
➤ Model, 182
Status command, 274–275
status (Dimstyle command), 97
status line, 288
stereolithography, exporting,
148
.STL file extension, exporting
to, 148
STLOUT command, 148
STRETCH prompt, 136
Stretch command, 71, **275–276**
Style command, **276–277**
styles. *See also* dimension
styles; text styles
editing for attribute, 16
for Mtext, 183
for multiline objects, 177, 178
substitute fonts, location of, 285
subtract, with solids, 267
Subtract command, **279**
Subtract mode, for Area
command, 8
surface, drawing by extruding
curve in straight line, 299,
300
surface curve, changing type,
65
surface density, of mesh, 207
surface polygon mesh, 3D, 114
surface settings, 239
Surfaces menu (DOS), ➤ 3D
Objects, 303
Surfaces toolbar (Windows)
➤ 3D Mesh, 305
➤ 3Dface, 304
➤ Edge, 113
➤ Edge Surface, 114
➤ Extruded Surfaces, 299

➤ Predefined Surface Object, 303

➤ Revolved Surface, 242

➤ Ruled Surface, 247

Surftab1 system variable, 114, 243, 292, 300

Surftab2 system variable, 114, 243, 292

Surftype variable, 207, 292

Surfu system variable, 207, 292

Surfv system variable, 207, 292

symbol fonts, 276

Symbols dialog box, 158, 310, 311

Syscodepage system variable, 292

system console, configuring, 40

system preferences, 223–224

system settings, file for, 1

system variables, **280–296**

Systemwindows command, **296–297**

T

Tab key, in dialog boxes, xiii

Tablet command, **297–299**

tablet menus, 298, 299

Tabmode system variable, 292

Tabsurf command, **299–300**

tag value, changing for attribute, 64

Tagged Image format, importing, 144, 146

tangent, circle zoom value and, 331

TArget (Dview command), *110*, 110

Target system variable, 292

Tbconfig command, **300–302**

Tdcreate system variable, 293

Tdindwg system variable, 293

Tdupdate system variable, 293

Tdusrtimer system variable, 293

tee, multiline options for, 176

template files
for Attext conversion, 18, 19
for Ddattext command, 47

templates, current drawing as, 191–192

temporary files
for AutoCAD, 127
location for, 40

Tempprefix system variable, 293

text. *See also* dimension text
appending to dimension text, 83
displaying properties of, 165
displaying as rectangular box, 229–230
editing, 50
justification, 64. *See also* justification
mirroring, 288
Mtext command for, 182–184
multiline, xiv, 182, 183
spell check of, 269–271

Text command, **106–108**

text definition, changing, 49–50

text editor
setting preferences, 225
specifying, 184

text files, exporting AutoCAD object and linked database to, 12

text styles
creating, 276–277
for dimension text, 57
importing from external reference, 341–342
list of, 64
for objects, 51
stripping unused from file, 339

text window, writing contents to log, 167

Texteval system variable, 293

Textfill system variable, 293
Textqlty system variable, 293
Textsize system variable, 293
Textstyle system variable, 293
thawing layers, 60, 61, 332
thick line, Trace command for,
    315
thickness
  in Modify dialog boxes, 63
  of objects, 34, 48, 52
    default, 115
Thickness system variable, 293
three. *See* "3" at beginning of
    index
thumbnail images, of
    drawings, 197
tick marks, size of, 85
.TIF file extension, importing
    files with, 144, 146
TIFFIN command, 146
tiled viewports, vs. floating
    viewports, 308
Tilemode system variable, 61,
    182, 187, 188, 293, **307–308**,
    335
time, system variables for, 293
Time command, **309**
title block, 190
tolerance, for fitting spline
    curve, 272
Tolerance command, **310–312**
tolerances, for dimension text,
    57
Tool Tip, xiv, 302, 315
Tool Windows toolbar, 312
Toolbar command, **312–315**
toolbars, xiv, *314*
  creating or modifying, 301
Toolbars dialog box, 300–301
Tools menu, 312
  ➤ Applications, 4
  ➤ Image
    Save, 241
    View, 241
  ➤ Slide, View, 337, 338

Tools menu (DOS)
  ➤ Calculator, 31
  ➤ Compile, 38
  ➤ External Database,
    Administration, 11
  ➤ Hide, 143
  ➤ Menus, 170
  ➤ Render, Render, 240
  ➤ Shade, 253
  ➤ Spelling, 270
  ➤ Toolbars, Predefined
    Options from Menu, 313
Tools menu (Windows)
  ➤ Customize Toolbars, 301
  ➤ Slide, Save, 181
Tooltips system variable, 293,
    302
topography, 3D models for,
    305–306
Torus command, 264
Trace command, **315–316**
traces
  erasing with Break
    command, 29
  solid fills for, 130–131
  UCS orientation based on, 323
Tracewid system variable, 293
transparent commands,
    316–317
Treedepth system variable,
    294, 317–318
Treemax system variable, 294
Treestat command, **317–318**
triangle, UCS icon as, 323
Trim (Chamfer command), 32
Trim command, xv, **318–319**
Trimmode system variable, 294
tripod rotation, *335*
TrueType fonts, xiv, 276, 278
  displaying, 293
TTR (Tangent, Tangent,
    Radius) option for circle
    definition, 36
Twist (Dview command), 111
two. *See* "2" at beginning of
    index

.TXT file name extension, 19
Txtfill system variables, 278
Txtqlty system variables, 278
Type 1 fonts, xiv

U

U command, **320**
UCS (user coordinate system),
   72, **320–323**
  and block written to file, 339
  image tiles of views, 73
  system variables for, 294
  trimming object to current
     plane, 318
  viewing angles relative to, 76
UCS Control dialog box, 72
UCS icon, display and location
   of, 323
UCS Orientation dialog box, 73
Ucsfollow system variable,
   209, 294, 322
Ucsicon system variable, 294,
   323–324
Ucsname system variable, 294
Ucsorg system variable, 294
Ucsxdir system variable, 294
Ucsydir system variable, 294
Undefine command, **233**
Undo (Select command), 252
Undo command, **325–326**
  Redo after, 234
Undoctl system variable, 294
Undomarks system variable,
   294
unerasing, 123
union, of solids, 267
Union command, 237, **326**
unit cell, in object array, 9, 10
Unitmode system variable, 295
Units command, **327–328**
Units Control dialog box, 74
unloading, menu group, 171

Unlock files (File Utilities
   dialog box), 127
unlocking layers, 60, 156
unparallel lines, joining, 31–32
updating cross-referenced file,
   346
user coordinate system (UCS)
  and copies, 42
  displaying view
     perpendicular to UCS, 209
User Positioned Text, cursor
   operation for, 86
user-defined hatch patterns,
   25, 139
Userin system variable, 295
Userrn system variable, 295
Usersn system variable, 295

V

Value, editing for attribute, 16,
   17
Verify (Attdef command), 14
version, identifying, 1
Vertical (Dimlinear command),
   94
vertical justification
  of dimension text, 56
  of tolerance values, 85
vertical text, 183
vertices, 203–205
  in 3D Mesh, 306
  multiline options for, 176
video display. *See* screen
   display
view
  copying, 43
  defining UCS parallel to, 321
View command, **329–330**
View Control dialog box, 75
View menu
  ➤ 3D Dynamic View, 108
  ➤ 3D Viewpoint, 333
  Rotate, 76

➤ 3D Viewpoint Presets, Plan View, 209
➤ Floating Viewports, Mvsetup, 188
➤ Named UCS, 72
➤ Named Views, 75
➤ Paperspace, 227, 308
➤ Preset UCS, 73
➤ Redraw View, 235
➤ Tiled Modelspace, 308
➤ Tiled Viewports, Preset, 336
View menu (DOS)
➤ Floating Model Space, 182, 308
➤ Floating Viewports, 186
➤ Pan, Point, 200
➤ Set UCS, Predefined UCS Settings, 321
➤ Zoom, Zoom, 348
View menu (Windows)
➤ Floating Model Space, 182
➤ Zoom, 348
View toolbar (Windows), ➤ Floating Viewports, 186
Viewctr system variable, 295
Viewdir system variable, 295
viewing point, setting, 333, *334*
Viewmode system variable, 295
viewpoint angles, 334
Viewpoints Presets dialog box, 76
viewports
  aligning locations, 188
  creating, 189
  displaying multiple, 336
  grid for multiple, 135
  ID number for, 283
  redrawing all, 337
  refreshing, 235
  tiled vs. floating, 308
  visibility of layers for, 332
Viewports command, 335–337
Viewres command, 330–331
Viewres Fast Zoom, 349
views, saving, 329–330
Viewsize system variable, 295

Viewtwist system variable, 295
virtual screen feature, 330
visibility
  of 3D face edges, 113
  editing, 65
Visretain system variable, 295
Vmax (Zoom command), 349
Vp Frz (Ddlmodes dialog box), 332
Vplayer command, **332–333**
Vpoint command, **333–335**
Vports command, **335–337**
Vpvisdflt (Vplayer command), 333
Vslide command, **337–338**
Vsmax system variable, 296
Vsmin system variable, 296

W

Wblock command, 28, 71, **338–339**
WCS. *See* world coordinate system
Wedge command, 264–265
width
  of multiline objects, 283
  of object, 64
  of polyline, 202, 211
wildcard characters, **340–341**
  for attribute specification prompts, 17
  in Layer command, 157
Window (Zoom command), 349
windows
  arranging, 296
  opening Aerial view, 105
  selecting objects in, 251
  setting preferences, 223
Windows Metafile format
  exporting to, 148
  importing, 146
Windows Notepad, 1

wire-frames
  planar view from, 111
  surface object display as, 304
.WMF file extension
  exporting to, 148
  importing files with, 144, 146
WMFIN command, 146
WMFOUT command, 148
word-processing documents,
      inserting, 153
world coordinate system
      (WCS), 322
  base point in, 24
  plan view of, 209
  returning to, 321
  viewing angles absolute to, 76
Worlducs system variable, 296
Worldview system variable,
      296
WPolygon (Select command),
      252

X

X axis, construction line
      parallel to, 343
X scale factor, 151
  for block insertion, 150
X Spacing edit box, 69–70
Xbind command, **341–342**
.XLG file extension, 347

Xline command, **342–343**
Xplode command, **343–344**
Xref command, **345–347**
Xrefctl system variable, 296
Xrefs, 124
XY plane, rotations in, 3

Y

Y axis
  construction line parallel to,
      343
  grid spacing in, 135
Y scale factor, 151
Y Spacing edit box, 69–70

Z

Z-axis elevation, default
      setting for, 115
Z buffer, 253
Z scale factor, 151
ZAxis (UCS), 321
Zero Suppression setting
Zero Suppression setting, 57
zoom, virtual screen for, 330
Zoom (Dview command), 111
Zoom command, 108, **348–349**
  Xp option, 190

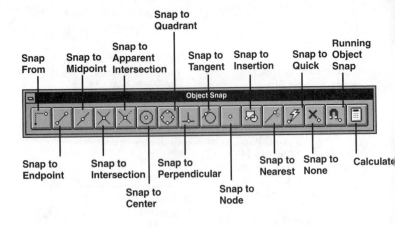

Object Snap toolbar

- Snap From
- Snap to Endpoint
- Snap to Midpoint
- Snap to Intersection
- Snap to Apparent Intersection
- Snap to Center
- Snap to Quadrant
- Snap to Perpendicular
- Snap to Tangent
- Snap to Node
- Snap to Insertion
- Snap to Nearest
- Snap to Quick
- Snap to None
- Running Object Snap
- Calculate

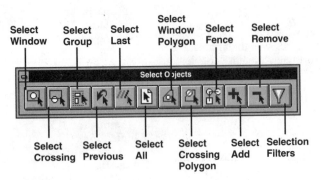

Select Objects toolbar

- Select Window
- Select Crossing
- Select Group
- Select Previous
- Select Last
- Select All
- Select Window Polygon
- Select Crossing Polygon
- Select Fence
- Select Add
- Select Remove
- Selection Filters

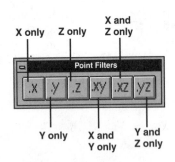

Point Filters toolbar

- X only
- Y only
- Z only
- X and Y only
- X and Z only
- Y and Z only